HISTORY'S WORST DISASTERS

HISTORY'S WORST DISASTERS

AND THE STORIES BEHIND THEM

Eric Chaline

METRO BOOKS
NEW YORK

METRO BOOKS
New York

An Imprint of Sterling Publishing
387 Park Avenue South
New York, NY 10016

METRO BOOKS and the distinctive Metro Books logo
are trademarks of Sterling Publishing Co., Inc.

© 2013 by Quid Publishing

This 2013 edition published by Metro Books, by arrangement with Quid Publishing.

Conceived, designed, and produced by
Quid Publishing
Level 4 Sheridan House
114 Western Road
Hove BN3 1DD
England

www.quidpublishing.com

ISBN: 978-1-4351-4583-2

For information about custom editions, special sales, and premium and corporate purchases,
please contact Sterling Special Sales at 800-805-5489 or specialsales@sterlingpublishing.com.

Manufactured in Singapore

2 4 6 8 10 9 7 5 3 1

www.sterlingpublishing.com

To Petey, Yoko, and Swell

CONTENTS

INTRODUCTION

The word "disaster" is made up of the Greek *astron* (star) with the negative prefix *dis*, meaning "ill-starred," and comes from a time when our ancestors believed that the heavens decided the fates of humans. There are few disasters, however, that are completely "natural," except the original star of ill omen that triggered the Cretaceous–Paleogene extinction of the dinosaurs (pp. 10–15) and maybe the Toba population bottleneck (pp. 16–20), which occurred when humans lived as small, scattered bands of hunter-gatherers whose actions did not affect the outcome of the disaster. The remaining disasters featured in this book can be classified either as "natural–human" or "human."

"Natural–human" disasters are those in which human activity and/or inactivity played a significant role in the causes, severity, and outcome of the disaster: When our ancestors began to build permanent cities, higher population concentrations meant that natural disasters would cause much greater material damage and casualties. Hence, the Santorini–Thera eruption (pp. 21–25) was much more disastrous than its prehistoric predecessors because it destroyed one civilization and fatally destabilized another. Similarly, the Great Kanto Earthquake (pp. 125–128), China Floods of 1931 (pp. 135–138), and Indian Ocean Earthquake and Tsunami (pp. 226–229) claimed between several hundred thousand and several million victims because of the high population densities in the disaster zones.

The major pandemics that feature in the book—the Black Death (pp. 41–46), the Spanish Flu (pp. 115–119), and HIV-AIDS (pp. 183–188)—present another type of natural–human disaster: The original cause is the spread of a pathogen from an animal species to humans, which then becomes transmissible between humans. Again, pandemics, while they have been classed as natural disasters because of their origins, could not occur without large population concentrations, as well as the human practice of long-distance travel. Famine presents a similar complication. The Great Irish Famine (pp. 87–91), for example, had a natural cause—the potato blight—but it was made far worse by the inaction of the British government that was responsible for its relief, so it is classed as a "natural–human" disaster. The next classification also includes famines, but of a different sort: man-made.

The "human" disasters category features events solely attributable to human actions: The Holodomor (pp. 139–144), which was a famine engineered by the Soviet state, and the postwar Great Chinese Famine (pp. 171–174), which was similarly a result of deliberate Chinese state policies; military actions, such as the sack of Rome of 410 CE (pp. 31–35), the first day of the Battle of the Somme (pp. 109–114), and the atomic bombings of Hiroshima and Nagasaki (pp. 160–164); political actions, such as the French revolutionary *Terreur* (pp. 83–86), the Cambodian "killing fields" (pp. 179–182), and the 9/11 attacks on New York (pp. 216–221); genocides, such as the Holocaust (pp. 149–155), and the Rwanda (pp. 207–210) and Srebrenica (pp. 211–215) genocides; economic disasters, such as the Great Depression (pp. 129–134) and the Lehman Brothers bankruptcy (pp. 234–240), which triggered a worldwide economic crisis; and industrial accidents, including the Bhopal gas leak (pp. 194–197), the Chernobyl nuclear accident (pp. 198–202), and the *Exxon Valdez* oil spill (pp. 203–206).

Rather than being a ghoulish catalog of death and destruction, this book will explore why some disasters have been incorporated into the historical narrative of our species, sometimes changing their meanings with the centuries, while others are now largely forgotten. The sinking of the RMS *Titanic* (pp. 100–103), for example, took the lives of just over 1,500 victims—not a vast figure when compared to the millions lost in floods, famines, wars, and earthquakes. However, *Titanic* is emblematic of a class of disasters directly attributable to human hubris (the "unsinkable" *Titanic*), stupidity and greed: the failure to provide sufficient lifeboats for all aboard. Another reason is scale. In contrast to the unimaginable size of events that killed millions, we find it easier to imagine 1,500 people in one place—a group the size of our home town or of the corporation that employs us—and for that reason, it affects us more.

The last entry addresses the issue of climate change (pp. 246–251), which is not yet a disaster but is predicted by the vast majority of climate scientists to be about to unfold. We do not know how many casualties have already been caused by changes to the earth's climate, directly attributable to human activity in the past two hundred years, but if the worst scenarios outlined by climatologists do play out in the next hundred years, then most of the disasters in this book will pale into insignificance by comparison: We are looking at the extinction event for our own species, made all the more tragic because it is of our own making.

A key lesson learned from history is that small changes in human behavior can improve the outcome of potential disasters. Therefore, if the earth is the planetary equivalent of the good ship RMS *Titanic*, and humanity its passengers, and our governments and major corporations its officers and crew, we could steer away from the obvious icebergs in our path and prevent the disaster ahead for generations of our descendants, rather than sail full-steam ahead with the words attributed to King Louis XV of France (1710–74) on our lips: "Après moi, le déluge!" ("After me, the flood!").

DISASTER

Extinction Event

Tectonic Event

Military Action

Fire

Pandemic

Famine

Political or Economic Event

Genocide

Flood or Storm

Industrial or Transport Accident

WHODUNIT?: CRETACEOUS–PALEOGENE EXTINCTION
ca. 65.5 million years before the present (BP)

Cause: One or more asteroid strikes

Event: Explosions millions of times larger and more destructive than the largest nuclear weapons; planet-wide megafires, megatsunamis, and an extended winter

Aftermath: Extinction of dinosaurs and many other forms of life; mammals become the dominant order of vertebrates on earth

Our present-day solar system is a quieter place, with impacts of the scale that killed the dinosaurs occurring only every 100 million years or so.

**Interview with George H. Reike,
Professor of Astronomy,
University of Arizona**

In the nineteenth century, naturalists realized that the petrified femurs, teeth, horns, and skulls that turned up in cliffs and bone fields all over the world were not the remains of an extinct race of biblical giants or of mythical dragons and griffins, but the fossilized skeletons of creatures that had existed on earth millions of years earlier. This realization led to the discovery of the two key processes that have shaped our understanding of life on earth: extinction and evolution. Until then, the churches had taught that God had created the earth between 5500 and 4000 BC, according to the Greek or Hebrew versions of the Bible, and creation was believed to have been a fixed, finished product. The subsequent discovery of thousands of species of giant reptiles upset the creationists and triggered the greatest murder hunt in scientific history: Who killed the dinosaurs?

The dinosaurs (land reptiles), mosasaurs, ichthyosaurs, and plesiosaurs (marine reptiles), and pterosaurs (flying reptiles) first appeared 230 million years BP and were the dominant vertebrates on earth for 135 million years, putting the hominids' current 4 to 5 million years into sharp relief. Paleontologists agree that dinosaurs became extinct 65.5 million years BP at the geological moment known as the Cretaceous–Paleogene (K–Pg) boundary, more commonly referred to as the K–T boundary. This is the division between two geological periods: Cretaceous, "K" (ca. 145.5–65.5 million years BP) and Tertiary, "T" (ca. 65.5–2.6 million years BP). We know that all large reptiles became extinct around that date because there are dinosaur bones below the K–T boundary and very few above.

The mass extinction was extremely sudden—possibly as rapid as a matter of days—and was almost total (sorry, fans of the plesiosaur theory of the Loch Ness Monster). The only reptilian survivors were the crocodilians (crocs and gators), turtles and tortoises, the smaller Squamata (snakes and lizards), and, of course, the birds—all species whose habitats, dietary habits, and sizes allowed them to survive alongside the mammals from which humans evolved millions of years later.

LOOKING FOR THE SMOKING GUN

What earlier generations of paleontologists could not explain, however, was what had caused the sudden mass extinction of most of the earth's reptilian mega fauna. They had corpses—by the fossilized thousands—but no smoking gun. It was a case for earth science's very own Hercule Poirot, though it was unlikely that the solution would be Colonel Mustard in the library with a blunt instrument. Extinction is not a particularly unusual phenomenon on earth, and humans were aware of it long before they had worked out a serviceable theory of extinction and evolution. As we shall see, Europeans realized their role in the extinction of the dodo (pp. 67–70) in the seventeenth century, but they weren't particularly concerned about.

Species extinctions have accompanied changes in the earth's climate over the past million years: For example, the regular cycles of cooling and warming associated with glacial and interglacial periods. However, while nature may cull its less adaptable species, like the mammoth, the American horse and camel, and the giant sloth (though prehistoric Native Americans may have also offered a helping spear), mass extinctions such as the K–T event are extremely rare. The disaster was so total that it was almost as if nature had decided to start again from scratch.

We can start by discounting the Christian fundamentalist explanations for the end of the dinosaurs: That they were washed away by the Great Flood a few thousands of years ago, that they never existed, and that their skeletal remains had been planted by God as a test of faith. Climate change was always in the frame as a possible cause of the K–T extinction, but such a major and sudden climate shift required a major catastrophe.

Until the 1980s, conventional scientific wisdom sought a terrestrial origin for the climatic shift. Fortuitously, geology had identified a prime suspect: Supervolcanic eruptions that lasted between one and two million years, creating the massive geological feature called the Deccan Traps in central India. The eruptions took place between 68 and 65 million years ago, so it was beginning to look bad for the Deccan volcanoes (which didn't have an alibi—where were you at the end of the Cretaceous?). As we know from more recent, and much smaller eruptions, volcanoes can throw up vast clouds of debris as well as greenhouse gases that can seriously affect the global climate. However, the evidence didn't quite stack up. The eruptions would have caused mass local extinctions, but could not really account for the extinction event that occurred simultaneously all over the planet and in a very short space of time.

Other possible suspects who were briefly considered but quickly rejected were us, meaning mammals. The first mammals evolved alongside the dinosaurs, and several biologists have suggested that our small, quick-witted, warm-blooded furry ancestors ate a lot of dinosaur eggs, and as the climate changed at the end of the Cretaceous, were more adaptable and better at surviving than the large, dumb, slow, cold-blooded dinosaurs. Later discoveries about the dinosaurs contradict this hypothesis. We now know that the dinosaurs were warm-blooded and therefore were not slow, and definitely not dumb. And, as with the Deccan supervolcano hypothesis, the time scale is all wrong. The dinosaurs did not die out slowly over millennia because of a slow shift in the climate or mammal predation of their eggs, but were killed by the evolutionary equivalent of a bullet in the back of the head.

In 1980, Walter Alvarez (b. 1940) and his team of earth scientists (aka CSI Planet Earth) came up with a radically new solution to the extinction whodunit. The K–T boundary consists of a thin layer of iridium-rich sediment, which is found all over the planet. The element iridium is rare on the surface of the earth, because, like most of the other heavier elements, it sank to the planet's core early in earth's history. The presence of iridium on the surface, at a recent geological date, Alvarez reasoned, indicated that its origin must be extraterrestrial. He was not suggesting aliens had murdered the dinosaurs, sprinkling iridium dust as they left, but that an asteroid containing iridium had collided with the earth, causing a supermassive impact that deposited a layer of vaporized iridium-rich material all over the planet's surface.

PRIME SUSPECT

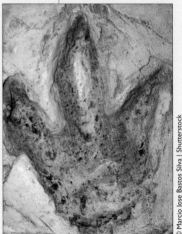

© Marcio Jose Bastos Silva | Shutterstock

FOSSILS
Dominant for 135 million years, all that remains of the dinosaurs is their bones and footprints.

When Alvarez first proposed the impact theory, he was lacking one vital piece of evidence: The asteroid would have created a giant crater, which he thought would have to be at least 160 miles (250 km) in diameter. The movements of the earth's crust and erosion over the past 65.5 million years would have partially hidden the crater, but they wouldn't have obliterated it. In 1978, unbeknownst to Alvarez, two geophysicists employed by the Mexican state oil company who were looking for drilling sites off the coast of Yucatán had identified a huge underwater feature in the shape of an arc, which they described as being of "extraordinary symmetry." They traced the buried remains of a crater 111 miles (180 km) across to the Mayan village of Chicxulub on land and out to sea.

During the 1990s further research into the Chicxulub crater found the geological evidence confirming that it had been created by the impact of an asteroid about 6.2 miles (10 km) in diameter, which generated an explosion two million times greater than the most powerful nuclear weapon ever tested. Scientists had finally managed to identify the smoking gun, the bullet, and the entry wound. The asteroid, roughly the size of Manhattan, crashed into the ocean, generating megatsunamis that washed thousands of miles inland, drowning everything in their path; what wasn't drowned would have been incinerated in worldwide megafires caused by superheated debris thrown up by the explosion that rained onto the

earth's surface; the shock waves from the impact would have triggered volcanic eruptions and earthquakes worldwide. Any organism that managed to survive the initial impact would have had to contend with the sudden onset of an extended winter caused by the particulate debris thrown up into the atmosphere that blocked out the sunlight.

ENTRY WOUND
One or more asteroid strikes triggered a chain reaction which proved fatal to the dinosaurs.

As the world entered into years of perpetual winter and darkness, most plants that depended on photosynthesis died out, followed by the vegetarian dinosaurs that fed on them, and finally, by the large carnivores that predated the plant-eaters. It is a testament to the resilience of life that any organism larger than bacteria managed to survive at all. The survivors—insects, fish, smaller reptiles, birds, and mammals—were small, so did not suffer as much from the sudden drop in temperature, and were able to live off carrion and rotting vegetation, of which there would have been an extremely plentiful supply—a century's worth of barbecued dinosaur ribs!

**THE GOOD,
THE BAD, AND
THE UGLY**

Since the discovery of the Chicxulub crater and the spectacular collision of the Shoemaker–Levy 9 comet fragments with Jupiter in 1994, asteroids and comets have not gotten good press. Worse still, recent finds on earth suggest that Chicxulub might have been just one of several impacts that led to the K–T extinction event, possibly from the pieces of a single asteroid that broke up in a collision in the asteroid belt, which then sent the fragments speeding toward earth. The stars, which our ancestors thought of as pretty lights stuck to the vault of heaven, suddenly began to look like a gang of muggers looking for an innocent planet to set upon. And there are so very many of them—between 700,000 and 1.7 million asteroids with a diameter of 0.6 mile (1 km) or more just beyond the orbit of Mars, which in astronomical terms is over there, yonder.

The asteroids don't deserve all of the bad press that they get: Their colliding with the earth in the distant geological past may have brought the water that created our planet's unique oceans, as well as rare elements, which together made possible the appearance of life on earth. While asteroids can bring destruction on a planetary scale, they may also have brought life to what might have otherwise remained a dry, desolate hunk of rock.

Since its discovery, the Cretaceous–Paleogene impact—one of the two truly "natural" disasters featured in this book—demonstrates that there are cosmic events on a scale so huge—planets colliding, stars going nova, black holes swallowing whole solar systems—that were one of them to involve the earth, there is nothing that we could do to save ourselves from destruction. However, had one or more asteroids not collided with the earth 65.5 million years ago, the dominant life forms on the planet would be the reptilian descendants of the dinosaurs, who might have evolved into sentient beings, instead of the rather unpromising bunch of small, furry mammals that barely managed to survive in their giant shadows—squeak!

DISASTER

Extinction Event

Tectonic Event

Military Action

Fire

Pandemic

Famine

Political or Economic Event

Genocide

Flood or Storm

Industrial or Transport Accident

GOING IT ALONE: TOBA POPULATION BOTTLENECK

ca. 70,000 years BP

Cause: Supervolcanic eruption (VEI 8)

Event: Extended volcanic winter and possible long-term planet-wide cooling

Aftermath: Extinction of several hominid species; near extinction of *Homo sapiens*, with the collapse of the population to between 3,000 and 10,000 breeding pairs; a drastic reduction in genetic variability in our species

The largest magnitude explosive eruption that took place during the late Quaternary was associated with the eruption of Toba, northern Sumatra. This eruption dwarfs, both in scale and magnitude, all other volcanic eruptions during the Quaternary and may have profoundly affected global climate.

Alastair Dawson,
Ice Age Earth, 1991

© Beboy | Shutterstock

Fifty or so years ago, the story of human evolution appeared straightforward. We had few hominid remains, and those that we had found seemed to indicate a well-pruned ancestral tree, indicating that over 4.5 million years the hominid family had gotten taller, brainier, and balder, until it gave birth to *Homo sapiens*, the "Naked Ape." The past decade has overturned this one-track evolutionary journey with the discovery of several new species of hominids, such as the pygmy *H. floresiensis*—known in the popular press as "hobbits." Genetics has also revolutionized the study of evolution. With the increased ease of mapping human genomes, geneticists have been able to trace the links between different modern populations; identify our oldest common male and female ancestors; and examine possible interbreeding between *H. sapiens* and other hominid species such as *H. neanderthalensis*.

This presents an unexpected picture of the life of early humans. *H. sapiens* evolving in near-isolation from other hominid species may more realistically be revised to a complex picture of interactions between different species of hominids, including interbreeding until the relatively recent past. Although we have surviving relatives among the great apes—the gorillas, chimps, and orangutans—these lived in isolated populations a long way away, especially from the ancient human populations of Europe and the Near East. Our historical ancestors developed their cultures, beliefs, and views of themselves and of other animals on the assumption that humans were unique, and quite unlike any other species on the planet. The Western world's attitude to animals was formed by the book of Genesis, in which God gave "dominion" over the animals to Adam, to use as he and his descendants saw fit.

© iStockphoto

EXTINCT
The supervolcanic eruption may have led to the extinction of several hominid species.

Imagine a different world where several other species of intelligent hominids existed, recognizably different in appearance and abilities. The superficial divisions of skin, hair, and eye color among otherwise genetically identical humans might be thought to create the same effect, but in significant periods of development, the human "races" existed in isolation and did not interact. What I am hypothesizing here is the existence of other hominid species worldwide, evolving alongside *H. sapiens* as they developed their first civilizations. Although it is a fascinating "what if," it did not happen.

According to recent genetic research, there was a drastic reduction in genetic diversity in *H. sapiens* around 70,000 years BP. The technical term for what our species experienced is a "population bottleneck," meaning such a sudden collapse in the human population that all subsequent humans are the descendants of a small group with clearly identifiable genetic markers. Anthropologists long ago worked out that *H. sapiens* evolved in Africa between 250,000 and 200,000 years BP and began to migrate at a time when other intelligent hominid species existed worldwide. We cannot be sure how our ancestors interacted with these other hominids, but there is evidence that we interbred with at least one species, the Neanderthals.

The human population bottleneck occurred so long ago that scientists are unable to pinpoint an exact event that might have caused it. We could posit a world pandemic, but pandemics, as we shall see, require certain factors that were not present during that period to develop. Another asteroid impact of the same magnitude as the K–T event would have been too destructive and probably wiped our ancestors out as comprehensively as the dinosaurs. What is required is a global event destructive enough to eliminate many populations but not set evolution back millions of years. The kind of event that might trigger a sudden shift in the climate is a major volcanic eruption, and the geological record features one supereruption around 70,000 BP, in Lake Toba (now Sumatra, Indonesia).

THE BIG BANG THEORY

Before examining the Toba supereruption, its classification as a "tectonic event" should be explained. "Tectonic" refers to movements of the earth's crust. You might imagine that the earth we are standing on is solid all the way down, but what feels like immutable ground to us is actually floating on a mantle of molten rock. The crust is divided into seven major tectonic plates and dozens of smaller plates that are all moving in relation to one another. If we could slow ourselves to geological time, we would see the continents whizzing around the earth's surface like excited puppies. There are three different types of boundary movement affecting the plates: convergent, when the plates are colliding, and one is slipping (or subducting) under the other; divergent, when they are moving apart, creating new crust; and transform, when they slide (or grind) past one another. Although the plates are moving only a few fractions of an inch a year, the movements are enough to generate huge forces that have created mountain ranges, and triggered earthquakes and volcanic eruptions.

A volcano is a vent into the mantle that is opened by tectonic movement, often at the boundaries of plates, through which gas and lava can escape. There are many different kinds of volcano and volcanic eruption, and in one classification—the Volcanic Explosivity Index (VEI)—the magnitude of the eruption is graded according to the amount of material expelled on a scale of 0 (Hawaiian) to 8 (supervolcanic), in which the ejected material is greater than 240 cubic miles (1,000 km³). Toba is one of the few known eruptions rating an 8, so it ejected a vast quantity of ash, rock, and gas, some of which fell in a layer 6 inches (15 cm) thick over a large part of Asia, and enough of which remained suspended in the atmosphere to block out the sun's heat and light.

According to the bottleneck theory, the human population was reduced to between 3,000 and 10,000 breeding pairs, based on genetic evidence that all living humans are descended from the same small population ca. 70,000 years ago. The disaster would have also killed off many other hominids with whom we shared the planet. However, the theory is not universally accepted and other scientists have proposed different hypotheses to explain the bottleneck. Although the eruption took place, and there is a strong probability that there was a bottleneck in the human population at around the same time, that does not prove a causal link between the two.

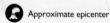 Approximate epicenter

VOLCANIC IMPACT
Geological records show a supereruption around 70,000 BP in Lake Toba (now Sumatra, Indonesia).

Regardless of exactly how or why the human population crashed, *H. sapiens* would henceforth live and develop alone. The surviving humans quickly multiplied and initiated a second human colonization of the earth. But something else of great importance occurred after the eruption, though exactly when it is hard to pinpoint. *H. sapiens* evolved around 200,000 years BP, and for much of that time there was little to differentiate them from other hominids. Then, between 75,000 and 50,000 years BP, humans made a huge cultural and technological leap, and achieved what social scientists call "behavioral modernity"—a set of intellectual and cultural traits and technological advances such as cooking food, fishing, the ritual burying of the dead, an increasingly sophisticated toolset, music making, personal ornamentation, and figurative art, which taken together indicate a quite dramatic shift in the way early humans thought and behaved.

Although, again, there is no evidence to link the changes in human behavior to the Toba supereruption and its aftermath, the achievement of behavioral modernity may have been delayed by the disaster, or conversely precipitated by it. The volcanic winter would have transformed a relatively benign environment into a much more difficult one, with less vegetation, and a corresponding fall in the animal species that depended on plants, including *H. sapiens* who, like later hunter-gatherers, probably obtained more of their regular calorific intake from the gathering of plant materials, edible insects, and shellfish than from the hunting of large animals. With food supplies dwindling, and starvation facing hominids worldwide, it is likely that only the most innovative and adaptable survived.

WITHOUT A TRACE: SANTORINI-THERA ERUPTION

ca. 1500 BCE

DISASTER

Extinction Event

Tectonic Event

Military Action

Fire

Pandemic

Famine

Political or Economic Event

Genocide

Flood or Storm

Industrial or Transport Accident

Cause: Volcanic eruption (VEI 6–7)

Event: Destruction of the island of Santorini-Thera; tsunamis and earth tremors devastated the Aegean region

Aftermath: Decline and ultimate downfall of Crete's Minoan civilization within 50 years of the eruption

But at a later time there occurred portentous earthquakes and floods, [. . . .] and the island of Atlantis in like manner was swallowed up by the sea and vanished; wherefore also the ocean at that spot has now become impassable and unsearchable, being blocked up by the shoal mud which the island created as it settled down.

**Plato, *Timaeus*,
4th century BCE;
trans. W. Lamb, 1925**

© Triff | Shutterstock

In two philosophical dialogs, *Timaeus* and *Critias*, the Athenian philosopher Plato (424–348 BCE) described Atlantis, locating the fabled island empire somewhere beyond the Pillar of Hercules (Straits of Gibraltar) in the Atlantic Ocean. The dialogs describe a circular island with three broad concentric moats crossed by bridges and linked by a canal, a magnificent palace and walled city, and a great harbor for Atlantis' fleet. Once exemplars of virtue, piety, and good government, the Atlanteans became corrupt, greedy, and violent, and set out to conquer the known world. To punish them, Zeus, the king of the gods, decreed the island's destruction by earthquakes and floods. In the space of one night Atlantis was destroyed and sank beneath the sea, leaving only mud shoals to mark its former location. According to Plato, knowledge of Atlantis and its fate was preserved in ancient Egypt—then, as now, considered to be the source of most esoteric knowledge. He dated the destruction of the island to 9,000 years before the time of the Athenian lawgiver Solon (638–558 BCE) hence ca. 9600 BCE (or 11,600 years BP).

© Creative Commons

STORYTELLER
The first reference to Atlantis is found in Plato's philosophical dialogs.

Time to compare the legend with the known facts: 11,600 years ago humans had not begun to build cities or large ocean-going vessels; they were in the process of inventing agriculture; and it would be thousands of years before the first writing systems would be devised. The earliest urban settlements of any size were built inland in Anatolia, Turkey, during the ninth millennium BCE—about 1,400 years after the supposed destruction of Atlantis. Although Plato's Atlanteans were not technological superbeings, even the level of sophistication that he described would have taken centuries, if not millennia, to achieve. Exhaustive geological surveys of the Atlantic ocean's floor have proven beyond doubt that there has never been a large landmass in the Atlantic, and what islands there are—the Cape Verde Islands, Canary Islands, and Azores—are small, barren volcanic archipelagos with no remains of advanced ancient civilizations.

Plato did not retell the Atlantis story as historical fact, but, like many of the other myths he used in his writings, as a story to illuminate the relationship between humanity and the gods, the nature of virtue, and the form of the ideal state. He probably did not invent the Atlantis story, though he rewrote it in accord with his own world view, depicting an island not unlike the

Greek city-states of his own time. We should not reject Atlantis as pure fiction, however. Archeology furnishes us with several examples of what were once thought to be fantastic legends but turned out to be distorted versions of real places and historical events. The biblical Tower of Babel is based on the ziggurats of Mesopotamia; the Minotaur and his labyrinth, on the Minoan palace-city of Knossos on Crete; and Troy, on a real city in Asia Minor. Hence, could the Atlantis story be a fictitious rendering of a historical event so significant that it survived the centuries as an evolving oral tradition before it was finally written down? That is certainly the case of the *Iliad*, the story of the Trojan War, which is based on events that took place around 1300 BCE but was written down around 750 BCE.

Suggested locations for Atlantis have spanned the globe, including the Mediterranean, the Near East, Britain, the North Sea, the Americas, India, Southeast Asia, Antarctica, and the North Pole. By the twentieth century, serious archeologists had decided that Atlantis was one ancient myth that did not have a historical basis—until, that is, a chance discovery on the Aegean island of Santorini, known as Thera to the ancient Greeks, located between Crete and the main group of Greece's Cycladic islands.

MEET THE ATLANTEANS

Atlantis

North Atlantic Ocean

South Atlantic Ocean

AT SEA
For centuries Atlantis-hunters searched for the fabled island in the Atlantic Ocean.

The Aegean sits atop a small tectonic plate between the much larger Eurasian and African plates, making it a zone particularly subject to tectonic events. Although earthquakes are fairly commonplace in the area, there has not been a major volcanic eruption for 3,500 years. This ancient eruption, which ranked among one of largest in recent earth history with a VEI of between 6–7 (see p. 19), literally blew Santorini-Thera apart, creating a large volcanic caldera crater flooded by the sea where there had once been dry land. Although there are no confirmed contemporary records of the eruption, it left its signature on the geological, climatic, and archeological records.

What was unknown until 1967 was that Santorini-Thera had been the home of an advanced urban civilization with close links to Minoan Crete. Led by a local resident, archeologist Spyridon Marinatos (1901–74) discovered the remains of a town with three-story houses decorated with frescoes

© UIG | Getty Images

FRESCO
A period painting of Santorini-Thera as it appeared before the disastrous volcanic eruption.

and served by a sophisticated underground drainage system on what remained of the island, preserved under a thick layer of volcanic ash and pumice. During the latter part of the Bronze Age (3650–1170 BCE), Minoan Crete rivaled Egypt and Mesopotamia as one of the superpowers of the ancient world—through the peaceful arts of civilization and trade.

The Santorini-Thera eruption not only destroyed the civilization on the island, it was of such magnitude that it triggered major tsunamis. In their path, the palace complexes of the northern coast of Crete, including Knossos, were seriously damaged, and the trading fleets on which the Minoans depended destroyed. A major eruption could also have cooled the climate, reducing agricultural production for several years, causing further economic and social dislocation. Although Minoan civilization survived the Santorini-Thera eruption, it entered a period of decline, culminating in an invasion from mainland Greece ca. 1450 BCE.

Although we have identified a major tectonic event that destroyed most of an island, what other evidence do we have that links it to the Atlantis myth? In terms of the physical description of Atlantis, a fresco discovered in one of the buried houses of Santorini-Thera shows a flotilla of ships sailing toward a city built on an island within what might be a lagoon before the eruption. Although itself not the center of an empire, Santorini-Thera was part of the Minoan hegemony that dominated the Eastern Mediterranean. The advanced culture on the island would certainly have overawed its more primitive neighbors on the other Cycladic islands and mainland Greece. Santorini-Thera's prosperous seafaring culture also matches the Atlantis story—though there is no evidence that the island's residents were warlike and entertained dreams of global conquest. Quite to the contrary, the frescos decorating the walls of their houses show peaceful scenes of fishing, agriculture, and elegantly dressed female goddesses that do not suggest a power-crazed militaristic state.

If Santorini-Thera is the island of Atlantis itself, then the cataclysmic end of the Atlantean "empire" could be the mythologized memory of the decline and fall of Minoan civilization in the decades after the eruption. If this interpretation is correct, there would have been many survivors and witnesses of the eruption and its aftermath, creating a strong oral tradition that could have morphed into the Atlantis myth recorded by Plato more than a thousand years later. The Santorini-Thera eruption is a classic example of a "natural–human" disaster.

Although the eruption had a VEI of between 6 and 7, this is relatively minor in purely geological terms. What made it particularly devastating was the presence of a large settled population on the island and the neighboring landmasses. The absence of human remains in the ruins suggests that the population had been evacuated before the final stages of the eruption blew the center of the island into the stratosphere and buried the rest under a sterilizing layer of volcanic ash and pumice. They were perhaps fortunate that their numbers were relatively small, and that they had enough vessels at hand to carry the whole population to the relative safety of Crete or the neighboring islands. Nevertheless, unlike later peoples who refused to leave their properties and possessions despite a very clear and present danger, such as a hurricane or a major forest fire, they left, preferring to save their lives rather than their material goods. And, as we have seen, the houses on Santorini-Thera were not mere shacks, but luxurious multi-story dwellings that would not look out of place in a modern seaside development. Perhaps the Atlanteans were an advanced race of superhumans after all.

DISASTER

Extinction Event

Tectonic Event

Military Action

Fire

Pandemic

Famine

Political or Economic Event

Genocide

Flood or Storm

Industrial or Transport Accident

THE FIRST "DARK AGES": BRONZE AGE COLLAPSE
ca. 1200–1150 BCE

Cause: Appearance of the Sea Peoples in the eastern Mediterranean

Event: Violent destruction of many major Bronze Age cultures

Aftermath: Social and economic dislocation, and the end of civilization and literacy in many areas for several centuries; first "Dark Ages" of human civilization

My father, behold, the enemy ships came; they burned my cities, and they did evil things in my country. Does not my father know that my army and chariots are in the Land of Hatti and my ships in the Land of Luka? Thus, the country is abandoned to itself. May my father know this: The seven ships of the enemy inflicted much damage upon us.

**Letter from King Ammurapi of Ugarit
to the ruler of Cyprus, 12th century BCE**

Many ancient cultures believed that humanity's happiest times were in the past, and that the future was dark and uncertain. The ancient Greek poet Hesiod (fl. mid-eighth century BCE) described four ages that predated his own "Iron Age." The first, the "Golden Age," was the happiest, when humans lived in harmony with the gods, did not work, grow crops, or wage war, and enjoyed long lives without illness or old age. This was succeeded by the "Silver," "Bronze," and "Heroic" Ages, each one a little harsher than its predecessor; until his own time, when humans had become evil, impious, and violent, and forsaken by the gods, their lives exemplified the much later saying "nasty, brutish, and short." A strong strand of pessimism was built into ancient Greek philosophy and religion: There was no heavenly reward for the virtuous, but only a dark, dreary, unchanging Underworld where the shades of the dead passed eternity in regret and sadness for their time on earth.

The irony that we can appreciate today is that Hesiod was alive at the beginning of one of Ancient Greece's most glorious epochs. Although he himself lived during Greece's Archaic period (800–480 BCE), this was to be the prelude to the great flowering of Hellenic civilization that we know today as Classical Greece (480–323 BCE), when the Greek city states, notably Athens, the birthplace of democracy, produced some of the world's greatest drama, art, architecture, and philosophy. For many later scholars, Western civilization's Golden Age was not some mythical past but Classical Athens under Perikles (ca. 495–429 BCE).

© UIG | Getty Images

IRONMAN
Nomadic invaders armed with superior iron weapons may have wrecked the Bronze Age empires.

Hesiod's pessimism as he surveyed his own time, was perhaps not entirely misplaced. The history of civilization is neither an inexorable slide into barbarism and decadence, as the Greeks saw it, nor an unstoppable progression toward universal health, wealth, and happiness, as the moderns believe. Both contrasting views are equally mistaken. Like the biological history of our planet, which we have glimpsed in the first two entries, the history of human civilization, in addition to its advances, has witnessed many sudden reversals and encountered many dead ends. To use a biological metaphor, human civilization has also experienced its own extinction events.

The term "Dark Ages" is applied to the period of European history that began after the collapse of the Western Roman Empire in 476 and lasted until the foundation of the Holy Roman Empire in 800. Although the period is now known more neutrally as the "Early Middle Ages," the popular impression remains of three centuries of barbarism when literacy and high culture vanished from Western Europe. But while Greco-Roman civilization did disappear from certain regions, in others the Church succeeded in preserving ancient learning in its monastic libraries, where it would be rediscovered by later generations.

There is a far darker time in the historical record than Europe's Dark or Early Middle Ages, when, across large parts of the Eastern Mediterranean, civilization was utterly destroyed; when pleading voices were silenced forever; when cities were sacked and burned, and their inhabitants slaughtered and scattered, so that even their names were forgotten for millennia. These were human civilization's first Dark Ages, and they were far grimmer for those who lived through them than the second, which themselves witnessed death and destruction on an epic scale. The event that triggered the first Dark Ages has been dubbed the "Bronze Age Collapse," which was not a slow imperial decline and fall, but a sudden human cataclysm that took less than fifty years, between 1200 and 1150 BCE.

"NO LAND COULD STAND BEFORE THEIR ARMS"

The historical Bronze Age (ca. 4th–1st millennia BCE) has nothing to do with Hesiod's mythical chronology. The terms "Stone," "Bronze," and "Iron" Ages, which make up the traditional chronology used to define the periods from prehistory to the Classical age, were devised in the early nineteenth century by the Danish antiquarian Christian Thomsen (1788–1865). He charted the history of civilization through the progression from stone tools and weapons, through copper, bronze, and finally iron and steel—although again this progression was more apparent than real and was based more on nineteenth-century preconceptions about progress than on the available archeological evidence.

Hesiod was not altogether mistaken when he characterized the Bronze Age as a time of military strife when brazen warriors were devoted to the god of war, Ares. During the preceding Chalcolithic (copper and stone) period human civilization underwent a dramatic transformation through its increasing use of and dependence on metals. Advances in technology and improvements in agricultural production allowed an unprecedented development of urban civilization in Egypt, the Near East, Asia Minor, and the Aegean region, giving rise to the world's first great empires, which became inextricably linked in complex trade networks, while at the same time they fought the first imperialist wars.

Much like mid-nineteenth-century Europe, when there was a balance of power between the major states, Bronze Age Egypt, Hatti (the Hittite Empire), Babylonia, Assyria, Minoan Crete, and Mycenaean Greece fought wars, but these were rarely all-out wars of conquest and annihilation, as these would have been far too costly and damaging for all. The bronze technology on which elites depended for their wealth and power imposed a certain level of cooperation between rival states. Bronze is an alloy of tin and copper, two metals that are rarely found together. The Bronze Age was the first period of globalization, with tin, copper, and other natural resources and manufactured goods traded across networks that spanned the whole of Europe, North Africa, and the Near East.

The previous entry showed how fragile these civilizations were when they experienced a major tectonic event: The Santorini-Thera eruption fatally weakened the Minoan economy, and in around 1450 BCE the Mycenaean Greeks conquered Minoan Crete. Historians believe that it was in the late Bronze Age that an alliance of Greek states besieged and destroyed the city of Troy in Asia Minor (now Turkey), an event immortalized in the *Iliad*, written by one of Hesiod's contemporaries, the poet Homer. But while Egypt, Hatti, and Assyria fought for dominion in the Levant, this little bubble of civilization was about to be burst by the first great man-made cataclysms of human history. Henceforth, humanity would rival volcanoes, floods, and earthquakes when it came to sheer destructiveness.

The Germanic and Scandinavian barbarians who conquered the Roman Empire are as well known to us as they were to the Romans. But in the thirteenth century BCE one or more peoples arrived in the eastern Mediterranean not to trade but to pillage and destroy. Known collectively as the "Sea Peoples," we can glimpse them in the records and chronicles of those states that survived their attacks, notably ancient Egypt. The Egyptians listed the Teresh, Ekwesh, Sherden, Shekelesh, Tekrur, Peleset, and Luka, which historians have tried to match to known Western European and Aegean peoples of the period, such as the ancient inhabitants of Sardinia, Sicily, and Italy, the Achaean Greeks, and the biblical Philistines. But beyond these possible identifications, little is known about the invaders, their motives, or their fate after the collapse.

Although they left no written records, the Sea Peoples were not savages in animal skins but had acquired military and seafaring capabilities that were at least equal or maybe even slightly superior to those of the Bronze Age states. An earlier generation of historians suggested that the Sea Peoples had iron technology that out matched the bronze weapons of their settled enemies. The end of the Bronze Age could be explained in terms of technological change. The archeological record, however, does not bear out this techno-positivist view of history. Iron technology was known to the great Bronze Age civilizations, but for a number of cultural and technological reasons, they themselves chose not to develop it.

SURVIVORS
Egypt was one of the few Bronze Age powers that managed to repulse the "Sea Peoples."

The Sea Peoples sacked and destroyed, usually abandoning their conquests, and more rarely settling among the ruins. In about half a century, the palace cities of Mycenaean Greece and the Aegean, the Hittite Empire, Cyprus, and the coastal states of the Near East had all been destroyed. The city of Ugarit, whose desperate last king, Ammurapi, is quoted on the opening page of this entry, was an important Bronze Age trading center on the Syrian coast with links to Egypt, Hatti, and the Aegean region. No one answered the king's pleas for help, because his allies were also under attack. Ugarit was sacked; its palaces, temples, and libraries burned—its very name forgotten until its ruins were rediscovered in 1928.

Greece entered a four-hundred-year period known as the "Greek Dark Ages," when urban culture and literacy disappeared. Only Assyria and Egypt survived, though much impoverished and weakened. Urban civilization and literacy re-emerged, and global trade resumed after centuries of darkness and chaos, but the citizens of this new age of gray iron tools and weapons half-remembered an earlier age of high art and learning, which, if not "golden," shone with the glow of another gilded metal, bronze.

THE END OF ETERNITY I: ALARIC'S SACK OF ROME

410 CE

DISASTER

Extinction Event

Tectonic Event

Military Action

Fire

Pandemic

Famine

Political or Economic Event

Genocide

Flood or Storm

Industrial or Transport Accident

Cause: Migration into the Roman Empire of Germanic and Scandinavian peoples, including the Goths, known to the Romans as "barbarians"

Event: First sack of Rome in eight centuries, by the Visigoths under their King Alaric I

Aftermath: Decline and collapse of the Western Roman Empire; the end of Classical antiquity; and the beginning of the Early Middle Ages

At the hour of midnight, the Salarian gate was silently opened, and the inhabitants were awakened by the tremendous sound of the Gothic trumpet. Eleven hundred and sixty-three years after the foundation of Rome, the imperial city, which had subdued and civilized so considerable a part of mankind, was delivered to the licentious fury of the tribes of Germany and Scythia.

Edward Gibbon,
The History of the Decline and Fall of the Roman Empire,
volume III, 1781

© Shutter1970 | Dreamstime

There are events of such symbolic importance that they resonate throughout history, sticking in the collective conscious in a manner that far outweighs the loss of life or material damage caused. Cities have been besieged, have fallen and been sacked since cities were first built, but very few are remembered: Homeric Troy, Jerusalem during the First Crusade, Paris in 1940, and the subject of this entry: Rome. In its long history, from its traditional foundation date of 753 BCE to its liberation from the Nazis in 1944, Rome has fallen to conquerors many times, but there is one sack of the "Eternal City" that still captures the communal imagination today: its first sack by barbarians in 410 CE.

© Creative Commons

VANDALISM
The Goths attacked the symbols of Roman power, including the Tomb of Augustus.

To understand the full significance of the sack of 410 CE, we have to look not just at what was going on in the fifth century, but also at what the event signified to the historians and political thinkers of later centuries, when Rome was no longer the capital of ancient empire, but the headquarters of the "Bishop of Rome"—the Pope, head of the Roman Catholic Church—and later still, during the Enlightenment, when its ancient system of government had become a political and social model. We also have to take account of our own prejudices and preconceptions. For the benefit of generations of children, history books have oversimplified the event, creating the following narrative: The barbarians invaded the decadent Roman Empire; they took Rome; the empire came to an end; the Dark Ages began. Of course, even a young child might pause to think: "If I am English, French, or German (or American, Australian, Canadian, etc. of European descent), then the savage barbarians—Angles, Franks, and Goths—who destroyed the Roman Empire are also my ancestors, of whom I am supposed to be proud."

We have quite a few threads to unravel, which will take us from late antiquity to the Age of Enlightenment, so we might as well begin with the historical background to the fall of Rome. The Roman Empire at the end of the fourth and in the early fifth centuries was very different from what it had been in its heyday in the first and second centuries CE under successful emperors such as Augustus (63 BCE–19 CE), Hadrian (76–138 CE), and Marcus Aurelius (121–180 CE). The Empire had not lost much territory, but it had suffered from severe economic, political, and social buffeting that almost saw its collapse during the "Crisis of the Third Century" (235–284), through a combination of civil wars, economic crises, and barbarian incursions.

The Emperor Diocletian (244–311) saved the empire and set it on a new course by dividing power between four rulers known as the "Tetrarchs." Although the system was unwieldy and did not survive the emperor's lifetime, it established the principle of divided imperial authority, which later became formalized in the division of the Western and Eastern Empires, with the border running roughly through the modern states of the former Yugoslavia. Although Rome was the capital of the western half, and retained its preeminent cultural and historical position as the birthplace of the empire, it had a strong rival in Constantinople (now Istanbul, Turkey), the "New Rome" founded in 330, and the capital of the Eastern Empire from the year 395.

The second major change that had taken place in the fourth century was the Christianization of the empire under Constantine the Great (272–337), who established religious toleration within the empire in 313. What this meant in practice was the promotion and protection of the formerly persecuted Christian minority, to that within eighty years Christianity would become the exclusive religion of both empires. These far-reaching transformations had not occurred peacefully, and the many civil wars of the period left the door open for Germanic and Scandinavian peoples to migrate into the empire, often because they themselves were being displaced by nomadic tribesmen from further east, such as the Huns. Although known as "barbarians" by the Romans, the Goths, Vandals, and Franks were far from the uncouth savages portrayed by unsympathetic Roman historians. In many cases they had been in contact with the empire for generations, sometimes employed as mercenaries by the Romans and invited to settle within the empire to bolster its falling population. Many were Christians, though not necessarily of a brand of Christianity considered orthodox by the Church: The Visigoths, for example, were Arians, a sect that the Church condemned as heretical.

The Visigoths were *foederati* (confederates), that is, not full Roman citizens but with a recognized status within the empire. They had served as mercenaries in Rome's civil wars and, as the empire in the West failed, their

PAGANS, CHRISTIANS, AND HERETICS

influence grew. Although successive emperors employed and depended on tribes such as the Goths, they treated them badly. The Emperor Theodosius the Great (347–395), the last to rule over a unified Roman world, had used the Goths under their leader and later king, Alaric I (370–410), as "catapult fodder," that is, using them as his shock troops, hoping not only to defeat his enemy but also to weaken the Goths themselves. In one battle, Alaric had lost 10,000 men, without getting what he felt was sufficient recompense or recognition from Theodosius.

In the early fifth century, feeling disgruntled, discriminated against, and mistreated, Alaric rebelled against Theodosius' two sons, who had divided the empire between them. After pillaging his way through Greece, he invaded Italy on three occasions, besieging Rome each time. On the first two occasions, he was satisfied with extorting money from the Senate. Alaric had no wish to destroy the empire: he merely wanted recognition for his past services and the grant of a secure homeland for his people. But by the third siege, Alaric wanted to teach the Romans a lesson. His third attempt to take Rome succeeded, either by a surprise attack, or according to Edward Gibbon (see quote on p. 31), when slaves opened one of the city's gates.

© UIG | Getty Images

WORLD'S END
The sack of Rome was seen as a sign of the impending end of the world.

The city fell and was looted. Compared to later sacks, however, it seems to have been a relatively mild event. The Visigoths were Christian, and they spared the main Christian churches and shrines and those who had sought refuge in them. They burned down the Roman Forum and desecrated the tombs of Rome's pagan emperors. After three days, Alaric withdrew his troops from the city and moved south, planning to invade Roman North Africa, but he died of fever en route.

THE CITY OF GOD

Rome is known as the "Eternal City" and a holy place of pilgrimage, but in the fifth century, despite the presence of the papacy, it stood for paganism and the old Roman order. Both pagans and Christians used the fall of Rome, the first in eight centuries, to claim the superiority of their respective faiths; the pagans blamed the sack on the neglect of the old gods; the Christians countered that it proved their impotence. But even among Christians, the event was seen as momentous. Christianity was still imbued with millenarianism, and many Christians saw the fall of Rome as the beginning of the "End of Days." According to Saint Augustine (354–430), with Rome, the "City of Man," in ruins, the only hope left to humans was to be found in the heavenly "City of God."

Although the empire staggered on for another sixty-six years, coming to an end with the abdication of the last ruler of the Western Empire, the psychological damage had been done. In the modern period, an event of similar magnitude might be the 9/11 Attack on the World Trade Center (pp. 216–221). Although itself not an event heralding the immediate end of U.S. power, 9/11 was for many an omen of the decline and ultimate fall of the "American Empire."

The 410 sack of Rome was an event that continued to resonate for centuries. In Europe, "Rome" had several contrasted political meanings: During and after the Reformation, "Rome" as the headquarters of the Roman Catholic Church, was equated with religious and political tyranny. But during the Age of Enlightenment, "Rome" the classical state was adopted as a model by those European countries that saw themselves as the true heirs of Classical values. In *The History of the Decline and Fall of the Roman Empire* the English historian Edward Gibbon (1737–94) managed to combine his admiration for the ancient Roman state with a violent attack on Catholicism, while still managing to defend the "noble" Germanic barbarians who were the ancestors of England's Germanic royal dynasty and her Protestant allies in Europe. In his description of the sack of 410, he compares the restraint shown by the Visigoths with the much more violent and bloody sack of the city in 1527 by the Spanish troops of the Catholic Holy Roman Emperor Charles V (1500–58).

Over the centuries, the sack of Rome has had many interpretations, serving many different, sometimes completely opposite political, social, and religious ends. The sack of the former imperial capital and subsequent breakup of the Western Empire can be considered as a disaster, because it signaled the transition from a multi-cultural, multi-ethnic, and relatively tolerant state to a group of intolerant, xenophobic, and racist kingdoms, whose endless political, social, and religious conflicts have cost millions of lives over the past 1,600 years.

DISASTER

Extinction Event

Tectonic Event

Military Action

Fire

Pandemic

Famine

Political or Economic Event

Genocide

Flood or Storm

Industrial or Transport Accident

LOST: COLLAPSE OF CLASSIC MAYA

800–900 CE

Cause: Overpopulation and ecological collapse; warfare; and social upheaval

Event: Destruction and abandonment of Classic Maya cities; population migration from the Petén to northern Yucatán

Aftermath: End of Classic Maya civilization; origin of Post-Classic Maya civilization

It has become increasingly evident that the Classic Maya were not a utopian peaceful people and that, in fact, the overall cultural trajectory of the Maya was directly related to warfare. Changes in frequency, techniques, and goals of warfare both parallel and impact Maya cultural development.

Arlen and Diane Chase,
Classic Maya Warfare and Settlement
Archaeology at Caracol, Belize, 2002

Two intrepid explorers, the American John Stevens (1805–52) and his British companion Frederick Catherwood (1799–1854), visited the Maya heartland, drawn by tales of fantastic "lost cities" in the rainforest. Stephens' *Travels in Central America, Chiapas, and Yucatan*, published in 1841, documented and illustrated many Classic Maya (ca. 250–900 CE) sites for the first time, and caused a sensation in the U.S. and Europe.

To say that the Maya had been "lost," however, was a little bit of an exaggeration—especially when their descendants still lived in the area; Post-Classic Maya (900–1550s) cities still existed in northern Yucatán at the time of the Spanish conquest; and several abandoned Classic sites were known from the beginning of the colonial period. It is very difficult to mislay a whole civilization, though there may be political, religious, or cultural reasons to do so. The Spanish conquistadors and colonial authorities (see pp. 52–57), who systematically destroyed the indigenous cultures of Central and South America, did not want anything to remind their Native American subjects of their glorious past achievements.

From the earliest days of the conquest to the present, Classic Maya civilization has been the most misrepresented and misunderstood culture on the planet. The Spanish, who saw them as idolatrous devil-worshippers, destroyed as much of their material culture as they could find, including their scientific and mathematical texts. European scholars who visited Classic and Post-Classic sites from the eighteenth century onward refused to believe that the ancestors of the surviving Maya, who were politically oppressed, deliberately impoverished, and forcibly converted to Catholicism, had been capable of producing an advanced civilization; instead, they invoked Egyptian, Mesopotamian, or even wandering Israelite migrants as the true architects of the Maya cities, whose buildings they compared with the Old World's pyramids and ziggurats. Without excusing it in any way, we should not be surprised at this shameful racism, as these scholars were part of an imperial-colonial establishment seeking to justify its own subjugation of Native American peoples on the grounds of the white man's supposed cultural and racial superiority.

In more enlightened times, the academic pendulum swung to the other extreme. While finally conceding that the Maya (and other pre-Columbian peoples) had developed independently from any external influences, Western scholars, critical of their own destructive imperialist-colonialist pasts, sought to characterize Classic Maya civilization as a rainforest Utopia—a peaceful confederation of city-states living in harmony with its natural environment—whose astronomer-priests spent their days studying the heavens from atop their gorgeously stuccoed and painted pyramids, creating a complex calendar for the sheer pleasure of astronomy and pure mathematics. This begged an important question: Why, after 750 years of this idyllic existence, had the Maya abandoned their cities and migrated *en masse* northward, where they had established a second civilization which, as can be clearly seen from its architecture and iconography, was undeniably aggressive and warlike? For the most diehard Utopian Mayanists, this suggested a natural or human disaster—an extended drought or pandemic, or an outside invasion—that had fatally upset the equilibrium of Maya life.

Although archeologists have long abandoned this rose-tinted view of the Classic Maya and what led to the collapse of their civilization, we need to mention yet another type of misrepresentation, whose latest manifestation is the much-publicized "2012 Maya Prophecy." These fantasies tie in with preposterous claims that the Maya a) were the descendants of refugees from Atlantis and/or b) had been visited and civilized by an advanced race of space aliens. Never mind that we have complete sequences of Pre-Classic buildings, tracing their evolution from simple Pre-Classic earth platforms to the elaborate Classic pyramid-and-palace complexes. Unfortunately, careful archeological research, unlike an unsupported claim that an image engraved on a Maya king's sarcophagus lid shows him "piloting a spacecraft," does not sell books.

THE COLLAPSE HABIT

The last thirty years of research into the Maya, though it does not claim conclusively to solve the puzzle of the Classic Maya collapse, has definitely come up with a range of plausible explanations. It's worth noting that archeology and history are not exact sciences, and that there are many much more recent events that we cannot fully explain or understand, but that do not cause us to invoke the intervention of survivors from imaginary lost continents or aliens in flying saucers.

One of the most interesting discoveries about the Maya is that they had experienced an earlier collapse at the end of the Pre-Classic period in the first centuries CE. Just as in the Classic collapse, the major urban centers of the Pre-Classic were abandoned and never reoccupied. The greater historical distance makes the interpretation of the evidence even more difficult than with the Classic collapse, but some archeological finds suggest that similar processes may have been at work in this earlier collapse event.

A good place to start is to explore the ecology of the Petén region. Although it is now under threat from deforestation, for most of the past millennium the area has been covered by rainforest. Although furnished with several rivers and lakes, the area is extremely short of dependable water supplies during the dry season. The soil is thin, and the traditional mode of agriculture is slash-and-burn cultivation, in which an area, once planted and harvested, must be left fallow for several years to recover its fertility. Such environments can only support small numbers of inhabitants, and the current population of the Petén is 337,000.

The Classic Maya heartland is far from being ideal agricultural land, and ecological collapse, caused by overexploitation of the area's resources, aggravated by a natural disaster such as a drought, has always been in the frame to explain the abandonment of Classic sites. The Maya, however, managed to survive in this unpromising environment for thousands of years. They built huge networks of cisterns to store water during the dry season, and they must have found ways effectively to manage the land to maximize production, through irrigation, crop rotation, and soil enrichment (i.e., recycling human waste).

WARLORDS
Far from being peace-loving astronomers, the Maya were bloodthirsty warriors.

The most recent population estimate for the height of the Classic period of around 10 million shows how successful they must have been. However, there must have come a point when even the best agricultural practices were no longer sufficient, and the productive ecology of the area was strained to breaking point. The landscape would not have been one of patches of open ground around the major cities and fields within the dense forested canopy as we see today, but the entire region would have been cleared and turned over to farming and settlement. After the forest had been cleared, natural food sources would have disappeared, leaving the Maya to depend entirely on what they could grow themselves. At this stage, even a minor drought could have caused significant problems, leading to famine, epidemics, and social dislocation.

While ecological collapse through overexploitation must be the primary reason why the Maya abandoned their homes and left the region en masse, we need to explain why, when faced with a worsening situation, the rulers of the various cities did not get together and agree, in the interests of all, that a certain proportion of the population would migrate, allowing some settlement of the area to continue. This presupposes that Maya rulers were capable of cooperation and altruistic behavior. Sadly, the available evidence points to the exact opposite. Maya society was organized around warfare in order to obtain captives for ritual sacrifice. Unlike the Aztecs of Mexico, who had a democratic approach to human sacrifice—preferring quantity over quality—the Maya believed that only noble blood, and royal blood in particular, had the potency required to nourish the gods.

© Thinkstock

LOST AND FOUND
Not so much lost as forgotten, the Maya's cities have now been cleared.

In short, the Maya elites were completely incapable of cooperating in the interests of the greater good. When faced by shortages of food, land, water, and natural resources, their solution was to go to war with their neighbors and take what they lacked. In 629, Tikal, one of the two superpowers of the Classic Petén, established a military outpost, Dos Pilas, specifically to control trade routes in the area and raid neighboring states. Dos Pilas broke away from Tikal, but it never developed an agricultural or trading infrastructure of its own, and, until its destruction, lived by predating on weaker states, including its own parent, Tikal.

By the eighth century, the whole Maya area was experiencing a major systemic collapse. Warfare continued, ever more violently, as many cities were destroyed and abandoned, and others erected makeshift fortifications. But when all were starving and there was nothing left to steal, it is thought that the hitherto silent majority—the peasants who fed and clothed the divine Maya kings and built their elaborate palaces and pyramids—rebelled and slaughtered the masters who had failed them so badly. By the year 900, all the major Classic sites had been abandoned apart from a few squatters living among the ruins. Soon even they would shun the dead cities and leave them to be reclaimed by the rainforest.

"A THIRD OF THE WORLD DIED": BLACK DEATH

1346–51

Cause: Outbreak of bubonic plague thought to have begun in Central Asia

Event: Death of up to one-third of the global population

Aftermath: Persecution of religious minorities, including the destruction of many Jewish communities in Europe; chronic labor shortages increased social mobility and speeded up the monetization of the economy; the Church lost its absolute hold on the population

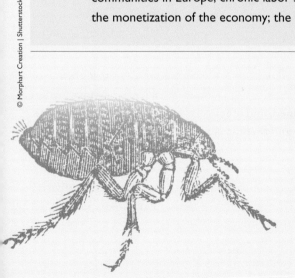

© Morphart Creation | Shutterstock

Clement VI calculated the number of dead in Christian Europe at 23,840,000. With a preplague population of about 75 million, Clement's figure accounts for mortality of 31%—a rate about midway between the 50% mortality estimated for East Anglia, Tuscany, and parts of Scandinavia, and the less-than-15% morbidity for Bohemia and Galicia. And it is unerringly close to Froissart's claim that "a third of the world died."

Robert Gottfried,
***Black Death,* 1985**

The particularly chilling title of this entry, "A third of the world died," is taken from the work of the French chronicler of England and France's Hundred Years' War (1337–1453), Jean Froissart (ca. 1337–ca. 1405). Following Froissart, Pope Clement VI (1291–1352) estimated that the fourteenth-century outbreak of the plague *(Yersinia pestis)* known as the "Black Death" killed almost 24 million Europeans within five years from when the disease reached Sicily, in 1347, until 1351, when the plague had burned itself out in Western Europe.

If the one-third mortality rate is the total losses from a pandemic thought to have begun in the late 1330s in Central or East Asia, then global mortality may have been as high as 150 million victims, given a world population at the time of 450 million. Even if the Black Death only killed 10 percent of the population (45 million souls), we are still dealing with apocalyptic human losses, the scale of which would not be matched until the wars of the twentieth century. To those living through the outbreak, it must have seemed that the calamitous predictions of the book of Revelation were coming to pass. To put these numbers into a contemporary context: One-third of the current population of the U.S. is 105 million, one-third of the population of the EU, 167.5 million, and one-third of the global population, 2.3 billion.

© Creative Commons

INFECTED
Without proper disease control, the pandemic ran riot throughout medieval towns.

Like other disasters that are sometimes classed as "natural," the Black Death is more correctly a "natural–human" disaster. A natural disaster is one in which human action or omission of action is irrelevant to the causes or outcome of the event. Hence, an asteroid strike on December 21, 2012, however unlikely, would be a completely natural disaster. But an epidemic, much less a pandemic, could not occur without the intervention of humans, and their severity has often been affected by human action or inaction. Infectious diseases caused by bacteria or viruses have always afflicted humans but their prevalence and virulence was transformed by an event that took place worldwide some 10,000 years BP, when humans began to settle and farm rather than live as nomadic hunter-gatherers. With widespread settlement came two factors promoting the transmission of pathogens: the concentration of population itself and inter-community trading networks. Other factors affecting a disease outbreak are the state of medical knowledge at the time, the availability and effectiveness of medical treatments, and the imposition of quarantines and other disease-control measures.

The World Health Organization (WHO) does not use the terms "epidemic" and "pandemic," but prefers the term "disease outbreak." The WHO defines a disease outbreak as "the occurrence of cases of disease in excess of what would normally be expected in a defined community, geographical area or season [....] caused by an agent not previously recognized in that community or area, or the emergence of a previously unknown disease." It may be medically accurate, but it fails to express the magnitude of the Black Death, so let's refer to it as a pandemic.

If you'd lived in the fourteenth century, a minor parasitic skin irritation wouldn't have registered on your health radar. The animal hosts of the plague bacillus, *Yersinia pestis*, are small mammals, including rodents, and their fleas. The plague comes in three deadly variants: "bubonic," in which the bacteria are transmitted via the bite of infected fleas, resulting in swollen lymph nodes known as buboes; "septicemic," the blood-borne form of the disease without buboes; and "pneumonic," the rare but deadly airborne form of the disease. Incubation of the plague takes between three and seven days, and untreated cases have a mortality rate of 30–60 percent.

We have records of several major "plagues" before the Black Death, but these were probably not caused by *Yersinia pestis* but by other pathogens such as measles, influenza, and smallpox. "Plague" derives from the Latin *plaga*, meaning "blow" or "wound," which later took on the meaning of an outbreak of any infectious disease. But there is one ancient epidemic that many scholars now believe was an early outbreak of bubonic plague: the "Plague of Justinian," named for the ruling emperor of the day, Justinian I (483–565).

THE END OF THE ROMAN DREAM

We left the wreck of the Western Roman Empire in the smoking ruins of Rome in 410 (see pp. 31–35), but the Eastern Roman or Byzantine Empire, with its capital in Constantinople (formerly Byzantium), would endure for another thousand years. With a more compact territory made up of the wealthiest provinces of the old Roman world, the Byzantines recovered from the chaos of the fifth century and once again became the dominant power in the Mediterranean. The Eastern emperors had never abandoned their claim to suzerainty over the whole Roman Empire, and Justinian intended to make good his claim with military might. In a series of brilliant campaigns, Justinian's leading general, Belisarius (ca. 500–565), regained much of North Africa, Italy, and southern Spain for his master.

We can imagine another intriguing "what-if" scenario: Had Justinian and his successors managed to reconquer and hold the whole of Western Europe, the damaging schism between the Greek Orthodox and Roman Catholic Churches might never have taken place, and a stronger, united Christendom might have been able to resist the rise of Islam and Arab wars of conquest (632–750). At this critical juncture, however, there occurred one of those terrible events that shake the very foundations of civilization. In 541, the plague arrived in Constantinople, probably from Egypt. At its height, the disease was killing between 5,000 and 10,000 people a day in the capital. Historians estimate that up to 40 percent of the city's population and 25 percent of the population of the eastern Mediterranean perished in the initial outbreak.

Although there are many other factors—social, cultural, economic, political, and military—that prevented the reunification of the two halves of the Roman Empire in the sixth century, the Plague of Justinian must rank high as a cause of the subsequent decline of the Byzantine state, which lost much of its territory to militant Islam during the seventh and eighth centuries and only began to recover in the ninth.

RING A RING O' ROSES

Although modern scholarship now discounts the link between the singing game "Ring a Ring o' Roses" and the Black Death, the image of a group of children dancing in a ring and falling down, as if struck dead, remains a powerful image that is evocative of the sudden death that took the lives of millions—young and old, fit and sickly, rich and poor, without distinction. The Florentine poet Boccaccio (1313–75) lamented: "How many valiant men, how many fair ladies, breakfasted with their kinfolk and the same night supped with their ancestors in the next world! [….] They sickened by the thousands daily, and died unattended and without help."

Historians have traced the origins of the European outbreak of the worldwide plague pandemic to the Mongol siege of the Genoese trading port of Caffa in the Black Sea in 1346. The Mongols, a nomadic people from Central Asia, conquered a vast empire stretching from China to Eastern

Europe during the thirteenth and fourteenth centuries. Their conquest not only allowed an unprecedented flow of trade and ideas along the Silk Route between China and the Near East, but also gave free passage to Central Asian rodents and their plague-carrying fleas. When the plague broke out among the besieging army, the Mongols catapulted the corpses of plague victims into the city in an early attempt at biological warfare.

The Genoese took to their ships and sailed back to Europe, carrying the plague with them. They first infected Constantinople in 1346 and then Sicily in 1347. The effects of the Black Death were immediate and catastrophic. There are no exact statistics for the death toll from the outbreak, but 30 percent mortality would match the WHO's lower morbidity figure quoted above. Medieval historian Philip Daileader gave a much higher estimate, claiming that about half of the European population perished between 1347 and 1351, but with large variations between town and country, as well as between different European countries: as high as 80 percent in Italy, Spain, and Provence, and as low as 20 percent in parts of England, the Netherlands, and Germany.

© Creative Commons

THE GREAT LEVELER
Young and old, male and female, rich and poor—the plague spared none.

As concentrations of humans are particularly vulnerable to epidemic diseases, the overcrowded, unsanitary cities of Medieval Europe were very badly affected, with half of the population of Paris, Florence, and Hamburg perishing in the first few years. Germ theory would not be discovered until the nineteenth century, and medieval doctors believed that epidemic diseases were spread by "miasma" (foul-smelling or bad air). To protect himself from the plague the "beak doctor" wore a floor-length coat, leggings, boots, gloves, and hat made of waxed leather. His sinister outfit was topped with a mask in the shape of a bird's head, complete with a long curved beak. The mask was a kind of primitive respirator, and the beak was packed with dried flowers, herbs, spices, and camphor, that were believed to prevent contagion.

Like modern New Age practitioners who put their faith in positive thinking, pseudo-science, and magic, the beak doctor had no effective treatments to offer. The victims, often weakened by hunger and other diseases, died quickly. With no disease-control laws in place, when the plague struck

QUACK!
The sinister bird mask was
packed with herbs supposed
to prevent infection

**EUROPE
REBORN**

a city, civic authority disappeared. The beleaguered citizens either locked themselves away in their homes to pray and hope the epidemic would spare them, or engaged in an orgy of hedonistic debauchery to enjoy what little time was left to them. Many fled the cities, carrying the plague with them to uninfected areas. If there ever was an object lesson on how not to deal with a major pandemic, the Black Death remains the one shining example.

Unfortunately, there was worse to come. To the medieval mind, an epidemic must either be the work of an angry deity or of evil men. Groups of religious fanatics, known as the "flagellants" from the whips they carried to scourge themselves, attempted to assuage divine anger by shedding their own blood. Others blamed the Jews, accusing them of spreading the plague by poisoning wells, which led to massacres of Jewish communities all over Western Europe. In an aside, people slaughtered domestic cats as potential plague carriers, killing the main predators of the rodents that were the real hosts of the disease.

It would take the European population a century and a half to recover from the Black Death. But Europe, once the epidemic had burned itself out, emerged reinvigorated from the disaster. For all its apparent energy and self-confidence, Europe in the first half of the fourteenth century was a civilization in deep crisis. Overpopulation combined with a "little ice age" had caused widespread famines; society was politically oppressed by the feudal nobility and intellectually repressed by the Church.

The sudden collapse in population broke the vicious cycle of famine and economic stagnation. Historians point to the post-pandemic period as the starting point of Western capitalism. Labor was in short supply, and peasants, once tied to the land, were now hired for wages, which led to the monetization of the economy, and improved living standards for the peasantry; the high mortality rates across all classes promoted social mobility; and the failure of the Church to avert the disaster put its absolute authority into question. Together these factors would lead to the flowering of art, philosophy, science, and technology known as the European Renaissance.

DISASTER

Extinction Event

Tectonic Event

Military Action

Fire

Pandemic

Famine

Political or Economic Event

Genocide

Flood or Storm

Industrial or Transport Accident

THE END OF ETERNITY II: MEHMET THE CONQUEROR TAKES CONSTANTINOPLE

1453

Cause: Conquest of the provinces of the Byzantine Empire by the Ottoman Turks

Event: Capture of Constantinople after a six-week siege; sack of the city; death of Emperor Constantine XI

Aftermath: End of the Byzantine Empire and of the Christian East; Ottoman advance into Eastern Europe; Byzantine scholars flee to Europe, bringing with them many ancient Greek texts unknown in the West

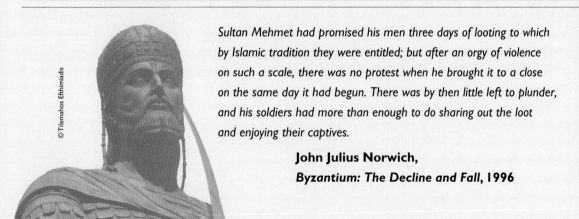

© Tilemahos Efthimiadis

Sultan Mehmet had promised his men three days of looting to which by Islamic tradition they were entitled; but after an orgy of violence on such a scale, there was no protest when he brought it to a close on the same day it had begun. There was by then little left to plunder, and his soldiers had more than enough to do sharing out the loot and enjoying their captives.

John Julius Norwich,
Byzantium: The Decline and Fall, 1996

We have reached the third entry that features the "end" of the Roman Empire—along with the entry on the sack of Rome (pp. 31–35) and the previous sixth-century Plague of Justinian, which ended the dream of a

reunited Roman world. The empire, as befits such a significant and long-lasting state, took a long time to die. Depending on where you draw the line, the empire spanned either 500 years or 1,500 years. Many historians date the demise of the empire to 476 CE, with the abdication of the last Western emperor. But for "Romans" living in the eastern half, the empire survived for another millennium.

PROTECTOR
For 700 years, the Byzantine Empire was the West's bulwark against Islam.

Although the state religion of the empire had changed, an emperor still sat on the throne by divine right, reigning with the support of a senate in accordance with legal codes set down by the emperors of a united Roman Empire. While they could see the radical breaks with the past, they could also see the continuities with Classical Rome's values, art, and ideals.

The Eastern Empire gradually substituted its Latin linguistic culture with Greek—the mother tongue of the majority of the citizens of the Hellenized eastern Mediterranean. But the emperor in Constantinople, while he might have replaced the Latin *imperator* with the Greek *basileus*, remained *basileus Rhomaion*, "emperor of the Romans," until the sixteenth century. After the conquests of Justinian (483–565), the empire entered a protracted period of decline. Historians point to the devastating plague that struck the empire during his reign, and also to the economic exhaustion caused by his efforts to reconquer the West. Nevertheless, the empire, referred to as Byzantine Empire (from Byzantium, the former name of Constantinople), remained the major power in the Mediterranean.

While its fortunes in the West waxed and waned, the empire's main military adversary was Sassanid Persia. The two empires—Christian Byzantium and Zoroastrian Persia—fought war after war for over a century. Each side scored major successes against the other, until the Emperor Heraclius (ca. 575–641) finally ended the conflict with a decisive victory at the Battle of Nineveh in 627. Persia sued for peace and Heraclius was fêted in Constantinople as the new Julius Caesar. The Byzantine triumph was short-lived, because within a few years the armies of militant Islam had overrun Egypt and the Near Eastern provinces of the empire, and in the next century threatened the capital on two occasions. Each time the Arab armies were repulsed by Constantinople's defensive walls, and also the Arab fleets by "Greek fire"—a now lost cocktail of petroleum, asphalt, and other inflammable ingredients that was the napalm of its day.

The Byzantines never recovered Egypt or North Africa, but they managed to hold off the Arabs armies and shield Western Europe. A series of able rulers such as Emperor Alexius I (1056–1118) stabilized and reorganized a much smaller empire, centered on Constantinople and encompassing Thrace, Greece, and parts of Asia Minor (now Turkey). This more defensible and socially homogeneous empire was able to resist any further incursions from the east, including the Mongol invasions of the thirteenth century. But by then the greatest threat to Byzantium was not from the Islamic East but from an ungrateful Christian West.

The Greek Orthodox Church, led by the Patriarch of Constantinople, and the Catholic Church, led by the Pope in Rome, had been diverging for centuries. It was not just a question of language, though this played a major part, but also of dogma, and, of course, politics. While the papacy had been dependent on Constantinople for its survival, it had toed the imperial line in all matters religious. But when the Pope had crowned an emperor of his own, he saw no need to kowtow to Constantinople. The rift between the two churches became official with the Great Schism of 1054. Henceforth, the two Christian churches and their sectarians each viewed the other as heretics that were just as feared and hated as the common Muslim enemy.

The mutual distrust and occasional hostilities between the Western European states and the empire culminated in the greatest betrayal of one Christian power by another, when during the Fourth Crusade (1202–4), Western European crusaders, led by the Doge of Venice, took Constantinople, mercilessly sacked the city, including its holiest shrines, churches, monasteries, and convents, and established the Latin Empire of Constantinople. This event has gone down through history as the "Great Betrayal of 1204." The Byzantines set up their own successor states in Asia Minor and Greece, and managed to retake Constantinople and re-establish a semblance of their former empire in 1261. Byzantine power,

THE GREAT BETRAYAL OF 1204

however, had been broken just when the empire had to face a new threat from the East, the Ottoman Turks.

The Turkic Seljuk Sultanate of Rum (Rome), which ruled much of Anatolia, began to disintegrate in the second half of the thirteenth century, making way for a number of successor states, including an emirate led by Osman I (1258–1328), for whom the Ottoman Dynasty and Empire are named. Originally a Central Asian Turkic tribe, the Ottomans were unknown in Europe until 1227 when the Seljuk sultans employed them as mercenaries. Osman was a visionary who conceived of a vast empire encompassing North Africa, Europe, and the Near East. His own conquests were fairly modest but his heirs expanded Ottoman power in Anatolia and the Balkans until they had surrounded Constantinople—the ultimate prize and the future capital of their empire.

The city could have fallen to the Ottomans as early as 1400, but they were thrown into confusion when their sultan was defeated in battle and captured by another would-be world conqueror, Timur (better known as Tamerlane; 1336–1405). It took the Ottomans fofty years to recover fully from the defeat and ensuing civil war. The true heir of Osman's vision of empire, Mehmet II (1432–81), dubbed "The Conqueror," ascended the throne in 1451. His priority was to take Constantinople, which in his eyes was tantamount to being recognized as the rightful ruler of the whole Roman Empire.

Byzantine emperors were aware of the danger they faced, and in a dramatic reversal of fortune, several incumbents traveled to Europe in the early fifteenth century to beg the Pope and European sovereigns for help against the Ottoman threat. Having no money or power of their own, they offered the only thing that could sway the Pope: an end to the schism between the Greek and Latin churches, on the Pope's terms. Even with their city threatened by Muslims, the Byzantines resisted the proposed church union, one of their leaders declaring: "Rather the sultan's turban than the cardinal's hat!"

Although the city was impoverished and depopulated, it still possessed some of the most superb natural and man-made defenses of any major city of the medieval world. Constantinople is surrounded on three sides by water: a broad inlet to the north called the Golden Horn that could be closed off with a massive chain strung from the city walls to the fortified

Genoese suburb of Galata on the opposite shore; the headland juts into the Bosphorus; and to the south is the Sea of Marmara—the whole coastline is defended by a sea wall, the treacherous currents, and the small fleet that the Byzantines still had at their disposal.

Sections of the land walls—actually two walls with moats built by Theodosius the Great (347–395)—can still be seen today, though they have now been swallowed by the city sprawl of modern Istanbul. With the exception of the capture of the city in 1204, the walls had proved effective against ancient barbarians, Arabs, Bulgars, Russians, and, in the early fifteenth century, an earlier five-year siege by the Ottomans. But Mehmet was determined to succeed where other would-be conquerors had failed. He fielded an army of around 80,000 and a fleet of 90 ships against Emperor Constantine XI's (1404–53) army of 7,000 Byzantine, Genoese, and mixed Western European allies and his fleet of 26 warships. Although the odds seemed to be overwhelmingly in Mehmet's favor, several historians have argued that Constantinople's fall was not a foregone conclusion because of the city's superb defenses.

© Art Renewal

CONQUERORS
With the best defences of the period, the fall of the city was not a foregone conclusion.

There are several detailed descriptions of the siege, two of which are cited in the Further Reading section (pp. 252–256), which will take you on an emotional roller coaster. Mehmet famously deployed the largest cannon of the age in his attack to try and breech the land walls, but in the end it was the sheer determination of the Ottoman infantry that won the day. The last emperor of the Romans died fighting to save his capital, and the city was given over to the traditional sack by the victorious army.

RIP the Roman Empire—finally—as all later claimants to the title were spurious. But, as with the Black Death, the effects of the fall of Constantinople were not all disastrous: The Ottomans achieved their dream of an empire that stretched from the Atlas to the Caucasus, which would endure until 1922, and the West gained immeasurably as fleeing Byzantine scholars brought with them priceless knowledge and Greek manuscripts preserved from antiquity. If the Black Death had prepared the ground for the European Renaissance, the Byzantine refugees of 1453 brought with them many of the literary, scientific, and philosophical seeds that would grow and bear fruit in the following decades.

DISASTER

Extinction Event

Tectonic Event

Military Action

Fire

Pandemic

Famine

Political or Economic Event

Genocide

Flood or Storm

Industrial or Transport Accident

THE BLACK REALITY: DEMOGRAPHIC COLLAPSE IN THE AMERICAS

16th century onward

Cause: Invasion and colonization of the Americas by Europeans

Event: Continent-wide pandemic of Old World diseases; massacres by settlers; use of Native Americans as slave labor; deaths from starvation, suicide, and mistreatment

Aftermath: Collapse of Native American populations to between 5 and 10 percent of their pre-Columbian levels

Later, when the Spaniards had inflicted extraordinary abominations on the city of Mexico and the other cities and towns, over a surface of fifteen or twenty leagues, killing countless Indians, they pressed forward to spread terror and lay waste the province of Pánuco, where an amazing number of people were slain.

Bartolomé de las Casas,
The Devastation of the Indies:
A Brief Account, 1552

The history of the European conquest and colonization of the Americas involved every major Western European maritime power—from the Protestant north to the Catholic south—but it was the Spanish who reached the Americas first (if you the ignore the contested landings by Vikings and Irish monks), and it fell to them to be the first to make contact with the sophisticated urban cultures of the Americas. The first phase of colonization saw the Spanish and Portuguese settle Central and South America, and the second, the French, Dutch, and English, the northern half of the continent. Although the Native American population in North America was far smaller and more dispersed, the demographic collapse was just as marked and tragic in both halves of the continent.

The year 1492 witnessed two major points in world history: Christopher Columbus (1451–1506), "sailed the ocean blue," and the Crown of Castile completed the *Reconquista* (Reconquest) of Spain, expelling the last Muslim ruler of Granada. A self-confident, victorious, militaristic Castile was ready to go on the offensive against the Muslim world; but instead of a crusade against Islam, it found itself in possession of a vast new continent, initially mistaken for East Asia. The Treaty of Tordesillas (1494) between the crowns of Spain and Portugal reserved the eastern route to the East Indies for Portugal, and granted the still non-existent (Western) passage to the East to Spain.

© De Agostini | Getty Images

ON TRIAL
Disappointed by the lack of gold in the West Indies, the Spanish crown put Columbus on trial.

Initially, the Spanish must have been disappointed with their new realm, which effectively blocked the westward trading route to Asia. The West Indies, or Greater and Lesser Antilles, including Hispaniola (now Haiti and the Dominican Republic), Puerto Rico, Jamaica, and Cuba, had neither spices nor the vast quantities of gold that Europeans believed were to be found in Asia. Instead they encountered Native Americans, who were not interested in becoming good Catholic subjects of the Spanish Crown. There are no reliable figures for the pre-Columbian population of the Antilles. According to Bartolomé de las Casas (1474–1556), Bishop of Chiapas, and the author of the *Brevísima relación de la destrucción de las Indias* (usually translated as The Devastation of the Indies: A Brief Account) published in 1552, the Taino Native American population of Hispaniola crashed from 3 million to 60,000 between 1494 and 1508. Several modern population studies have revised the figure downward, estimating the island's population before the arrival of Columbus to be between 100,000 and 1 million.

Regardless of the actual numbers involved, the Antilles established the tragic pattern of European–Native American relations that would be followed throughout the conquest and colonization of the Americas, both North and South. Although, in the early years of colonization, there would have been far too few Europeans to resist an all-out assault by the native peoples of the islands, the Spanish skillfully exploited tribal and ethnic divisions to divide, conquer, rule, and then exterminate.

Once established and supported by native allies, the Spanish indentured most of the population through the *encomienda* system, which, though represented as a reciprocal arrangement of labor in exchange for protection, care, and education, was really a form of slavery. The Taino and other native peoples of the Caribbean realized too late that their new masters expected nothing less than total submission and the extinction of their culture, religion, and way of life. The subsequent Native American rebellions were ruthlessly repressed with mass executions and massacres. Fatalities from military actions and mistreatment probably accounted for tens of thousands of deaths, but the real cause of the Taino population collapse was disease.

THE COLUMBIAN EXCHANGE

In the earlier entry on the Black Death (pp. 41–46), we saw the devastating killing power of a plague pandemic, when a single outbreak of the disease killed around 30 percent of the population of Eurasia. And the plague was only one of the many epidemic diseases that regularly visited the Old World, along with typhus, smallpox, whooping cough, measles, mumps, cholera, and influenza, though these were not on the scale of the Black Death. Many epidemic diseases have animal hosts or vectors—the rat flea, for example. And in Eurasia, pre-modern humans lived in close proximity to their animals, and were therefore prone to animal-to-human infections. A modern example is the H1N1 avian flu virus, which many fear will cause the next major pandemic. Over the centuries, however, repeated exposure to epidemic diseases, though it killed millions, at the same time created a population that was, if not immune, at least much more resistant to infectious diseases.

In contrast, in Central America there were no large herds of domesticated animals. The Aztec and Maya had no sheep or cattle for meat, milk, and wool, and no horses, donkeys, or bullocks for transport or plowing. This put them at a serious disadvantage: Their diet was more restricted, which made them less resistant to disease than Europeans and lowered their fertility, while at the same time they had much weaker immunity to diseases transmitted by animal vectors.

The land bridge between Siberia and Alaska—the main human migration route into the Americas—became impassable around 15,000 years BP. Even if the far north of the continent had been visited by Vikings in the tenth century, they had not established permanent settlements, and their impact on the Native American population was minimal, especially in terms of the transmission of European diseases. For all intents and purposes, Native Americans developed in isolation from the rest of the world. As the colonization of the Americas predated agriculture and urban settlement, it also predated the major epidemic outbreaks associated with large population concentrations in Eurasia, though there were also epidemic diseases associated with Native Americans once they, too, had ceased being nomadic.

© Creative Commons

Medical knowledge in Europe had not advanced since the Black Death, and infectious disease was still understood as being caused by polluted air, triggering an imbalance in the body's four "humors." The common treatments of the day— bleeding, cupping, and various purges—were more likely to kill the patient than help him recover. Native American medicine, while maybe more benign, was just as ineffective against bacteria and viruses. With no quarantines, vaccinations, or disease-control mechanisms, Europeans infected with the full Pandora's Box of Old World diseases, including smallpox, plague, and cholera, arrived in the Antilles, quickly infecting the native population. The Taino, already demoralized, oppressed, and half starved, died in their hundreds of thousands or, as some accounts say, millions.

FAIR EXCHANGE
While Europeans took deadly diseases to the Americas, Europe had gotten syphilis in exchange.

The Europeans, however, did not escape retribution. There were epidemic diseases in the Americas to which they had never been exposed, including the sexually transmitted infection syphilis. Exposure to a totally new pathogen increases its virulence and morbidity. Large numbers of Europeans contracted syphilis and died, but not before bringing it back to Europe, where it quickly took on epidemic proportions. Syphilis, or the "pox," was the HIV-AIDS of its day because it was sexually transmitted, and, until the discovery of antibiotics, incurable. This cross-infectivity between Europe and the Americas is known as the "Columbian Exchange"—a name suggesting a rather jolly form of cultural activity rather than the transmission of deadly pathogens between the Old and New Worlds. Unfortunately, in this one instance, the Old World gave a lot more than it took.

Driven by dreams of El Dorado, the conquistadors smashed their way into Central America in 1519, and the Andean region a decade later. In each case the Spanish strategy was the same: Exploit divisions among the ruling elites and different ethnic groups; overawe the native peoples with superior technology; and terrify them with genocidal atrocities. At the same time their silent and deadly allies, the epidemic diseases, rode with them. The most reliable population estimates for the Mexica-Aztec Empire is around 15 million, and six million for the Inca Empire. Estimates for mortality rates from military actions, mistreatment, and disease have been calculated to be as high as 90 to 95 percent in the most badly affected areas. The Native American population of the Caribbean was almost totally wiped out, and had to be replaced by imported slave labor from Africa (see pp. 62–66). In Mexico, the native population dropped to around 1 to 1.5 million, with a similar reduction in the most populated areas of Yucatán and the Andean region.

BURIED MY HEART AT WOUNDED KNEE

The situation north of the Rio Grande was scarcely better, though the isolation, lower population densities, and hunter-gatherer lifestyles of many Native North Americans and First Peoples meant that the deadly progress of epidemic diseases was slower than in Mexico and Peru. In the early conquest and colonization of North America, in addition to many of the abuses seen in the Spanish New World, there was the added complication of competing European powers—the French and British, and for a short time the Dutch—using Native American allies to attack one another.

Smallpox in particular killed many of the Native North American peoples of the United States and Canada, and settlers, often aided by national or state governments, completed the process of ethnic cleansing and expropriation of Native American land. Although doctors would not identify the viral causes of smallpox until the middle of the nineteenth century, there is one well-attested story, during a mid-eighteenth-century war against the Pontiac people of American colonists and British army officers conspiring to send blankets used by smallpox victims to Native Americans in the hope that they would become infected with the disease.

The demographic collapse in the Americas is a human disaster unmatched until the genocides carried out by totalitarian regimes during the twentieth century. Although now it should rank among the great genocides and ethnic cleansings of all time, it rarely merits more than a historical footnote. The reader could argue that this is because of the historical distance between the sixteenth century and our own time, but collective guilt might well play a part. Any Europeans or Americans of European descent are implicit in the destruction of pre-Columbian Native American civilizations and the huge loss of life that accompanied it. Could it be another case of to the victor, the spoils, and to the winner, the right to write the history books?

BUILDING ON SAND: SHAANXI EARTHQUAKE

1556

Cause: Earthquake (MMS 7.9–8)

Event: Deadliest earthquake in history, with a death toll estimated at 830,000 victims

Aftermath: 520-mile (840 km)-wide area destroyed, in which up to 60 percent of population killed; Shaanxi and China took decades to recover from the loss of life, property, and infrastructure

Mountains and rivers traded places and roads were destroyed. In some places, the ground suddenly rose up to form new hills, or it sank abruptly, creating new valleys. In other areas, streams burst out in an instant, or the ground broke and new gullies opened up. Huts, government buildings, temples, and city walls suddenly collapsed.

Qin Keda,
Eyewitness account of the Shaanxi earthquake, 1556

I am indebted to Lucy Jones of the United States Geological Survey (USGS) for the following "peanut butter-and-jelly-sandwich" earthquake-fault experiment that will enable the reader to recreate the three types of earthquake faults: "normal," "thrust," and "strike-slip." Take three slices of bread and cover the two outer slices liberally with your favorite fillings before assembling your triple-decker sandwich model of the earth's crust. Then make a diagonal cut (i.e., holding the knife at 45 degrees) through the sandwich, dividing it into two halves.

Like volcanoes, earthquakes are tectonic events caused by the movements of the earth's crust. As in the earlier entry on the Toba supereruption (pp. 16–20), the earth's tectonic plates move in different ways in relation to one another, leading to three types of earthquake faults where the plates meet. Holding up the two halves of the sandwich model together, so that the two halves stay in contact, slide one half downward to create a normal fault, which occurs where the plates are pulling apart, as in rift valleys. Put the two halves together again. Keeping both halves in contact, slide one half upward to create a thrust fault, which occurs where the plates collide, creating mountain ranges. Finally, slide the two halves sideways relative to one another to recreate a strike-slip fault, the most famous of which is California's San Andreas Fault.

HEARTLAND
Shaanxi is the cradle of Chinese civilization and the home of its first imperial dynasties.

Our earthquake 101 will conclude with a survey of the history of the detection and measurement of earthquakes. The first functional earthquake detector was Zhang Heng's (78–139 CE) "Instrument for measuring the seasonal winds and the movements of the earth" built during the Eastern Han Dynasty (25–220 CE), which is contemporary with the Roman Empire. Zhang's device consisted of a large bronze vessel, with a pendulum mechanism inside that was sensitive enough to pick up distant seismic waves. When an earthquake occurred, the mechanism was able to detect its location and caused a ball to drop out of the mouth of one of the eight dragons that indicated the cardinal points of the Chinese compass.

Pendulum mechanisms were used to measure seismic events until they were replaced by more sensitive electronic detectors. Until the mid-twentieth century, the Richter Scale (ML) measured the magnitude of earthquakes. Created by Charles Richter (1900–85) in 1935, it was superseded in the 1970s by the Moment Magnitude Scale (MMS or MW),

© Yang Xiaofeng | Shutterstock

more accurate for larger earthquakes. The Richter scale remains in use for smaller tremors.

**"MOUNTAINS
AND RIVERS
TRADED
PLACES"**

This entry takes us to East Asia for the first time, to the country that features so prominently on lists of megadisasters that a whole book could be entitled *Chinese History's Worst Disasters*. There are good reasons why China has experienced so many tragic episodes. China is one of the cradles of human civilization and has had high population densities since the earliest times. With a rich literate culture, we also have very good records stretching back thousands of years. However, many of history's worst disasters are little known in the West because they took place in China.

The province of Shaanxi in China is perhaps best known for the city of Xi'an (ancient Chang'an), which was the first capital of a united China under Emperor Qin Shi Huang (259–210 BCE), who is famously buried outside the city, guarded by his vast terracotta army. The city's other claim to historical fame is as the eastern terminus of the Silk Road that linked China with the Near East and Europe. The Silk Road was the main conduit for East–West trade from the Hellenistic period (323–31 BCE) until the Age of Discovery (fifteenth century onward), when Europe established direct maritime routes with East Asia that bypassed the Ottoman Empire (pp. 47–51).

In China, the area is famous for a much darker reason, as the location of history's worst earthquake by death toll and sheer destructiveness. Estimated to be at the top end of both the Richter and the Moment Magnitude scales, the Shaanxi earthquake of 1556 affected a vast area, covering counties in ten of the most densely populated Chinese provinces. The magnitude of the earthquake alone does not explain the estimated death toll of 830,000 victims. A great part of the province forms part of the Huangtu Plateau, an area of loess sediments that is not only very fertile but also geologically unstable and highly prone to erosion and landslides.

The reader can imagine that this is not a soil capable of providing solid foundations for buildings of any size. Worse, the traditional house type in the area, the *yaodong* (cave house), was a dwelling excavated into the side of a hill or sunken into the ground with underground chambers around a central courtyard. Although *yaodong* have excellent insulation from both the summer heat and the winter cold, they are very vulnerable to earth movements and landslides. Combine this with an area of tectonic instability and you have a recipe for a megadisaster. The Shaanxi earthquake and its aftershocks destroyed or damaged most of the surface buildings over a large area, but it annihilated the yaodong, burying their inhabitants alive. Those who survived the earthquake had to face major fires, as the earthquake struck in winter, upsetting braziers, lamps, and cooking stoves; and looting and banditry on a grand scale, as any form of civilian and military authority quickly broke down.

China is used to major disasters of this kind, and we shall return to the country several more times in the course of this book, but this one disaster that wiped out up to 60 percent of the population in the worst affected area must have had profound political, social, and economic effects on the whole country for decades. The disaster was catastrophic, but what is just as shocking is that it is so little known outside China. We are deluged with documentaries and films about the sinking of the RMS *Titanic* (pp. 100–103) and other disasters, yet an event that wiped out the equivalent of the population of San Francisco in a matter of seconds merits only a few paragraphs in rather stuffy geological histories.

Approximate epicenter

Shaanxi province

Provinces affected

UTTER DESTRUCTION
The Shaanxi Earthquake had a drastic impact on population numbers and destroyed or damaged inhabited buildings.

DISASTER

Extinction Event

Tectonic Event

Military Action

Fire

Pandemic

Famine

Political or Economic Event

Genocide

Flood or Storm

Industrial or Transport Accident

THE FATAL MIDDLE WAY: TRIANGULAR TRADE

16th–19th centuries

Cause: The Portuguese began importing African slaves to the Americas to make good the labor shortfalls after the demographic collapse of Native American populations; the British controlled much of the trade from the seventeenth century onward

Event: Manufactured goods shipped to Africa where they were traded or exchanged for slaves; slaves were transported to the Americas where they were traded or exchanged for raw materials to be taken back to Europe

Aftermath: Deaths of 2 million Africans attributable to the sea passage and 4 million from the institution of slavery; ongoing problem of racial discrimination

I got them by barter; and gave in exchange
Glass beads, steel goods, and some brandy;
I shall make at least eight hundred percent,
With but half of them living and handy.

Heinrich Heine,
The Slave Ship, ca. 1843

© Thinkstock

When European explorers reached sub-Saharan Africa in the fourteenth century, they discovered a continent that was as vast and as alien as the Americas. Africa, however, had always formed part of the Old World, with trading links with the Mediterranean and Near East since antiquity. When the Portuguese made landfall in West Africa, there had been Muslim kingdoms in the region for over seven centuries. In the Americas, in addition to the disruption of the conquest and the huge loss of life caused by European diseases, the native population experienced a culture shock of a magnitude that is difficult to imagine. In contrast, in Africa, there was no culture shock when the Portuguese arrived and no population collapse caused by new diseases.

The "Africa–Europe disease exchange" worked very much in Africa's favor, and thousands of Europeans died of diseases to which Africans had much better immunity and resistance. Another important factor was that technologically Africa was not as disadvantaged as the Americas. It possessed iron and steel metallurgy and gunpowder weapons. As a result, while the Portuguese established several African colonies, these were territorially insignificant when compared to the vast landholdings of Spain's American Empire, or Portugal's Brazilian enterprise. The great African land grab would take place much later, in the nineteenth century, led by the Belgians, British, and French.

The West Indies, or Antilles, played a central role in the colonization of the New World. They were the first place Europeans landed, and they became a way station and supply base for further exploration and conquest. Although the Antilles had a large Native American population when Columbus first landed, within a few decades the Taino and other Native Caribbean peoples were almost extinct. There were not enough settlers arriving from Europe to make up for the shortfall, and many immigrants were drawn to New Spain (now Mexico). The islands experienced an acute labor shortage, and history, religion, and the nascent Capitalist market provided a solution: demand in the Americas + supply in Africa = a transfer of labor between the two continents. Of course, no one thought that Africans could be induced to leave their ancestral home of their own free will, so the only practical alternative was slavery. The first African slaves to reach the Americas arrived on the island of Hispaniola with Columbus in 1501.

THE LAW OF SUPPLY AND DEMAND

Slavery is an extremely ancient social institution dating back to the Bronze Age (3600–1200 BCE) or earlier. The great cultures of the ancient world—Egypt, Greece, and Rome—were all slave economies. There were so many slaves in the Hellenistic and Roman worlds that slavery was a recognized social status, not just with its rather onerous duties but also with a limited number of rights. A slave was not a mere chattel like an inanimate object or an animal that could be killed or injured without consequences, though they could be bought and sold, and most slaves did experience lives of unremitting drudgery and hard labor. The Church had no objection to the institution because slavery existed in the Bible, and the Spanish had experimented with the indenture system known as the encomienda, first in conquered Muslim lands in Spain and then in the New World. A very similar indenture system would be employed in Britain's North American colonies, though this fell out of use after the foundation of an independent United States of America, to be replaced by full slavery.

Portugal began to settle Brazil from 1500. After the Portuguese had established sugar cane cultivation in the 1540s, they began transporting large numbers of African slaves to the colony to replace the Native American population that was succumbing to European diseases. Anyone visiting Brazil's northern states today will be struck by the high percentage of the population that is of African descent, and the rich cultural mix that the arrival of West African peoples has produced in the cities of Salvador, Recife, and Natal. The Portuguese maintained a monopoly on the African slave trade until the seventeenth century, when they faced the challenge of the rising power of the northern Europeans—French, Dutch, Scandinavians, and English—who had acquired their own New World interests, in the West Indies and North America, which required a large, static, indentured labor force that would not eat into plantation owners' profits with demands for better conditions and higher wages, as workers were beginning to do in the industrial towns of Europe.

THE FATAL MIDDLE WAY

The seventeenth and eighteenth centuries witnessed a worldwide competition between two broad alliances: Team Protestant Work Ethic, led by England, with occasional Dutch and German backing, versus Team Catholic Tradition, headed by France, with Spain and Portugal in train. The rivalry was played out in a series of wars that started in Europe and gradually spread worldwide, culminating in the victory of British interests

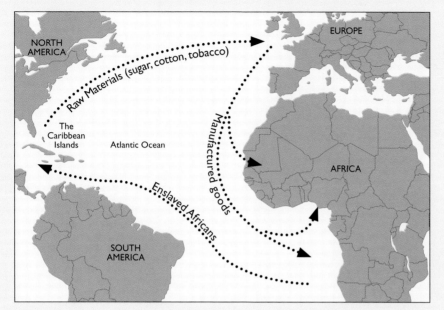

NORTH AMERICA

Raw Materials (sugar, cotton, tobacco)

EUROPE

The Caribbean Islands

Atlantic Ocean

Manufactured goods

AFRICA

Enslaved Africans

SOUTH AMERICA

SHIPS OF DEATH
The passage between Africa and the Americas was the costliest in terms of lost African lives.

in the Americas. For the British, losing the American colonies in 1783 was made up by the gains in the West Indies at Spain's and France's expense.

The vast agricultural monocultures that would define the economies of Brazil, the United States, and the West Indies—sugar cane, coffee, tobacco, and cotton—required a huge workforce that could not be recruited from Europe or locally because of the continuing decline of the Native American population. When they became the dominant sea power, the English quickly dominated the transatlantic slave trade with North America and the West Indies, using their economic, military, and colonial might to create an extraordinary tri-continental trade, known as the "triangular trade." It would have been an admirable early attempt at globalization had it not been for the dreadful cargo carried on the second leg of the trade, the "Middle Passage"—human beings kidnapped and sold into slavery.

The first side of the triangle took manufactured goods from the mills and workshops of Lancashire, England, to Africa. With one cargo sold, the ships were loaded with a fearful cargo of human misery—Africans kidnapped and enslaved by African and Arab intermediaries who sold them to European slavers. Men, women, and children were packed onto ships, the men chained together and to the decks so that they could not attack their captors or jump overboard to their deaths, and then had to endure the arduous 6- to 12-week sea passage on short rations, mistreated by the crew, and suffering outbreaks of epidemic diseases.

There are no reliable figures for the total number of Africans kidnapped, enslaved, and forcefully transported from Africa to the Americas between the sixteenth and nineteenth centuries, but the figure most often quoted is in the region of 12 million people, 40 percent of whom were taken to Brazil.

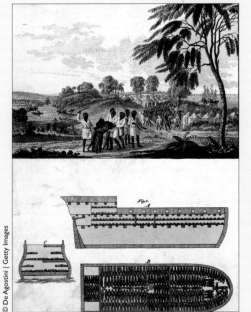

© De Agostini | Getty Images

CARGO
Slaves were packed tightly and chained to one another to prevent them from jumping overboard.

Likewise the number of deaths attributable to the slave trade is very difficult to calculate. Abolitionists naturally quoted high figures, while apologists for the trade (and later revisionist historians) have given lower estimates. Again, going by the most usually quoted figures, the losses during the Middle Passage have been estimated to be around 2 million, with another 2 million fatalities divided between the deaths caused by the effects of the trade in Africa, and those who died soon after their arrival in the Americas.

Slavery was abolished in the British West Indies in 1838, in the French West Indies in 1849, and in the U.S. in 1865 after the Civil War, whose calamitous one million-plus fatalities could also be added to the dismal calculation of the human cost of the Atlantic slave trade. Although the slave trade and slavery were abolished in the Caribbean and North America in the mid-nineteenth century, the legacy of racial discrimination endured for another century until finally confronted in the United States by the Civil Rights Movement.

We cannot attribute all of the racial problems of present-day America and Europe to the Atlantic slave trade; however, the complex web of intellectual, religious, and moral constructs that allowed the slave trade to develop and sustained it for hundreds of years created deep fissures within our societies: delusions of racial superiority on the far right and a destructive sense of social exclusion and hopelessness among certain ethnic and cultural groups.

THE HUMAN TOUCH: HOLOCENE EXTINCTION

ca. 1662

DISASTER

Extinction Event

Tectonic Event

Military Action

Fire

Pandemic

Famine

Political or Economic Event

Genocide

Flood or Storm

Industrial or Transport Accident

Cause: Colonization of the planet by humans

Event: Human activities such as hunting, deforestation, agriculture, animal husbandry, and species introduction

Aftermath: Extinction of an estimated 140,000 species a year

The end of the Pleistocene saw many extinctions, especially of the mega fauna, a group of large, slow animals with low reproductive rates. The theory that excessive hunting by humans was the major contributing cause to the extinction of these species is known as the overkill hypothesis.

Paul Martin,
Quaternary Extinctions, 1989

©Thinkstock

Over the past 3.6 billion years, extinction has been more biological rule than exception. The average lifespan of a species ranges from 1 to 10 million years, and scientists estimate that 98 to 99 percent of recorded species are now extinct. Biologists have identified fifteen or so lesser extinctions, one of which is the subject of this entry: the Holocene Extinction with which humans are intimately associated. The Holocene interglacial period began 12,000 years BP with the end of the last glacial period. It is known as an "interglacial," because the chances are that this is only a temporary warm period during an ongoing Quaternary Ice Age (2.58 million years BP–present). The end of the last glaciation, which triggered the retreat of the ice sheets and sea level rise, resulting in a major climate shift, accounts for some loss of species in a broader "Quaternary extinction event," but the warmer, more benign conditions on earth also contributed to another important event: the Neolithic Revolution (ca. 10,000 BP), when humans developed agriculture and established permanent settlements.

For most of human prehistory, our ancestors lived as hunter-gatherers, and let's dwell on the "hunter" part of the term here. Among the more idealistic eco-campaigners there is a romanticized notion of a human "Golden Age" when our ancestors existed in balance with the ecosystem, in a state of "nature." However, the Holocene coincides with the extinctions of many species of mega fauna worldwide, which brings us to the first major mechanism for extinction: overkill from human hunting. The two characteristics that have made our species so successful are our ability to make tools and weapons and our sociability: Whereas one unarmed human is pretty harmless, ten humans armed with stone-tipped spears are quite a different matter. Humans have also been very good at boosting their hunting skills by employing animal allies: dogs for their tracking and killing abilities and horses for long-distance travel, transport, and speed. Finally we have one terrifying weapon in our arsenal, sure to panic any wild animal: fire.

Another human characteristic is our propensity for conspicuous over-consumption. Today it's fashion bling, fast cars, and Crystal champagne; in the Stone Age it was driving a herd of mammoths over a cliff, producing more mammoth kebabs than a band of hunter-gatherers could eat in a year. Many species of mega fauna—horses, camelids, sloths—died out in the Americas after the arrival of humans around 14,500 BP, a situation reproduced in Europe, Australia, and several parts of Asia. To this day, overexploitation of animal species, using an ever more sophisticated arsenal of tools and weapons, remains a major cause of species extinctions.

Although hunter-gatherers helped bring about the extinction of larger animals, both large herding herbivores and rival carnivores, the real damage began after we had begun to settle and farm. The first major impact on the environment from settlement was deforestation. During prehistory, all the areas of the planet that were climatically suitable would have supported dense forests—rainforests in the tropics, deciduous forests in temperate zones, and evergreen forests farther north. Our ancestors felled the forests to build settlements and to plant crops, and their grazing and browsing animals ensured that the trees never returned. The open country that we see all over temperate Europe, and which we identify as the "natural" environment, is in reality an artificial human construct.

Deforestation alone probably accounted for the extinction of thousands of animal and plant species that depended on the woodland habitat—a process that is continuing to this day with the clearance of rainforests. The introduction of large-scale monocultures, such as cereals, rice, cotton, sugar cane, coffee, and tobacco, in different parts of the world further reduced biodiversity, eliminating another group of species whose habitats were drastically reduced or destroyed altogether. Finally, the development of large-scale industry and the resulting extraction and use of natural resources in the past two centuries have caused further habitat loss and a massive increase in all forms of pollution. Although the oceans have not experienced the kind of settlement seen on land, marine species have witnessed an equivalent high rate of extinctions from the overexploitation of food species and from pollution.

© Creative Commons

INEDIBLE
The dodo was not hunted to extinction as its flesh was said to taste terrible.

The last set of human-related variables leading to extinctions is illustrated by our headline extinct species, the dodo *(Raphus cucullatus)*. A native of the Indian Ocean island of Mauritius, the dodo was first sighted by Europeans in 1507, when a Portuguese ship called in at the island on its way to India. Taxonomically, the dodo is a giant, flightless pigeon. Its ancestors would have flown to the uninhabited island, where they found a bird paradise: no predators and a plentiful supply of food at ground level.

THE PROVERBIAL DEATH

With no pressing evolutionary need to fly, the dodo decided to give up the high life and settle on the ground, growing larger and larger until it was incapable of taking to the wing.

Indian, Arab, and East African mariners had known about Mauritius since the tenth century CE, and, like the Portuguese, used it to replenish supplies of water and fresh food, but they probably spared the dodo, whose flesh, according to those who ate it, was foul-tasting and tough. For this reason, the Dutch, who finally settled the island in the early seventeenth century, nicknamed the dodo the "loathsome bird." For once, it was not our predilection for BBQ dodo wings or *dodo-au-vin* that caused its extinction within eighty years of human colonization. Human activities, such as farming and building, would have destroyed the dodo's habitat, but what really killed off the species were the fellow-passenger and "stowaway" species that accompanied human settlers on their worldwide travels: pigs, goats, cats, dogs, monkeys, mongooses, weasels, and that supreme animal freeloader, the rat. As predators, they were too small to threaten an adult bird, but the eggs and chicks of the ground-nesting dodo would have made easy pickings for feral pigs, cats, monkeys, and rats.

Introduced animal and plant species have caused havoc in hitherto isolated ecosystems, such as islands that had no rodents or grazing or browsing herbivores, and, on a much larger scale, on continents isolated from the rest of the world, such as the Americas and Australia before European settlement. Additional human-related factors leading to extinctions in closed eco-systems are introduced diseases and insect pests, as well as an increased fire risk from human activities.

A human population that has just topped 7 billion, combined with accelerating deforestation for settlement, the extraction of raw materials, and agriculture, has led to a worst-case-scenario estimated extinction rate of 140,000 species a year. Tragically, as many of these species exist in the rainforests that are disappearing at an alarming rate, we have potentially already lost a great deal of biodiversity that could have provided a priceless genetic bounty for the ever-growing human population.

DEATHTRAP: GREAT FIRE OF LONDON

1666

DISASTER

Extinction Event

Tectonic Event

Military Action

Fire

Pandemic

Famine

Political or Economic Event

Genocide

Flood or Storm

Industrial or Transport Accident

Cause: Overcrowded city with many wooden buildings and stores of inflammable materials; no dedicated firefighting force; failure to enforce anti-fire-hazard legislation

Event: Slow response allowed the fire to burn for four days, developing into a firestorm

Aftermath: Destruction of most of the historic City of London, the ancient medieval city within the Roman walls, including St. Paul's Cathedral, many churches, and most public buildings of the city authorities

We saw the fire as only one entire arch of fire from this to the other side the bridge, and in a bow up the hill for an arch of above a mile long: it made me weep to see it. The churches, houses, and all on fire and flaming at once; and a horrid noise the flames made, and the cracking of houses at their ruins.

**The Diary of Samuel Pepys,
Sunday, September 2, 1666**

In 1666 London was a medieval city of narrow winding lanes and wooden thatched houses. The City of London (then as now the financial district of the English capital), still enclosed by its Roman walls, and its western and southern suburbs beyond them, sheltered a population of about half a million. The king's palace, Parliament, and great offices of state were in Whitehall, outside the city walls to the west of the City. There was only one bridge, London Bridge, itself lined with inflammable wooden houses, linking the City to the suburb of Southwark on the south bank of the Thames. If you were to superimpose seventeenth-century London onto today's London Underground Map, it would cover less than half of Zone One, which is now considered to make up Central London. The levels of overcrowding in London made the city particularly vulnerable to the two major urban threats of the early modern period: outbreaks of the plague and fire.

BLOWN AWAY
The Tower of London was saved by the creation of firebreaks.

Fire was an ever-present danger in medieval and early modern cities, and London had experienced many conflagrations, including another "Great Fire" in 1123. As a result there was an attempt to ban the use of inflammable materials such as wood and thatch for construction, and exclude dangerous trades such as foundries and smithies from urban areas, but these regulations were ignored. In 1661, King Charles II (1630–85), just restored to the English throne after the country's only republican interlude, warned the Lord Mayor of the fire risk to the city, but the royal warning and attempt at legislation went unheeded.

The presence of hazardous trades in the center of London was not the major risk, as fire was the universal source of heating, lighting, and cooking, and therefore every house was a potential fire hazard. The streets, unchanged since the medieval period, were extremely narrow, made even narrower by the practice of building projecting upper floors, or "jetties," which meant that in the most densely populated neighborhoods the upper floors of the wooden tenement buildings almost touched one another. In addition to the use of inflammable construction materials, the city was packed with hazardous products, including tar, coal, tallow, gunpowder, and brandy and other liquors.

Compounding all these risks was the absence of any official firefighting force, though extinguishing fires was a duty entrusted to the forerunner of the police force, the city Watch. London was fortunate in that it was built on the Thames, which in theory could provide water to put out a fire, but the banks of the river were crowded with houses and businesses, which, once they were ablaze, would make access to the river impossible. The main method of fighting fires at the time was to demolish buildings in the path of the blaze in the hope of creating a firebreak, but the effectiveness of this depended on favorable weather conditions and prompt action. In short, London in 1666 was a firetrap.

We are extremely fortunate in having the eyewitness account of the Great Fire by one of the most entertaining and engaging writers of the day, the diarist Samuel Pepys (1633–1703), who at the time was employed by the Navy Board, and was directly involved not only as a witness but also as a participant communicating with the king in Whitehall and the Lord Mayor in the attempts at extinguishing the blaze. The fire broke out in a bakery in Pudding Lane, just north of London Bridge, in the small hours of Sunday, September 2. Pepys records that his maidservant woke him up to tell him about the fire, but as fires were not uncommon, he did not consider the matter particularly urgent or dangerous and went back to sleep.

At this point, had the Lord Mayor, Thomas Bloodworth (1620–82), taken prompt action to create firebreaks around the affected area, the fire might have still been contained despite a strong easterly wind. Bloodworth refused to allow the demolition of houses until the owners could be found. The delay proved fatal: Fanned by the wind, the fire quickly spread westward toward the center of the city, and along the northern bank of the Thames. London Bridge, which was covered in wooden tenements, was ablaze, and the fire would have spread to Southwark had not a firebreak partway along the bridge halted the flames.

Pepys, who lived east of Pudding Lane, rose at seven on Sunday morning and inspected the fire from the vantage point of the Tower of London. Realizing that the fire was out of control, he took a boat to the Palace of Whitehall, the river being the only way to reach the western part of London, and conferred with the king's brother, James, Duke of York (1633–1701), about the measures to take to contain the fire. He returned with orders from the king to the Lord Mayor to demolish as many houses

BURYING HIS PARMESAN CHEESE

as necessary to create a firebreak to protect what was left of the city to the east, and the areas outside the walls to the north and west. Although his orders were followed and houses were demolished, the fire was so intense that the firefighters could not keep pace with the blaze, which consumed the heart of the city, including St. Paul's Cathedral. The fire, pushed westward by the wind, was also spreading east toward Pepys' home. Although he had already sent his wife away with many of his possessions, his money, and papers, including his diaries, he decided to bury his Parmesan cheese, then an expensive delicacy, and his wines in his garden to save them from the flames.

With the fire nearing the Tower of London, which contained a large store of gunpowder, the Tower's garrison, having failed to receive orders from the Duke of York who was working to save the west of the city, took matters into their own hands and used gunpowder to demolish houses in the path of the fire to create a firebreak that stopped its eastward spread. By Wednesday, the wind had dropped, and large enough firebreaks were in place to contain what was still burning. By Thursday, the conflagration was at an end, and all that was left was to apportion the blame and count the cost. Three-quarters of the city had been destroyed, including its Cathedral, many historic churches, and civic and commercial buildings, as well as a part of the western suburbs (now the area around Fleet Street).

Strangely, considering the huge loss of buildings and property, the death toll from the fire itself was recorded to be between four and eight victims. However, modern historians reject this figure as much too low, and explain that at its height the fire was so intense that the bodies of the dead would have been almost completely consumed apart from the bones. There were also indirect casualties among those made homeless and destitute by the fire, as well as French and Dutch residents of the city who were lynched as firestarters because England was at war with the Netherlands at the time, and almost perennially at war with France.

WITNESS
The diarist Samuel Pepys was instrumental in fighting the Great Fire.

SHAKING FAITH: LISBON EARTHQUAKE AND TSUNAMI

1755

DISASTER

Extinction Event

Tectonic Event

Military Action

Fire

Pandemic

Famine

Political or Economic Event

Genocide

Flood or Storm

Industrial or Transport Accident

Cause: Earthquake (MMS 8.5–9)

Event: Destruction of city of Lisbon and Atlantic coasts of Portugal and Spain; tsunamis reaching North Africa, British Isles, Atlantic islands, and West Indies

Aftermath: Economic crisis in Portugal; philosophers of the Enlightenment criticized simplistic views of divine providence; start of seismology and quake-proof architecture

And can you then impute a sinful deed
To babes who on their mothers' bosoms bleed?
Was then more vice in fallen Lisbon found,
Than Paris, where voluptuous joys abound?
Was less debauchery to London known,
Where opulence luxurious holds the throne?

Voltaire, *Poème sur le désastre de Lisbonne*
("Poem on the Lisbon Disaster"), 1756

© Mana Photo | Shutterstock

There has been no shortage of large, destructive earthquakes in Europe and the Near East since antiquity. For most of history, earthquakes, like volcanic eruptions, epidemics, droughts, and floods, were not seen as "natural" disasters but as acts of god or of the gods. In the polytheistic religions of antiquity, the idea that a god punished a city or country for some evil deed did not present any major theological difficulty. The ancient gods of Greece and Rome, in addition to being immortal, shared with humans their many foibles and faults. Their actions, like our own, could be noble and just, or petty and unfair. When Zeus destroyed Atlantis (see pp. 21–25), he acted to punish the Atlanteans' violence and impiety, but other plagues, floods, and visitations by monsters could just as readily be a manifestation of divine pique at some imagined slight on the part of humans, or the result of a scrap between two rival gods vying for influence over the same city.

For the polytheistic world view the problem of evil in the world did not present insurmountable problems, because pagans accepted that the gods

could be as just or as unjust as themselves, and there was always another god to appeal to. Both gods and humans were endowed with free will, and there was no concept of absolute good and evil. The evolution of Christian monotheism from Judaism changed the relationship between the human and divine, and good and evil. From the earliest times, Christians wrestled with the idea of an omnipotent, omnipresent, and omnibenevolent god who allowed the existence of

WAVE POWER
Devastated by the earthquake, Lisbon was hit by a 60-foot tsunami.

evil in the world. Resolving the problem of evil is known as "theodicy," and the solution comes in two major Christian flavors: God made the world perfect, but when Adam and Eve ate the fruit of the Tree of Knowledge, evil came into the world as a punishment for their disobedience. A slightly more sophisticated version explains that God allows evil to exist so that humans, who are endowed with free will, are able to attain salvation through their own moral choices.

In the view of many medieval and early-modern Christians who had not benefited from a theological education, disasters, natural and human, were a sign of God's displeasure, and a direct punishment for some transgression of his commandments on the well-established biblical principle of "smite the city or spoil the congregation." Sometimes they examined their own behavior but often they sought a readily identifiable group to blame: In medieval Europe that usually meant persecuting the Jews.

At 9:40 a.m., on November 1, 1755, an earthquake estimated at between 8.5 and 9 on the Moment Magnitude Scale (MMS, see p. 60) occurred in the Atlantic 125 miles (200 km) off the coast of the Iberian peninsula. November 1 is All Saint's Day, which is a Holy Day of Obligation in many Roman Catholic countries, when anyone who was fit enough to walk was expected to go to church. The churches of Portugal and Spain's Atlantic coastal communities would have been full of the faithful attending one of the many masses that would be celebrated throughout the day. The massive initial shock destroyed and damaged many buildings and started fires in those that had not collapsed, so that those who were not crushed to death were burned alive.

DIVINE IMPROVIDENCE

But worse was to come: The earthquake had taken place out to sea, and the sudden boundary movement between the Eurasian and African tectonic plates released a huge amount of energy into the water above. The ocean was literally sucked away from the coast only to return minutes later as a massive wall of water. The burning city was hit by a 60-foot (20 m) tsunami that completed the destruction caused by the quake and fires, which together with the tsunami destroyed 85 percent of the city. Tsunamis radiated from the epicenter in every direction, with giant waves devastating the Atlantic coasts of Portugal, Spain, and Morocco; abnormally large waves were recorded as far north as Ireland, in Cornwall on England's south coast, and across the Atlantic in the West Indies.

As with many other early modern disasters, we only have estimates for the death toll, which range from 40,000 to 50,000 casualties. The human losses would have been particularly high in Catholic Spain and Portugal because many people were packed into churches, many of which collapsed on their congregations. King Joseph I of Portugal (1714–77) had a lucky escape, having gone to Mass early so as to grant one of his daughters' wish to spend the holiday outside the city. Returning to his devastated capital, the king thereafter refused to live in a building of any kind and spent the remainder of his life in a luxurious tented camp at Ajuda in the hills overlooking the city. Ajuda is now the site of a palace built on the royal campsite by

Joseph's daughter. There were also incalculable cultural losses. The crown of Portugal, like other European monarchies, had amassed vast collections of priceless artworks, furniture, tapestries, and manuscripts, including the archives of Portugal's extensive maritime explorations since the fourteenth century. Finally, if one considers the economic losses caused by the 2008 Indian Ocean quake and tsunami (pp. 226–229), the economic cost to Portugal must have been crippling.

In addition to the loss of life and the cultural, material, and economic damage caused, the Lisbon quake and tsunami occurred during a critical period in the Western world's intellectual history, the Age of Enlightenment (mid-seventeenth to late eighteenth centuries). Like the Black Death, which had shaken the absolute authority of the Roman Catholic Church in the fourteenth century, the Lisbon disaster caused considerable personal disquiet among the Catholic faithful of Europe and skeptical speculations among the Enlightenment philosophers. The fact that the event had taken place on a Catholic holiday, and that the death toll was particularly high because people were in church, was used by Voltaire (1694–1778), quoted on page 75, to criticize simplistic notions of divine providence, and also by believers, such as the German philosopher Leibniz (1646–1716), who claimed that humans lived "in the best of all possible worlds." The quake also played an important formative role in the intellectual development of Immanuel Kant (1724–1804), one of the key thinkers of the German Enlightenment. Finally, the greater emphasis on reason and scientific research during the period led to the first serious attempt to understand the causes of earthquakes and tsunamis, which is recognized today as the beginning of modern seismology. The disaster also marks the beginning of earthquake-proof architecture in Europe, which was used in the reconstruction of Lisbon.

A QUESTION OF SUPPLY: BENGAL FAMINE

1769–73

DISASTER

Extinction Event

Tectonic Event

Military Action

Fire

Pandemic

Famine

Political or Economic Event

Genocide

Flood or Storm

Industrial or Transport Accident

Cause: Succession of bad harvests compounded by the economic and taxation policies of the British East India Company

Event: Famine across British-administered Bengal

Aftermath: Death of 10 million people, or one-third of the population of Bengal, from which the region took decades to recover

The first duty incumbent upon the government in a case like that of the failure of the winter rice-crop of 1769, was to do away with all hindrance to the importation of food into the province. One chief cause of the far-reaching distress wrought by great Asiatic famines has been the almost complete commercial isolation of Asiatic communities.

John Fiske,
The Unseen World, 1869

© Thinkstock

The initial cause of a localized food shortage can be entirely natural: a prolonged drought, flood, or a disease that destroys the main staple of a region. But to develop into a full-blown disaster in which people die in large numbers for want of food, a food shortage needs concerted human intervention. It is inconceivable that there was a national shortage of food in the United Kingdom during the two "Great Famines" that devastated Ireland during the eighteenth and nineteenth centuries; equally, in eighteenth- and nineteenth-century India, the whole continent was not starving. Hence, the natural causes were supplemented by human actions or omission of action that greatly aggravated the existing crises. As John Fiske pointed out in an essay that compared the Bengal famines of 1770 to that of 1866 (see p. 79), the real problem was one of supply and distribution and not of an absolute shortage of foodstuffs.

© Getty Images | Thinkstock

UNHEARD
The starving millions could only pray to the gods as the British authorities did not listen.

In the sixteenth and seventeenth centuries, the Indian and Chinese empires were the richest, most populous, and culturally and technologically most advanced nations on earth. They looked with considerable scorn, distaste, and derision at the antics of the uncouth, unwashed, and bigoted European explorers and traders who began to visit their shores from the early sixteenth century, seeking to circumvent the Ottoman stranglehold on the trade with the East. As we saw above, this led to the Spanish colonization of the Americas, with disastrous consequences first for the Native Americans (see pp. 52–57), and then for enslaved Africans who were forcibly sent there to replace them (see pp. 62–66). The Chinese, Japanese, and Indians were aware of what had befallen the Native Americans, and were rightly suspicious of Western visitors, but they were self-confident enough in their own abilities and strengths to believe (wrongly) that no latter-day Cortés would storm Beijing's Forbidden City or Delhi's Red Fort.

Early modern India was vast, fabulously wealthy, and ruled by the Mughal Dynasty (1526–1857), Muslim descendants of the Mongols, who gradually expanded from their northern Indian strongholds to conquer the Muslim sultanates and Hindu kingdoms of central and south India to create a united Indian empire. Like other vast, ethnically, culturally, and religiously diverse empires, Mughal India looked far more formidable and stable than it really was, and the power of the dynasty depended on the personality of the ruling emperor and the loyalty he could inspire in his many vassals. The Mughal Empire was a complex feudal pyramid with the emperor at the top. If the emperor were weak, his wealthier and more powerful vassals would assert their independence while paying lip service to the imperial government.

The Portuguese, French, and British, who arrived in India as traders, began to play an ever-increasing role in the politics of the subcontinent, exploiting rivalries between leading Mughal vassals, and encouraging rebellions among the empire's majority Hindu subjects, while at the same time attacking one another's outposts when their home countries were at war. By the mid-eighteenth century, the British East India Company (1600–1874), headquartered in Calcutta, was in the anomalous position of being the dominant power in northeast India—imagine Amazon or Microsoft running the U.S. Northwest from Seattle. After the battles of Plassey (1757) and Buxar (1764), the company was the de facto ruler of Bengal, then a vast area covering the modern Indian state of West Bengal, parts of Indian Assam, Bihar, and Orissa, and Bangladesh, with its capital in Calcutta, and with an estimated 30 million inhabitants, for the most part farmers.

Bengal was one of the wealthiest parts of India, described by the Mughals as the "Paradise of the Nations." It was a major producer of rice and of the Darjeeling teas that the British are still so fond of. With the effective collapse of Mughal rule, the emperor was maintained as the nominal ruler in Delhi, where the last Mughal emperors exercised their very limited authority. A large corporation, however, is not the ideal ruler of a nascent colonial empire. Its primary responsibility is to maximize the profits of its stockholders. Even the Spanish Crown, under whose aegis the most terrible deeds were done in the Americas, attempted to correct the greatest abuses of the conquest, although for the vast majority of the population of the Caribbean and Central America it was a case of much too little, much too late.

"PARADISE OF THE NATIONS"

The British East India Company did not have a sovereign state's conscience, or even much care for its own reputation. It controlled one of the richest provinces of the Mughal Empire, which was now effectively cut off from the rest of India, with which the company was often at war. The region suffered a bad harvest in 1768, but this was not an unusual event in a pre-modern agricultural economy. But a severe drought struck again the following year, causing major shortages of food in rural areas. People began to die of starvation in large numbers in early 1770, but the company ignored their pleas for assistance and refused to lift import controls on rice, whose trade was a company monopoly.

In order to ensure a maximum return from its new holdings, the company raised the land tax from 10 to 50 percent in the first few years of its rule, and even in the famine year of 1770 implemented a further 10 percent taxation hike. At the same time, it ordered farmers to plant cash crops such as opium and indigo instead of rice, further reducing supplies, and it enforced draconian measures against "hoarding," which prevented rice merchants and farmers from keeping grain in reserve to tide the population over. Despite a brief respite with a good harvest in 1770, the situation remained critical. There were further bad harvests until 1773, by which time 10 million, or one-third of the population of Bengal, had starved to death. Unconcerned by the massive death toll, the company continued to extort ever-higher land taxes and duties on rice, actually doubling its profits from the area between 1765 and 1777.

EMPIRE
Bengal was acquired by the East India Company to further its commercial interests.

The famine, however, had not gone unnoticed in Britain, and in 1773 the government took the first legislative steps to establish the sovereignty of the Crown over the company's Indian landholdings, and its control over the company itself, which culminated in the 1813 East India Company Act that completed the Crown's takeover, while leaving the company with limited trade monopolies and political responsibilities in India. The British often compare their rule in India with Spanish rule in the New World, contrasting their own much more benign, paternalistic treatment of the Indians with the wholesale slaughter and enslavement of Native Americans; however, the evidence of repeated famines that continued to occur throughout British rule in India, killing countless millions, should make them reconsider this rose-tinted view of their own colonial past.

LE DÉLUGE: FRENCH REVOLUTIONARY *TERREUR*

1793–94

DISASTER

Extinction Event

Tectonic Event

Military Action

Fire

Pandemic

Famine

Political or Economic Event

Genocide

Flood or Storm

Industrial or Transport Accident

Cause: National Convention established the Committee of Public Safety, ceding to it increasingly dictatorial powers

Event: Execution of 42,000 "counter-revolutionaries" in France; genocide in the Vendée region where between 117,000 and 400,000 people died during a pro-Royalist rebellion

Aftermath: Arrest and execution of Robespierre and his associates; consolidation of the Republic under the more moderate rule of the Directoire; ultimate failure of the Republic and Napoleon's rise to power

Power tends to corrupt, and absolute power corrupts absolutely. Great men are almost always bad men, even when they exercise influence and not authority: still more when you superadd the tendency or the certainty of corruption by authority.

**Lord Acton,
letter, 1887**

The Introduction (pp. 8–9) referenced a quote from King Louis XV of France (1710–74), who, realizing how badly he and his ministers were governing France, is reputed to have said, "Après moi, le déluge!" ("After me, the flood!"). The deluge was not long in coming, sweeping away France's absolute monarchy in the revolution of 1789, during the reign of Louis XVI (1754–93) and of his much maligned wife, Queen Marie-Antoinette (1755–93), she of "Let-them-eat-cake" fame. The French Revolution was the second revolt against monarchical rule triggered by the ideals of the Enlightenment, the first being, of course, the American Revolution. The two revolutions, though linked by the philosophical ideals that the revolutionaries espoused, were very different: The American Declaration of Independence of 1776 signaled the birth of a new nation, while the storming of the Bastille in 1789 heralded the beginning of the end of monarchical absolutism in Europe.

© Creative Commons

TERRORIST
Outside France, Robespierre was the most reviled person in Europe.

The French, having overthrown the *Ancien Régime*, or "old order," in 1789, had to devise new constitutional arrangements with the monarchy. In 1791, however, Louis fled Paris in an attempt to join the revolution's enemies, who had sworn to restore him to full power. The king was caught, deposed, and imprisoned, and the French assembly, the National Convention, declared the First Republic (1792–1804). France, however, remained in a perilous state, with an untested form of republican government, royalist revolts in the provinces, and at war with Austria and Prussia, which were soon joined by a grand alliance of Britain, the Netherlands, Spain, and the Kingdom of Naples, which all feared that the revolutionary contagion would spread to their own countries.

"FOR THE SALVATION OF THE PEOPLE"

Maximilien de Robespierre (1758–94), depending on your political affiliations, was either the man who saved the French Revolution or destroyed it. Robespierre was a political idealist steeped in the democratic ideals of the Enlightenment philosopher Jean-Jacques Rousseau (1712–78). He advocated universal (male) suffrage and a form of direct democracy based on ancient Greco-Roman models. As the revolution took its course, with the deposition of the king, Robespierre came to the fore because of his reputation for incorruptibility and his powers of oratory.

With the fledgling republic beset with internal and external enemies, the National Convention that had replaced the Constituent Assembly created the *Comité de Salut Public* (Committee of Public Safety) in the spring of 1793, electing Robespierre to be one of its members in July.

With France's foreign enemies moving in for the kill and defections among its leading generals, a rebellion broke out in western France's most traditional, Catholic area, the Vendée. The initial cause of the revolt was the Republic's moves against France's Catholic clergy, the majority of whom were staunchly traditionalist and monarchist. After the execution of the king in 1793, the Convention began closing churches and forcing priests to swear loyalty to the republic and to marry. All clergy who resisted were imprisoned and later executed. The rebellion quickly took on counter-revolutionary overtones, and the insurrection's insignia were inscribed with the words "Dieu, le roi" ("God, the king"). The rebels hoped to get help from the English and French *émigré* aristocrats, but, lacking any military strategy beyond expelling republican forces from their region, they did not consolidate their early victories. The Committee for Public Safety sent reinforcements, the *colonnes infernales* (infernal columns), which moved against the rebels, executing a genocidal policy targeting both armed rebels and the civilian population. The action continued until 1796, long after the downfall of Robespierre, and claimed the lives of between 117,000 and 400,000 victims. The upper figure would account for half the population of the Vendée.

In Paris, starting in the fall of 1793, Robespierre and his fellow committee members instituted an official rule of *Terreur* (Terror) as an instrument of state policy, prefiguring the actions of totalitarian regimes during the twentieth century. The adoption of the Terror, which we know from his own writing and speeches was a strategy designed by Robespierre and his closest associates, sits very oddly with the idealist who supported the abolition of slavery and of the death penalty, and initially opposed the war with Austria.

Robespierre advocated the Terror "for the Salvation of the People." The "people" to be "saved," however, did not include the 42,000 victims who went to the guillotine or were summarily executed after the briefest of trials by revolutionary tribunals. These included a small number of aristocrats, bourgeois, and clergymen accused of counter-revolutionary activities, but the vast majority were workers and peasants who were convicted of rebellion, draft dodging, desertion, or hoarding food. Another group of prominent victims included Robespierre's political enemies on the right, the moderate Girondins, and on the left, the *enragés* (enraged), who wanted even more extreme reforms of the state. An English cartoon of the day depicted Robespierre guillotining the state's executioner after having guillotined the whole population of France.

UNKINDEST CUT
The guillotine dispatched most of the *Terreur's* victims.

Robespierre's overthrow in July 1794 was engineered by a coalition of moderates and extremists, two groups that he had managed to alienate during his nine months in office. He attempted to cheat the guillotine by shooting himself before his arrest but he missed, injuring himself in the jaw. After a trial that made full use of the expedited justice of the Revolutionary Tribunal that he had employed to dispatch many of the Terror's victims, Robespierre and his close associates were guillotined the next day.

The Committee of Public Safety was slowly sidelined and then disbanded as the moderates gained the upper hand over their erstwhile extremist allies. The Convention drafted a new constitution establishing a complex bicameral system with an executive known as the *Directoire* (Directory). The system was unwieldy, inefficient and was soon mired in corruption. France, however, was beginning to win its civil and foreign wars, thanks to young generals such as Napoleon Bonaparte (1769–1821). The populist Napoleon seized power in a military coup in 1799, giving himself the ancient Roman title of First Consul, in imitation of Julius Caesar (100–44 BCE). The pragmatic Robespierre who believed that the most violent means justified his ends had, at last, found a worthy heir.

BLIGHTED LAND: THE GREAT FAMINE

1845–52

DISASTER

Extinction Event

Tectonic Event

Military Action

Fire

Pandemic

Famine

Political or Economic Event

Genocide

Flood or Storm

Industrial or Transport Accident

Cause: Potato blight destroyed the Irish potato crop several years in a row; lack of concerted action on the part of the British government

Event: Death by starvation and disease of between 1 and 1.5 million Irish Catholic subjects of the British Crown

Aftermath: Emigration of 1 to 1.5 million Irish Catholic to the mainland UK, to British colonies, and to the U.S.; drastic population fall in Ireland; legacy of bitterness between Ireland's Protestant and Catholic communities and against the British

Ochón, ochón	Alas, alas
Ochón, Aimsir an Drochshaoil	Lament the time of the Famine
Ochón, ochón	Alas, Alas
Ochón an Gorta Mór	Lament of the Great Hunger

Brendan Graham
Ochón an Gorta Mór
("Lament of the Great Hunger"), 2000

The Anglo-Irish "question," "problem," or "troubles," as the difficult relationship between the neighboring islands of Great Britain and Ireland has variously been known over the past two centuries, began in the twelfth century, when the Anglo-Norman King Henry II (1133–89) led a first English invasion of the island, after receiving a papal sanction recognizing his "Lordship of Ireland" in 1155. English dominance continued until the Black Death (pp. 41–46) decimated the mainly urban English-speaking settlers from the mainland, allowing the rural Gaelic-speaking Irish to regain their former ascendancy.

The next major chapter in Anglo-Irish relations began in the sixteenth century, when Henry VIII (1491–1537) could no longer use the Catholic Church to justify his invasion so declared himself king of Ireland in 1541, replacing the island's long defunct high kingship. He broke with the Roman Catholic Church over the pope's refusal to sanction his divorce from his first wife Catherine of Aragon (1485–1536). The majority of the Irish population were staunch supporters of the Catholic Church and determined to keep their allegiance to Rome, and this added a religious dimension to what had been a national and military conflict. Henceforth, the English invaders and colonizers would be mainly Protestant, ruling over a majority Irish Catholic population.

During the century-long subjugation of Ireland, English Protestant settlers were sent from the mainland and established in the north of the island in the six provinces of Ulster—still the stronghold of Protestant Unionism, and the last part of Ireland that still forms part of the United Kingdom. The former Catholic landowners were dispossessed and exiled. It mattered little whether the incumbent of the English throne were pro-Catholic or Protestant, as it was the Catholic sympathizer King James I (1566–1625) who started the settlement policy of "plantations" and systematic expropriations of Catholic lands in Ulster. Oliver Cromwell (1599–1658), the man who led England's eleven-year republican experiment (1649–60), enthusiastically pursued the policy of colonization. The Irish had sided with the royalists and rebelled, and Cromwell's response was to invade and put down the rebellion with "extreme prejudice," and then to pass legislation that discriminated against Irish Catholics. Discrimination long continued through to the abolition of the Irish Parliament under the 1801 Acts of Union which saw that Ireland sent its elected Protestant representatives to the British Parliament in Westminster.

The British have always compared themselves favorably to other European powers when it comes to the treatment of their colonial subjects. Contrasting their own behavior with that of the Spanish, Portuguese, Dutch, and French, the British have a view that after the necessary military subjugation of their colonial subjects, they provided them with all the benefits and comforts of Western civilization. Their first colonial experiences, however, were not in America, Asia, or Africa—in the far-flung corners of the world map that would later be stained red—but in the British Isles, in the neighboring Celtic realms of Wales, Scotland, and Ireland. Any illusion of benevolent paternalism quickly evaporates when one studies the history of Anglo-Irish relations, briefly sketched out above. One of the most tragic episodes, however, occurred after the Catholic Emancipation Act of 1829 had removed many of the constraints on the civil rights of English and Irish Catholics. The disaster, known in Irish Gaelic as *An Gorta Mór*, was the Great Famine, which lasted from 1845 to 1852.

The staple crop of the majority of Irish Catholic tenant farmers was the potato, a root vegetable that is not native to Europe but was introduced by the Spanish from the Americas in the sixteenth century. The potato is well suited to the climatic conditions of northern Europe and will also grow in poor soil. Its introduction led to a steady increase in northern Europe's population during the seventeenth and eighteenth centuries. The potato, however, suffered from one major drawback as a staple food crop. In the Americas, there are hundreds of varieties, creating a large genetic pool that provides good resistance to disease, but the varieties introduced to Europe came from a limited number of genetic stocks, making them much more vulnerable. This had caused crop failures ever since the potato's introduction, including a first "Great Famine" in Ireland in 1740–41.

In the 1840s a new and much more serious disease of the potato arrived in Europe from the Americas: *Phytophthora infestans*, more commonly known as "potato blight." The fungus-like blight caused infected tubers to rot into a foul-smelling, poisonous mush while they were still in the ground, and it could affect seemingly healthy tubers that had already been harvested and stored. As with India's Bengal famine (pp. 79–82), localized food shortages

© Creative Commons

DOWN AND OUT
Starving farmers were
evicted from their cottages
for not paying their rents.

**"A TENDENCY TO
EXAGGERATION"**

were not unusual in the rural areas of the British Isles and Europe in the nineteenth century. However, the severity of the blight, combined with social, political, and economic factors specific to the Anglo-Irish context, insured that a grave food shortage was transformed into one of nineteenth-century Europe's deadliest famines.

The bulk of the Irish Catholic population made a precarious living as the tenants of absentee Anglo-Irish landowners, who, detached from their lands and tenants, felt little duty of care toward them. They entrusted the collection of rents to unscrupulous agents, who did not hesitate to evict tenants in arrears with their rents. The best land was given over to pasture to raise beef cattle and to grow corn for distilling into alcohol or for export to the mainland. Tenancies were based on the "cottier" system in which farmers rented a cottage and a small patch of marginal land in exchange for labor on the landowner's estate or, less frequently, for the payment of a cash rent. Because the tenancies were short-term and had no security of tenure, the tenants were not motivated to make improvements to the land. The holdings were too small to grow anything but potatoes, and even in a good year, after the payment of rent and taxes, tenants had just enough food to keep their families fed. This dangerous dependency on the potato often led to severe food shortages in bad years.

In 1845, the blight reached Western Ireland and spread quickly throughout the island, drastically reducing the potato harvest on which 80 percent of the population depended. By 1846 the Irish potato crop had collapsed to one-fifth of its pre-blight levels. Alarming reports of starvation started to reach England from Ireland but the general opinion in London was that the Irish press always had "a tendency to exaggeration." The British were by no means all callous and uncaring, but in the mid-nineteenth century the welfare system was extremely basic. England's seventeenth-century Poor Law established a system of "outdoor" and "indoor" relief. Outdoor relief meant the giving of financial or food aid that allowed the recipients to continue farming their land, but this was considered expensive, and the landowners who paid for the system preferred the cheaper indoor relief, which entailed sending the poor to a prison-like "workhouse," where families were split up and the inmates were forced to work and live in terrible conditions. Many people preferred to go hungry rather than go to the workhouse, and many others were excluded from even this basic safety net by exemptions and loopholes designed to save the landowners money at the cost of human misery and lives.

Another factor that worsened the famine was the economic system of the day. Britain was in the process of moving from a protectionist economy, which sheltered its domestic markets by imposing high tariffs on imports, to a *laissez-faire* capitalist economy, in which everything was left to the workings of the market. The centerpiece of the protectionist system was the legislation known as the Corn Laws of 1815 that kept the price of grain artificially high in Britain. Although it went against the interests of his own party, the Tory (Conservative) prime minister Sir Robert Peel (1788–1850) used the Great Famine to repeal the Corn Laws in 1846. Although Peel instituted some limited measures to relieve the famine, these were largely ineffective, and they were abandoned by the next laissez-faire Whig (Liberal) administration, which believed that market mechanisms would deal with the problem. In the earlier Great Famine, food exports from Ireland had been banned and the island's ports closed, but during the 1840 famine, Ireland continued to be an exporter of foodstuffs while most of its population starved.

The outcome was disastrous: Between 1 and 1.5 million died of starvation and epidemic diseases between 1845 and 1852, and a further 1 to 1.5 million emigrated, establishing the large Irish diaspora in the U.S., UK mainland, Canada, and Australia. The population of Ireland, estimated to be between seven and eight million just before the famine, crashed to between four and five million a decade later. But in addition to the human cost of the disaster, the Great Famine created a legacy of bitterness against the British state and Protestant Irish that has endured to the present day, costing many more lives during the succeeding century of rebellion, civil war, and political dissent.

DISASTER

Extinction Event

Tectonic Event

Military Action

Fire

Pandemic

Famine

Political or Economic Event

Genocide

Flood or Storm

Industrial or Transport Accident

THE YEAR OF FIRES: PESHTIGO FIRE

1871

Cause: Long, hot summer; tree branches and cleared brush left to dry out after land clearance and timber felling; high number of lumber mills and woodenware factories with large timber stocks; practice of burning to clear land for agriculture, railroads, and building

Event: Smaller fires were fanned together into a huge firestorm by unfavorable winds; fires across the region surrounding Peshtigo, Wisconsin

Aftermath: Destruction of Peshtigo and the loss of between 1,500 and 2,500 lives; millions of acres of forest burned

So great was the violence of the wind that in less than one minute after the first house took fire the whole village was in flames. There was no prospect of checking the flames, for the smoldering forest presented one mass of fire. People could only flee to the river for safety.

Report of the Peshtigo Fire,
New York Times,
October 17, 1871

One of the key developments in the evolution of the human species is the control of fire. Archeological evidence from caves in South Africa suggests that one ancient hominid species, *Homo erectus* (1.8 million–300,000 years BP), may have used fire to cook food as far back as one million years BP, but the remains of ash and charred bones found in the caves along with early human stone tools do not conclusively prove that this was from the intentional use of fire for cooking. Archeologists have not found any kind of hearth, which would provide conclusive evidence of a prehistoric BBQ. Hearths are one of the technological advances associated with the behavioral modernity of humans, which occurred between 75,000 and 50,000 years BP, when archaic *H. sapiens* became the recognizably modern *H. sapiens sapiens*—a man or woman just like you and me, apart from the fur loincloth.

The control of fire gave our ancestors a huge advantage in the survival stakes. It allowed early humans to keep warm and to stay active at nighttime, as well as to live in deep caves where they could shelter from the elements; fire was also a formidable weapon that they could use against the largest prey and fiercest predators. When our ancestors put fire and meat together, creating the first roast dinner, they may have triggered an increase in brain size. Cooked food is already partially broken down, hence our bodies can get a lot more out of it with a much lower energy expenditure to digest it. This calorific gain, some scientists argue, was ultimately converted into larger brains. When humans settled to create the first agricultural civilizations around 10,000 years BP, fire became an even more useful adjunct in clearing forested land.

The great benefits that fire brought to our ancestors, however, also came with a high price tag. Settled communities of buildings constructed from wood and other organic materials, heated and lit by open hearths, candles, or oil lamps, were always at risk of fire, as we saw in the Great Fire of London (pp. 71–74). Right into the industrial age, fire remained a high risk, because cities were lit with explosive gas made from coal, and the infrastructure of pipes was much less robust and secure than it is today. Say the date October 8, 1871, and "fire" in the same sentence, and many readers will immediately think of the Great Chicago Fire that started on that day and burned itself out on October 10, having destroyed about one-third of the city and killed between 200 and 300 citizens. Although the loss of life was thankfully relatively small in terms of the total population of the city of some 300,000, the material damage was immense, with 100,000 made homeless.

The causes of the fire were not that different from those of the Great Fire of London two centuries earlier: wooden houses, boardwalks, and jetties built too close together, stores of inflammable materials in the center of town, naked flames used in homes for lighting, heating, and cooking, and strong winds to fan the flames into an inferno that jumped over rivers, and that the firefighters could not hope to contain with the equipment at their disposal. In the end, the wind dropped and it began to rain, bringing the conflagration under control. But the Great Chicago Fire was just one of four fires that broke out in the Great Lakes region that hot, dry October day, and while it probably caused the most damage in material terms, it was far from being the deadliest. The real human disaster that took place on October 8, 1871, is now mostly forgotten, except by the residents of the area who have good reason to remember it. This was the deadliest forest fire in the history of the U.S., which, in a matter of hours, wiped out the town of Peshtigo, Wisconsin, and most of its surrounding communities.

"PEOPLE COULD ONLY FLEE TO THE RIVER FOR SAFETY"

The fact that four fires occurred on the same day in the Great Lakes region has led several scientists to speculate that they had a common cause. For once, this is not any kind of conspiracy theory involving the Federal government or aliens, but fragments of a comet or large meteor re-entering the atmosphere. However, space scientists have discounted the idea because meteorite fragments landing on earth are usually too cold to start fires, and an airborne explosion would have been more destructive as demonstrated by the Tunguska event of 1908, which exploded between three and six miles (5–10 km) above the earth's surface, detonating with an explosive yield equivalent to a large thermo-nuclear device.

The actual causes of the fires are actually quite easy to explain if one studies the areas involved, the working practices of the day, and the climatic conditions for the summer of 1871. Peshtigo had been built in a forested area, and the inhabitants made a living from farming, logging, and the manufacture of woodenwares. The European immigrants to the area employed the tried-and-tested land-clearance technique known as "slash-and-burn" agriculture, in which virgin forest was cleared by controlled fires; another type of "slash"—the unwanted branches of trees cut down for logging—was burned on the spot or left in huge piles in the forest; and the local lumberyards and woodenware factories had large stocks of timber and vast quantities of waste from processing the lumber. Another fire risk were the railroads that were being built in the area: Trees and brush were not cleared but left by the side of tracks where stray sparks from the engines could set them alight. And finally, Peshtigo and the communities of the vicinity were built mostly of wood and other inflammable materials, with sawdust floors and streets. Couple these factors with a summer-long drought and strong winds blowing toward the town on the day, and you have the recipe for a firestorm of epic proportions.

© Wisconsin Historical Society

PERFECT STORM
Survivors had to jump into the river to survive the firestorm.

In the evening of October 8, a freshening wind fanned the slow-burning fires in the neighboring forests into a firestorm that raced toward the town. The fire spread so quickly, surprising the terrified residents of the area, that many burned to death in their homes or as they were preparing to flee. The heat was so intense that their clothes and hair caught fire as they ran from the flames. A few managed to survive the calamity by throwing themselves into the Peshtigo River, where they were forced to keep dousing their heads with water to prevent their hair from catching light, such was the heat from the fire on both banks. Even then, many perished in the cold water, either drowned or from hyperthermia. Estimates for the victims of the fire in Peshtigo and the surrounding communities range between 1,500 and 2,500, and between 1,875 and 2,355 square miles (4,860 and 6,100 km²) of forest and agricultural land were burned.

DISASTER

Extinction Event

Tectonic Event

Military Action

Fire

Pandemic

Famine

Political or Economic Event

Genocide

Flood or Storm

Industrial or Transport Accident

BIGGEST BANG:
KRAKATOA ERUPTION

1883

Cause: Volcanic eruption (VEI 6)

Event: Two-thirds of the island of Krakatoa was destroyed in the final eruptions

Aftermath: Pyroclastic flows destroyed communities 25 miles (40 km) away across the sea, killing 1,000 people; a 151-foot (43 m) tsunami killed an estimated 36,000 people; global cooling from ash in atmosphere and disrupted weather patterns for five years

The Kratataus [Krakatoa] were uninhabited—luckily so, for no one would have survived on the islands; there were no survivors from the 3,000 or so people on the island of Sebesi, 13 km away. Even the great tsunami was seen by very few.

Ian Thornton,
Krakatau: The Destruction and Reassembly of an Island Ecosystem, 1997

We return to tectonic events with the eruption of Krakatoa (Indonesian: Krakatau), an island volcano in the Sunda Strait between the two major Indonesian islands of Sumatra and Java. Krakatoa forms part of the Pacific "Ring of Fire"—actually more of a "bent horseshoe of fire," but that does not quite have the same *ring* to it—which features many of the planet's most recent major volcanic eruptions and most devastating earthquakes and tsunamis. In terms of the different kinds of tectonic boundaries and earthquake faults described in previous entries, the Ring of Fire has the full set. The left-hand (bent) side of the horseshoe starts in New Zealand and Tonga and then curls around toward Papua New Guinea and Indonesia, creating a convergent boundary where the Indo-Australian plate subducts under the Eurasian plate.

If you still have your "peanut-butter-and-jelly-sandwich" model of the earth's crust (p. 59), we can reproduce the type of volcano associated with a convergent boundary: when two tectonic plates are moving together. With the sandwich flat on the plate, push the half with the pointy bit of the cut at the bottom toward the other half to produce convergent "subduction"— that is where one plate goes underneath the other, causing the top to buckle upward. Convergence between two landmasses can lead to some pretty impressive results, for example the Himalayas; but when an oceanic plate subducts under a continental plate, it creates zones of extreme tectonic instability with the full set of earthquakes, volcanoes, and tsunamis.

Before we turn our attention to the Krakatoa eruption, a few words about the volcano shapes and sizes—a volcano identity parade, if you wish, or "Are you sure that this was the volcano that buried your city?" Volcanoes are a bit like adolescent acne: You get the sudden-onset spot that grows overnight and is ready to spew its contents in the morning, or the slow-progressing swelling that never seems to reach maturity and gets bigger and harder, until it finally bursts leaving a large crater. A "shield" volcano, named for an ancient warrior's flattened circular shield, is produced by lava that spreads out slowly and evenly like cream or custard over a cake. "Cinder cones" are built up of ash-like materials around a volcanic vent. "Stratovolcanoes" are what the average person thinks of as volcanoes: a steep conical mountain, made up of alternate layers of lava and cinders and ash with a great big hole in the middle, like Mount Fuji or Vesuvius. Finally, "dome volcanoes" are rounded protrusions made of thick lava

PROJECTILE
A giant block of coral flung
onto the island of Java by
the force of the eruption.

that cannot flow very far. The huge pressures involved in the creation of a dome mean that when it ruptures, you get an extremely violent eruption.

Although shield volcanoes can eject a lot of material, the eruptions are not violent. The most dangerous eruptions are, firstly, supervolcanic eruptions, such as the Toba supereruption of 70,000 years BP (pp. 16–20), which can trigger severe worldwide climate change. Fortunately for humanity, there have been no supereruptions in historical times. Next in line in the disaster stakes are stratovolcanoes and lava domes, two volcano types that erupt extremely violently, not only ejecting a great deal of lava, but also sending ash and droplets of sulfuric acid high into the atmosphere, blocking out heat and light and temporarily cooling the climate. Another Indonesian volcano, Mount Tambora on Sumatra, which erupted in 1815, was responsible for "the year without a summer" of 1816, when there were unseasonal snowfalls early in the year in the U.S. and a marked worldwide drop in temperature.

MAKE SOME NOISE

Krakatoa had erupted several times before, but the 1883 eruption was the first to be recorded and studied scientifically. The eruption began in May and ended spectacularly four months later with several supermassive explosions between 5:30 a.m. and 10:41 a.m. on August 27. Imagine the loudest noise you've ever heard and then multiply it several thousand times, you might begin to get an idea of what the explosions sounded like. According to contemporary reports, the final explosions were heard 2,000 miles (3,200 km) to the south in the city of Perth in Western Australia, and 3,000 miles (4,800 km) to the west on the Indian Ocean island of Rodrigues. The eruptions vaporized two-thirds of the island of Krakatoa, and the shockwave from the last blast ruptured the eardrums of sailors on ships in the Sunda Strait and registered on pressure gauges all over the planet.

The eruption produced pyroclastic flows, which are columns of superheated gas and ash. On land, these race down the volcano's slopes incinerating anything in their path. The Krakatoa flows were unique because they surfed over 25 miles (40 km) of open sea across the Sunda Strait and reached the coast of Sumatra, killing an estimated 1,000 people. A tsunami some 151 feet (43 m) high swept over the nearby island of Sebesi, killing its entire population of around 3,000, and went on to ravage the coasts of Java and Sumatra, claiming a further estimated 29,000 victims (though another estimate puts the death toll as high as 120,000). Tsunamis rocked ships on the East African coast, and unusually high waves were reported as far away as the English Channel. But the most spectacular effect was on the world's climate. In the year after the eruption, global temperatures fell by around 2.2°F (1.2°C) and weather patterns were disrupted for a further five years. At the same time, the ash in the atmosphere created the most extraordinarily colorful sunsets, tinting the sky in bright shades of day-glow red and orange.

Scientists think that most of the island fell into the magma chamber under the volcano during the eruption, creating a caldera volcanic crater that was immediately filled with seawater. In 1927, a new volcano began to emerge within the caldera. Anak Krakatoa (Child of Krakatoa) is now 1,000 feet (305 m) high, with a 300-foot (100 m) lava dome within the crater that suggests that the volcano is due another major eruption. If and when it occurs, the casualties and material damage will be much greater, as Indonesia now has a population of 237.6 million, and Java, on the western side of the Sunda Strait, is the most densely populated island in the world. We shall see how deadly a major tectonic disaster in the area can be when we examine the Indian Ocean earthquake and tsunami of 2004 (pp. 226–229).

© Creative Commons

DEAFENING
The final eruption of Krakatoa is thought to be the loudest noise ever heard on earth.

DISASTER

Extinction Event

Tectonic Event

Military Action

Fire

Pandemic

Famine

Political or Economic Event

Genocide

Flood or Storm

Industrial or Transport Accident

SHIP OF NIGHTMARES: SINKING OF THE RMS *TITANIC*

1912

Cause: Iceberg; the captain's failure to receive two crucial iceberg warnings; insufficient numbers of lifeboats for the total number on board; design faults

Event: Gash in the hull caused by the iceberg holed five watertight compartments, when the ship had been designed to withstand the loss of four compartments; the ship began to sink, dragging many victims down with her

Aftermath: 1,517 deaths; *Titanic*, the movie

We do not care anything for the heaviest storms in these big ships. It is fog that we fear. The big icebergs that drift into warmer water melt much more rapidly under water than on the surface, and sometimes a sharp, low reef extending two or three hundred feet beneath the sea is formed. If a vessel should run on one of these reefs half her bottom might be torn away.

**Captain Edward Smith,
interview before the *Titanic*'s maiden voyage, 1912**

We reach the fateful year of 1912, and one of the most infamous disasters in history, the sinking of the RMS *Titanic*, the "ship of dreams" featured in *Titanic*, the movie (1997). In the introduction, it was speculated as to why the sinking of this one passenger liner ranked so highly in the narrative of human disasters. Of course, as film director James Cameron realized, it makes for a "ripping yarn," even without the made-up love triangle between Rose (Kate Winslet), Jack (Leonardo DiCaprio), and Cal (Billy Zane).

As the movie starts, there is the buildup: The majestic, luxurious, awe-inspiring liner that dwarfs the passengers on the quayside at Southampton, causing Cal to turn to Rose and utter the fateful words: "It is unsinkable. God himself could not sink this ship!" With all safely aboard and underway, Cameron gives us intimations of the impending disaster, with the unheeded iceberg warnings, the Captain trying to please his employers, the White Star Line, by breaking the record for the transatlantic crossing—all preparation for the inevitable waterlogged conclusion. You would have to have been cut off from civilization not to know how the story climaxes—and not just the maudlin *liaison dangereuse* between Rose and Jack, but the tragic fate of the great ship herself. So are we just ghouls? Or is it alright, because there are so many mad, bad, or foolish passengers on board that they deserve to sink?

© Gorgios | Dreamstime

DREAM LINER
Titanic was the largest, most advanced, and most luxurious liner of its time.

There is a good deal of psychology at work here. After all, we all love a good disaster movie—the bigger the better, it seems—and watch in fascinated horror news reports and documentaries about real hurricanes, earthquakes, volcanic eruptions, and tsunamis in the comfort and safety of our own homes. Is it an expression of Sigmund Freud's (1856–1939) famous "death drive"? Or is it just a case of realizing how much better off we are than the benighted victims of faraway natural and human disasters? In addition, there must also be something particularly horrifying about imagining ourselves trapped on a doomed sinking ship far away from any hope of rescue.

RMS *Titanic* set sail from Southampton, England, on her maiden voyage to New York on April 10, 1912. An *Olympic*-class liner, she was the largest ship then built, at 882 feet 9 inches (269.1 m) long, 92 feet (28 m)

ON THE ROCKS

wide, and 175 feet (53.3 m) high from keel to funnel top, and probably the most technologically advanced ocean liner of her day. She set sail from her last port of call in Ireland carrying 2,240 passengers and crew, though she had been designed to accommodate more than 3,500. Apart from the shenanigans between the imaginary Cal, Rose, and Jack, the movie is pretty accurate about the details and timing of the accident and sinking, the technical shortcomings of the liner, and her less than adequate lifeboat capacity.

WATERY GRAVE
Titanic stayed afloat for two hours before she broke up and sank.

The British regulations of the day stated that a ship over 10,000 tons had to carry 16 lifeboats, plus extra rafts. *Titanic* was four-and-a-half times that tonnage, at 46,328 tons, and she carried 20 lifeboats, which was actually four more than the law required, but these only had a woefully inadequate capacity of 1,178. However, anticipating a change in the law, the owners, the White Star Line, had 16 large davits (crane-like devices that lower lifeboats over the side) fitted on the decks, each with a capacity to launch four lifeboats. Therefore, on future crossings, *Titanic* could have carried as many as 64 lifeboats, enough for 4,000 passengers and crew.

The hull of *Titanic* was divided into 16 watertight compartments that could be sealed from the bridge as soon as the ship began to take on water. She had been designed to stay afloat with four compartments holed, and she was also equipped with the latest in steam-pump technology. In theory, as long as the coal-fired furnaces powering the pumps were operational, they could cope with a four-compartment breech. The final safety feature was a wireless telegraph room fitted with the latest Marconi radio equipment, with two operators working in shifts around the clock.

The bridge received iceberg warnings during the first few days of the crossing, and the captain decided to change course, unfortunately into the path of more southerly icebergs. *Titanic*'s bridge failed to get two crucial warnings on April 14 because the wireless operators had been instructed to give priority to the messages of first-class passengers. At 11:40 p.m., the lookout sighted an iceberg dead ahead but the evasive maneuver ordered by the officer of the watch failed to prevent the collision. The iceberg buckled the side of the hull under the waterline, breaching five compartments—one more than the ship was designed to lose and remain afloat. The ship stayed afloat for another two hours until the pumps failed and then went down quickly, breaking into two as she sank. By then many of the lifeboats had been launched, many not filled to capacity. In the freezing waters of the Atlantic in April, life expectancy could be calculated in minutes. Very few who were pulled out of the waters by the two lifeboats that turned back to rescue people in the water survived the ordeal. A total of 1,517 passengers and crew perished in the sinking.

The loss of *Titanic*, while far from being the first disaster story, which begin in dimmest, darkest pre-biblical antiquity, did begin the disaster-movie genre, with two early movies about the sinking: *Night and Ice* (1912) and *Atlantis* (1913). The disaster movie has never gone away, reaching a hysterical zenith in the 1970s with movies such as *The Andromeda Strain* (1971), *Earthquake* (1974), and *Towering Inferno* (1974), and culminating in the apocalyptic EOTWAWKI ("End Of The World As We Know It") movie to end all movies, *2012* (2009). But in the introduction (pp. 8–9), I suggested another reason for the enduring appeal of the *Titanic* story.

So far in this book, disasters have been covered which killed millions, destroyed whole cities and civilizations, and changed the course of history and biology; and sadly, many more shall be covered. But just as with money, while it's easy to imagine holding $1,000 or even $10,000 (OK, be greedy!) in your hot little hands, $1 million, let alone $1 billion, is a lot more difficult to imagine—you'd need much bigger hands for starters. The death of 100,000 or 1 million people is pretty unimaginable, but 1,500 people is the size of a small town, or of a large high school, factory, or corporation. You might not know everyone in town, or all the people you work or study with, but you can easily picture 1,517 people standing in one place. Hence, we have a direct emotional connection to 1,517 people that we could not have with anonymous millions. And maybe, by extension, it is when we start thinking of living human beings as abstract numbers that the most terrible things can happen, as we are about to see in the next entry that deals with history's first recognized genocide.

DISASTER

Extinction Event

Tectonic Event

Military Action

Fire

Pandemic

Famine

Political or Economic Event

Genocide

Flood or Storm

Industrial or Transport Accident

THE FIRST GENOCIDE: ARMENIA

1915–23

Cause: Separatism and rebellions among the Armenian population due to historical oppression of non-Muslim minorities; dislocation of the Ottoman Empire; hostilities during First World War used as an excuse by the Turkish government to begin a systematic extermination of its minority populations

Event: Deaths of between 600,000 and 1,500,000 Armenians

Aftermath: Genocide denied in Turkey–referring to it as a criminal offence risks official prosecution and persecution, and the threat of assassination by Turkish ultranationalists

Deportation of and excesses against peaceful Armenians is increasing and from harrowing reports of eye witnesses it appears that a campaign of race extermination is in progress under a pretext of reprisal against rebellion.

**U.S. Ambassador Morgenthau,
telegram to the State Department,
July 16, 1915**

We come to the first disaster in this book that is defined as a true "genocide"—a term coined by Polish-born American jurist Raphael Lemkin (1900–59) in 1944. The International Criminal Court (ICC), which is now charged with the prosecution of the perpetrators of genocide, defines it as: "The deliberate and systematic destruction, in whole or in part, of an ethnic, racial, religious, or national group." In 1996, Professor Gregory Stanton of George Mason University refined the definition of genocide by outlining eight stages: (1) classification, (2) symbolization, (3) dehumanization, (4) organization, (5) polarization, (6) preparation, (7) extermination, and (8) denial. The first three serve to separate the victim group and make it into an "other"; the next three are concerned with the planning and preparation of the genocide; and finally, after the genocide has taken place, the eighth change: once the genocide is under way, the perpetrators will deny that it is taking place.

Of course, the definition owes a great deal to the Holocaust perpetrated by the Nazis during World War Two (pp. 149–155), when Lemkin was formulating his ideas, but he himself explained that he had developed the concept by studying an event thought by many to be the first genocide of the modern era: the extermination of the Armenian citizens of the Ottoman Empire between 1915 and 1923. The definition of the disaster as a genocide is still a bitterly contested issue, with the Turkish government using every means at its disposal to press its Western allies not to recognize it as such, as well as prosecuting its own citizens who try to write about or discuss it.

MEMORIAL
The genocide is not recognized in Turkey, where anyone discussing it risks prosecution.

The term "genocide" has been applied to human disasters before the twentieth century, but not all of these meet the criteria of in the Lemkin/ICC/Stanton definitions. Although the Assyrians, Egyptians, Greeks, and Romans would sometimes massacre the population of a town or a tribe, this was usually done as a punishment for rebellion or to encourage others to surrender, to kill every last person in a city or province would be a waste of human resources and of potential imperial slaves, subjects, or soldiers.

In Europe, during the Middle Ages and the early modern period, religion constituted a major cause for genocidal acts. The First Crusade (1096–99), for example, culminated in the massacre of the Muslim and Jewish population of Jerusalem in 1099. There were similar "crusades" in Europe,

© UIG | Getty Images

GENOCIDE
The massacres of Armenians in Turkey led to the legal definition of genocide.

which targeted heretical Christian sects. The Albigensian Crusade (1209–55) ended with the total extermination of the Cathars. Similar massacres of Catholics by Protestants, or of Protestants by Catholics, as in the Saint Bartholomew's Day Massacre in 1572, which claimed between 10,000 and 30,000 lives in France, blighted Europe during the Wars of Religion (1524–1648) triggered by the Protestant Reformation of 1517.

Long before the internecine struggles between Protestant and Catholic, Europe had persecuted one religious minority, the Jews, who were regularly dispossessed, exiled, and slaughtered, under various pretexts, such as the "Blood Libel," recorded from England in the twelfth century, and as agents spreading the plague during the Black Death (pp. 52–57). The European persecution of the Jews during the Middle Ages, however, stopped short of genocide. Jews were murdered, robbed, and driven from their homes, but there was no deliberate program of extermination until the Nazi "final solution." Several European countries forcibly converted or expelled their Jewish communities, such as Spain in 1492 — not entirely coincidentally, the same year as the discovery of the Americas and the end of the *Reconquista*. Many of Spain's Jewish population, who refused to convert to Catholicism, fled to the relative safety of the Muslim lands of North Africa and Egypt, and of the Ottoman Empire, creating the Sephardi community of European Jewry (from *Sfarad*, Hebrew for "Spain").

EUROPE'S "SICK MAN"

The founder of the Ottoman state, Osman I (1258–1328), dreamed of an empire that spanned Europe, North Africa, and the Near East, with its capital in Constantinople. It took his successor Mehmet II (1432–81) until 1453 to achieve the capture of the Byzantine capital, but once this was achieved the Ottoman Empire expanded exponentially, defeating Safavid Persia and seizing control of the Near East, Egypt, and North Africa. In Europe, the Ottoman advance seemed unstoppable. The Ottomans already controlled the former Byzantine provinces in the Balkans; now they conquered Bulgaria and Hungary, and threatened the Austrian capital of Vienna. The defeat of the besieging Ottoman army at the Battle of Vienna (1683), however, marked the apogee of the empire.

The reasons for Ottoman decline are complex, combining internal and external factors. Internally, the empire had expanded to such an extent that, like the Roman Empire before it, it had become too large and unwieldy to govern. Rebellious provincial governors exploited weakness in Constantinople to assert their independence. Early able sultans made way for weak incompetents, who were manipulated by their corrupt, power-hungry courtiers. Externally, the empire's European enemies were making huge strides economically and technologically. Wealth was flowing into Western Europe from the New World, and from the maritime trade that bypassed and impoverished the Ottoman lands that had once controlled all trade between Asia and Europe. From being one of the socially and technologically most advanced areas of the world, the empire was stagnating socially and intellectually, and fast becoming the "sick man of Europe."

During the nineteenth century, the Ottoman frontiers were gradually shrinking: Greece won its independence in 1832, followed by the rest of the Balkans and Ottoman Eastern Europe; the empire lost North Africa, Egypt, and retained only nominal control over Arabia. At the outbreak of World War One, the empire consisted of modern-day Turkey and parts of the Near East. In deciding to side with the losing Central Powers of Germany and Austria-Hungary, it would soon be subject to the same fate as the other two empires that would not survive the national aspirations of their component nationalities.

Independence for the empire's Christian European subjects stimulated demands among other minorities for independence and autonomy. The Armenians, who constituted one of the empire's largest non-Muslim minorities, lived mainly in the eastern provinces of the empire. Armenia had adopted Christianity as its state religion even before the Roman Empire did so, in 301 CE. As non-Muslims, the Armenians, like the empire's Greek and Jewish subjects, had a second-class status that left them vulnerable to abuse, violence, and exploitation from their Muslim neighbors or from provincial authorities when central authority was weak.

As the empire began to break up, the Armenian bid for equality under the law with their Muslim neighbors and a measure of autonomy changed into calls for revolution and independence—a trend encouraged by the Russian Empire that was expanding southward. The First World War saw the two empires on opposite sides, and the Russians invaded the eastern Ottoman provinces where they were welcomed as liberators by many

Armenians, some of whom joined the war fighting against their sovereign in Constantinople. Although there had been bloody pogroms targeting the Armenians throughout the nineteenth century, these did not amount to a concerted policy of extermination. What triggered the genocide was the outbreak of the war, and the fear by the government in Constantinople that the empire's Armenian citizens, peasants, and soldiers would join its enemies.

The first step of the genocide was to transfer all Armenian soldiers in the Ottoman armed forces to unarmed labor battalions in February 1915, on the pretext that they might defect to the Russian side. Once disarmed and separated from their Muslim comrades, the Armenians were executed by Turkish "special forces"—men released from prisons for the express purpose of providing personnel for killing squads. In April, leading Armenian figures, politicians, academics, professionals, and civil servants, were arrested in Constantinople and later in other major provincial towns and sent to detention camps near Ankara. Throughout this period, the Ottoman government was issuing propaganda accusing the Armenians of collusion with the enemy, and of fomenting rebellion.

With the Armenian community decapitated and defenseless, the killing squads moved into Armenian areas. Entire villages were rounded up, and their populations either drowned in the Black Sea or burned alive in churches. In moves that anticipated the Nazi Holocaust, the government set up 25 concentration camps, where deported Armenians were liquidated with poison or toxic gas, and burned alive. Armenian land and property was deemed "abandoned" and confiscated by the state—a policy that was codified into law by the Expropriation and Confiscation Law of September 1915. Those who had not met their deaths at the hands of the death squads were force-marched into the Syrian desert, without food or water, where they died of thirst, starvation, disease, or mistreatment at the hands of the Ottoman troops guarding them, or of Muslim citizens who were encouraged to attack, murder, rob, and rape the deportees. While many historians and around 20 countries now describe the events of 1915 as constituting genocide, the Turkish government continues in its denials. Without the collaboration of the Turkish authorities, it has been impossible to document the exact number of Armenian casualties but estimates range from 600,000 to 1.5 million victims of history's first genocide.

GOING FORTH: BATTLE OF THE SOMME

1916

DISASTER

Extinction Event

Tectonic Event

Military Action

Fire

Pandemic

Famine

Political or Economic Event

Genocide

Flood or Storm

Industrial or Transport Accident

Cause: Battle of the Somme was planned as the "Big Push" that would break through German lines on the Western Front in Flanders and northern France

Event: After an ineffective artillery bombardment, British forces attacked the German lines across no-man's-land

Aftermath: Casualties on the first day were the highest recorded for any British military action; the offensive continued until November when it had claimed 1 million casualties on both sides for maximum Allied territorial gains of 6–7 miles (9.5–11 km)

The British moved forward in line after line, dressed as if on parade; not a man wavered or broke rank, but minute by minute the ordered line melted under the deluge of high explosive, shrapnel, rifle and machine-gun fire.

John Buchan,
The Battle of the Somme, 1917

© Australian War Museum

For centuries, the principal military rivalry in northwest Europe was between the English and the French, who had been scrapping since the Norman Invasion of England in 1066. Dynastic claim and counterclaim embroiled the French and English crowns in the Hundred Years' War (1337–1453), which dovetailed neatly into the Wars of Religion (1524–1648) that saw Catholic France and Protestant England as natural enemies. During the reign of the Sun King, Louis XIV (1638–1715), France played the role of the continental bully, opposed by shifting alliances of Holland, England, and the German states which were nominally united within the Holy Roman Empire. The revolution of 1789 only worsened France's image, and she remained Europe's public enemy number one throughout the Revolutionary (see pp. 83–86) and Napoleonic Wars (1792–1815). But in 1871 everything changed with the unification of Germany after France's shock defeat in the Franco-Prussian War (1870–71).

The emergence of Germany as a second continental empire alongside the Hapsburg Austria-Hungary transformed European politics and upset the precarious balance of power that the great powers had managed to maintain since the defeat of Napoleon (1769–1821) in 1815. The German First Reich was founded amid Prussia's victory celebrations for her defeat of the Second French Empire, and enacted symbolically in the residence of the Sun King, the Palace of Versailles. France had been laid low and comprehensively defeated and humiliated. All of a sudden, there was a new hate figure in Europe, who was to prove even more troublesome to the British than the French.

The British and Germans had a long-standing common enmity with France; they were also united by Protestantism, and by family ties. The British royal family are of German descent: the House of Windsor was established by the German George I, Elector of Hanover (1660–1727), who, when he became king of England, could not speak English. Ties of kinship and marriage linked the German imperial family to the British royals: The Kaiser, Wilhelm II (1888–1941), was Queen Victoria's (1819–1901) grandson. In addition, Britain had a great colonial and maritime empire that preferred to avoid Continental entanglements, and the Germans calculated that the British would stay out of any future war in Europe.

Germany's crushing victory over France, her territorial ambitions in Europe and the rest of the world, her industrial and commercial might that rivaled British economic dominance, and her militaristic, anti-democratic ideology, however, would mean that it was Germany that Britain now feared as a rival and worked to contain, pushing her to ally herself with the old enemy, France, now in her Third Republic (1870–1940). The French were naturally keen to avenge their humiliating defeat of 1871, and recover the provinces of Alsace-Lorraine that they had been forced to cede to Germany. The Russians, worried about Germany's ambitions in the Balkans and Eastern Europe, had forgotten their former enmity with Britain and France, against whom they had fought the Crimean War (1853–56), and joined the "Triple Entente," as the Allies were known during World War One.

Military men are constantly accused of fighting "yesterday's war," meaning that they have carefully studied the mistakes that an earlier generation of soldiers made in past conflicts, so as to avoid them, hence making a whole new set of disastrous and costly mistakes. Unfortunately for the British, the last war they had fought against a European power was the Crimean War—a limited action, in a distant part of the no-man's-land between Asia and Eastern Europe in the mid-nineteenth century. Its one memorable action had been the "Charge of the Light Brigade" during the Battle of Balaclava in 1854—a typical piece of military insanity, which saw a British cavalry unit of 600 men charge a highly fortified Russian position, uphill, through a narrow valley, in full sight of enemy artillery. The last major battle the British had fought on European soil was even more ancient: the Battle of Waterloo in 1815.

YESTERDAY'S WAR

© Australian War Museum

EXPEDITION
The British Expeditionary Force succeeded in halting the German advance to the sea.

The reader might complain that it is easy to ridicule the British military preparations for the First World War with twenty-first-century hindsight, and that even they couldn't possibly have tried to fight a nineteenth-century infantry and cavalry war in the twentieth century. Well, the reader would be wrong. The first shot fired by a British soldier in France was fired by a cavalryman, and, in a repeat of the Light Brigade disaster of sixty years before, a British cavalry detachment charged a German infantry and artillery position in August 1914, losing 250 men and 300 horses in the ensuing carnage. The Germans and French, it must be admitted, also deployed cavalry, but with as little effect as the British. The British continued, however, in the face of the complete impossibility of using cavalry in trench warfare, to plan for its deployment as late as 1916, when it would be used to chase the Germans back to Berlin.

World War One is a war of many firsts: the first to involve every inhabited continent, with the exception of the southern half of the Americas, and the first to make full use of the many advances of the Second Industrial Revolution to mechanize the troublesome business of killing one's enemy. New technologies certainly made war deadlier, but they did not make it clean or clinical. The Germans had exploited the railways to move their troops during the Franco-Prussian War, and this time, all sides shared the ability to mobilize vast numbers of fighting men and get them to the front line quickly. In addition to trains, the combatants had the use of motor vehicles and airplanes, barbed wire, machine guns, radio, high explosives, and, of course, poison gas. The development of any one of these inventions would have had a serious impact on the fighting of a war, but combined, they completely transformed warfare from a giant chess game in which generals moved infantry, artillery, and cavalry units on the battlefield from the safety of a nearby hill, into a gigantic continent-sized stalemate in which the belligerents dug trenches and dugouts to avoid the other side's long-range, high-explosive artillery, protecting themselves with miles of barbed wire and machine-gun emplacements.

© Australian War Museum

MECHANIZED
The Somme saw the deployment of the first tanks and armored vehicles.

After an initial German advance into Belgium and France that was halted at some cost by the French and their British allies, the two sides fortified their forward positions and tried to think what to do next: Neither side had any real solution to the stalemate. The Germans had planned to repeat their victory of 1871, forcing a quick capitulation by charging across the French countryside, besieging Paris, and cutting off the British Expeditionary Force from the sea; the British strategy, if they had one at all, was to win a series of pitched battles and defeat the Germans as they had done one hundred years earlier against the French.

Fans of the hit BBC television series *Blackadder Goes Forth* (1989) will have some idea of the farcical horror that many soldiers faced on the Western Front. Although it has none of the gritty realism of the earlier movie *All Quiet on the Western Front* (1930), based on the 1929 novel of the same name, *Blackadder Goes Forth* satirically dramatizes the months before British forces go "over the top"—that is, out of the safety of their trenches, for the "final big push" through the German lines and on to victory. Of course, in order to engage the enemy, the troops would have to cross between 300 and 700 yards or meters of no-man's-land, covered in barbed wired, mined, deeply cratered by shells, and protected by artillery and machine guns.

The area chosen for the offensive was near the River Somme and would involve both British and imperial forces, under General, later Field Marshal, Douglas Haig (1861–1928), and French forces commanded by his French opposite number General, later Maréchal, Joseph Joffre (1852–1931). There was disagreement between the two high commands about the timing of the offensive. The French, under pressure from a major German attack on their fortress of Verdun in Lorraine, wanted to begin the offensive in June, but Haig wanted more time to train his troops, many of whom were fresh from England and the colonies, and also to bring in more heavy artillery to attack the strongly fortified German lines.

In the end, and after a heated argument during which the two generals almost came to blows, they compromised on a start date of July 1, 1916. The battle line was divided between the British in the northern sector and the French in the southern sector. The Germans, who had held the line since 1914, had constructed extremely good defensive works, with 30-foot (10 m) deep artillery-proof bunkers and an extensive network of trenches, protected by miles of barbed wire, heavy artillery, and machine-gun emplacements. They also had the advantage of the higher ground, which gave their guns a good field of fire, and made the attacking troops' task literally an uphill struggle.

Haig's "cunning plan" (to quote Baldrick's catchphrase in *Blackadder*) was for the infantry to open a breech in the German lines that would allow his cavalry to sweep through, chasing the retreating Germans, presumably all the way back to Germany. As was now the rule before any major engagement, a week long "shock and awe" artillery barrage preceded the assault, intended to clear the barbed wired from no-man's-land and

GENERAL HAIG'S "CUNNING PLAN"

destroy the German forward positions. Unfortunately, the British did not have enough heavy guns or the kind of shells that could penetrate the deep German bunkers, and the inexperienced British gunners even failed to clear the barbed wire. At zero hour, the British troops left their trenches, laden down with 66-pound (30 kg) packs that only allowed them to go at a steady walking pace. They emerged in ordered lines, marching slowly shoulder-to-shoulder.

The Germans, who had survived the shelling mostly unharmed and definitely unshocked and unawed in their dugouts, emerged to man their artillery and machine guns. Hampered by their packs over the uneven, muddy ground, impeded by the barbed wire that the shelling had only managed to tangle up even more, and with no cover for 300 to 700 yards/ meters of no-man's-land, the British troops were annihilated.

The first day of the Battle of the Somme, featuring an insane General Haig playing with toy soldiers, was re-staged for the series finale of *Blackadder Goes Fort*h, "Goodbyeee." The show, which ends with the main characters going over the top to their certain deaths, provided one of the most poignant and disturbing moments of British television—especially as it was the finale of a hit comedy show.

July 1, 1916, has gone down in history as the costliest single engagement for the British armed forces, which dwarfs the several thousand Allied casualties lost in this century's wars in Iraq and Afghanistan. On the first day of the battle, Britain and the empire alone lost a total of 57,470 men— 21,392 killed or missing in action, 35,493 wounded, and 585 taken prisoner. When he received the initial casualty figures, which underestimated the real carnage by 17,470, Haig is reported to have said, "This cannot be considered severe in view of the numbers engaged, and the length of front attacked." Not only was he not disciplined for the huge losses, let alone dismissed, Haig was promoted to the highest rank in the British Army, Field Marshal, a year later. The Battle of the Somme would go on for another four-and-a-half harrowing, bloody months of increasing stalemate, at the cost of 1 million casualties and for the gain of at best 7 miles (11 km) of enemy territory. Sadly, the Somme was only one of the costlier engagements of a disastrously murderous war, which saw an estimated 7,761,863 military casualties on the Western Front between 1914 and 1918.

MASS KILLER: SPANISH FLU

1918–20

DISASTER

Extinction Event

Tectonic Event

Military Action

Fire

Pandemic

Famine

Political or Economic Event

Genocide

Flood or Storm

Industrial or Transport Accident

Cause: Emergence of a particularly virulent pandemic strain of HINI influenza among a world population already weakened by the First World War

Event: Two waves of infections in 1918, the second much deadlier than the first

Aftermath: About one-third of the world's population was infected, and between 50 and 100 million died worldwide

The abruptness of the onset of the disease and the degree to which it overwhelmed the patient— the technical descriptive term is "fulminating"—seemed far too extreme to be attributed to influenza of any kind. After all, influenza, flu, grippe, grip—whatever you called it or however you spelled it—was a homey, familiar kind of illness.

Alfred Crosby,
America's Forgotten Pandemic, 2003

© CDC | Dr. Terrence Tumpey | PHIL

As far as deaths from infectious diseases are concerned, Westerners can count themselves extremely fortunate when compared to their forebears a few generations back. Even in the relatively recent past, Europeans and Americans were regularly struck down in large numbers with little or no remedy, such as the 150,000 North Americans who died in one cholera outbreak in the mid-nineteenth century, or the 80,000 victims of malaria who died yearly in Europe and North America in the early 1900s. Now a combination of vaccination, advances in healthcare and social welfare, and pest- and disease-control measures has almost eradicated infectious diseases from our cities.

© Library of Congress PPOC

VICTIMS
Most of the victims of the flu were otherwise healthy young men and women.

Citizens of the developed world now take this state of affairs so much for granted that today's major health scares—real and imagined—are about medications with dangerous side-effects, such as the Thalidomide disaster of the 1960s, and about vaccines, such as the panic caused by the MMR (mumps, measles, and rubella) controversy in the UK in 1998, when one maverick British researcher implicated the vaccine as a cause of autism. The predictable results of the false claim were epidemics of measles and mumps in the early 2000s, which led to unnecessary hospitalizations, high costs to the healthcare system, and, even more unfortunately, physical disabilities and deaths that would have otherwise been avoided. Although no medical procedure, including vaccination, is 100 percent safe, the only alternative is to accept the hundred of thousands of unnecessary deaths that continue to occur in the developing world.

Every so often, however, there is a major public-health crisis caused by a novel infectious disease, or, if not entirely new, its appearance in a part of the world where it has never been endemic. The prime example is the HIV-AIDS pandemic (pp. 183–188) that was first recognized in the West in the 1980s. But even when an undocumented illness does appear, it is not always a mass killer; for example, the SARS corona virus that first spread to humans from its animal hosts in 2002 and developed into a worldwide outbreak that claimed 775 victims. But, barring the appearance of a new "Black Death" of truly unexpected virulence, the real danger is not from an unknown pathogen but from familiar viruses that are genetically unstable and can mutate or combine with other viruses to create new, more dangerous strains.

The most dangerous of these unstable pathogens is perhaps among the most common and, for many in the West, the least remarkable: the influenza virus. To quote Alfred Crosby (see p. 115): Flu is a "homey, familiar kind of illness." We are so used to regular visitations from the flu that we don't even stop to consider why we need a different shot every year, while for most viral illnesses all that is required is a once-in-a-lifetime shot. Even "mild" seasonal flu, however, can be a very serious disease. In a completely naïve population, such as in the Americas in the sixteenth century, when it was one of the diseases introduced by the Spanish, even its milder manifestations, which would send us to bed for two or three days, were a killer. But even among a generally healthy modern population, the flu's regular visits should not be underestimated: It infects between five and 15 percent of the world population (350 million to 1 billion), and kills between 250,000 and 500,000 people among high-risk groups: the under-fives, over-65s, and people with underlying health problems. However, healthy adults usually shrug it off without developing any of the complications that will require treatment.

As well as the seasonal variety, strains of flu that exist in an animal host species can infect humans. Historically, the strains that cross the xenographic barrier have been far more dangerous to human health. The Word Health Organization (WHO) explains that, "During past pandemics, attack rates reached 25–35 percent. Assuming that a new virus would cause mild disease, the world could still experience an estimated 2 million to 7.4 million deaths." The WHO has established a six-level scale to monitor flu pandemics: At the lowest threat levels 1–2, the virus only affects animals, and there are no or very few cases of animal-to-human transmission; at levels 3–4 human-to-human transmission takes place at an increasing rate, and the disease begins to spread through the population of one WHO world region (a continent); at levels 5–6, the outbreak is declared a full-blown pandemic with efficient and sustained human-to-human transmission of the virus in at least two of the WHO's world regions.

The last time the WHO declared a level 6 flu pandemic was the outbreak of A/H1N1, quickly christened "swine flu" by the media, as it was originally a porcine strain of flu that jumped the species barrier; it broke out in Mexico in 2009, and quickly spread worldwide. Fortunately, although widespread, A/H1N1 was considerably more benign than seasonal flu in terms of fatalities. The other strain that the WHO has been monitoring carefully since 1997, which is currently rated as a level 3 pandemic, is the H5N1 influenza strain, the media's "bird flu." Although the strain is primarily found in wild and domesticated birds, especially poultry, the fear is that it will mutate or "re-assort" (acquire genetic material from another flu virus), and thus become much more infectious to humans and much deadlier. At the time of writing, the virus has infected 608 people, of whom 359 have died, giving it a very high mortality rate of 59 percent.

THE FORGOTTEN PANDEMIC

The WHO was criticized for the high threat level that it declared in 2009, causing governments to stock up on the unproven antiviral drug oseltamivir (Tamiflu) and generally mobilize their populations with dire warnings, when in fact nothing major happened. Although H1N1 killed around 17,000 worldwide, this was far fewer than the number of deaths from seasonal flu, and mercifully short of the apocalyptic predictions that were beginning to circulate in the media. However, the WHO was working with sound scientific, medical, and epidemiological data collected from the last major H1N1 pandemic that took place in 1918. Occurring in the last year of the First World War, its fatalities are often folded into the grim wartime total, and the outbreak is often called the "forgotten pandemic." The 1918 "Spanish Flu," however, remains the single most disastrous disease outbreak in world history, beating the fourteenth-century Black Death, as well as more recent pandemics such as HIV-AIDS.

As with the Black Death, although the disaster had an entirely natural cause—a viral pathogen—the pandemic would not have had the same impact at a time when humans still lived in isolated bands of hunter-gatherers. Human-to-human strains of flu, as we know to our cost, are highly infectious, but they depend for their lightning spread on large concentrations of settled humans, as well as on humans traveling quickly from place to place, to infect new populations. The 1918 strain, which came in two waves, the second deadlier than the first, was so infectious and deadly that had the world population not been so large and mobile at the time, it would have probably burned itself long out before becoming a global pandemic by decimating a more localized or isolated population.

However, with the rapid transcontinental movements of people associated with the First World War, and large concentrations of people in military, prisoner-of-war, and refugee camps and in hospitals, the disease found the ideal conditions to spread quickly. It reached every continent, including the Antarctic. Scientists estimate that up to one-third of the world's population, or 528 million out of a total of 1.6 billion, was infected. In modern terms, we would be looking at an infection rate of 2.31 billion. The mortality estimates range from 3 to 6 percent of those infected, or 50 to 100 million fatalities, or to put it in today's values, a staggering 230 to 500 million people wiped out in a single disease outbreak.

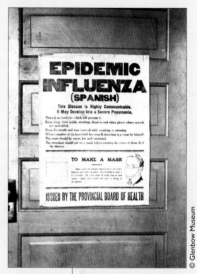

Although called the "Spanish Flu" at the time, because it was thought to have originated in Spain, the strain is now thought to have developed in East Asia, possibly China, just before the outbreak of the war. The pandemic had several unusual features: It began in January 1918 but continued to rage throughout the spring and summer of that year, finally abating in the fall; and it came in two successive waves of infections. The first was terrible enough, but the second, slightly mutated strain was even deadlier. Fortunately, by then many would have developed immunity because of exposure to the original strain, and disease-control measures were then in force, so the second wave was slightly less disastrous than it might have been.

ISOLATION
Without drugs to combat the pandemic, victims could only be quarantined.

Unlike seasonal flu that, as we saw above, affects the very young, the unwell, and the elderly, Spanish Flu affected mainly young, otherwise healthy adults. Modern researchers believe that the virus triggered a "cytokine storm," that is, an extreme reaction of the individual's own immune system that in many cases proved fatal. The reaction would not have been triggered in infants, the elderly, and those with compromised immune systems. Researchers believe that the same immune reaction was involved in the past decade's deaths of patients diagnosed with SARS and bird flu. Despite the vast numbers involved, and the social and economic dislocation it must have caused, the pandemic is now largely forgotten — its millions of victims no doubt added to the dreadful tally of 37 million civilian and military casualties caused by World War One.

DISASTER

Extinction Event

Tectonic Event

Military Action

Fire

Pandemic

Famine

Political or Economic Event

Genocide

Flood or Storm

Industrial or Transport Accident

THE WILL TO POWER: RISE OF FASCISM

1922–1933

Cause: Aftermath of the First World War; "*Revanchisme*" and the heavy reparations imposed on Germany; Great Depression; Bolshevik Revolution of 1917

Event: Fascist parties came to power across Europe, but particularly in Germany and Italy; Japan succumbed to ultranationalism and militarism

Aftermath: World War Two; the Sino-Japanese War; the Pacific War; the Holocaust

The receptivity of the masses is very limited, their intelligence is small, but their power of forgetting is enormous. In consequence of these facts, all effective propaganda must be limited to a very few points and must harp on these in slogans until the last member of the public understands what you want him to understand by your slogan.

> **Adolf Hitler,**
> *Mein Kampf ("My Struggle"), 1925–26*

Defeat in World War One is often put forward as one of the causes of the rise of fascism in the postwar period. Although the Treaty of Versailles of 1919 that officially ended hostilities between the Triple Entente and Central Powers is certainly a factor in Germany's subsequent descent into totalitarianism, the two countries that fought alongside Germany during World War Two, Italy and Japan, were on the winning side during the First World War. However, there are some interesting parallels between the three future Axis powers: the first being that not one of these countries existed as a fully functioning nation state before 1870.

The Italian peninsula was the heartland of the Roman world, but after the Western Empire's collapse in the fifth century CE, Italy remained divided into several successor states until the end of the nineteenth century. During the Renaissance, the most powerful of these were the city-states of Florence, Milan, and Venice in the north and the kingdom of Naples in the south; central Italy—Rome and the Papal States—was ruled by the popes as the temporal successors of Italy's ancient emperors, a situation that endured until the final reunification of the country in 1870, and the creation of the world's smallest sovereign state, Vatican City, in 1871. The architects of Italian unification—*Il Risorgimento* (the Renewal)—were the revolutionary Giuseppe Garibaldi (1807–82) and the more moderate but still liberal premier of the Kingdom of Sardinia-Piedmont, Count Cavour (1810–61).

Although something approaching the modern state of Italy had existed in ancient times, there had never been its German equivalent. In the Roman period, *Magna Germania* (Greater Germany) was a Roman fiction used to describe the home of many different tribal peoples, including the Goths and Franks, who went on to destabilize and ultimately conquer the Western Empire. Charlemagne (742–814), who is claimed by the French but could just as easily be considered German, founded the Holy Roman Empire covering much of modern-day France, Germany, Holland, Belgium, Austria, Switzerland, and Italy as far south as Rome.

Over the centuries, the empire shrank, grew, and broke up, finally re-forming in the post-Napoleonic era into the Austro-Hungarian Empire and the Swiss Confederation to the South, and the Kingdom of Prussia to the North, with a dozen or more independent kingdoms, principalities, dukedoms, and electorates-palatine in between, whose only commonality was the German language, or at least a Germanic dialect. After a failed attempt to create a liberal-democratic pan-German nation-state in the "Year of Revolutions," 1848, the German-speaking states outside Austria-Hungary and the Swiss Confederation were incorporated into a new Prussian-led German Reich by the authoritarian Prussian first minister, Otto von Bismarck (1815–98), in 1871.

Japan followed a quite different trajectory from her future Axis allies. As a culturally and linguistically homogeneous island nation, Japan became a unified state in the sixth century, ruled by emperors whose peripatetic capitals finally became fixed in the western city of Kyoto. But from the twelfth century, the emperor was relegated to an impotent ceremonial role, while his military protectors, the shoguns, who mostly based themselves in eastern Japan, in Kamakura and later Edo (now Tokyo), wielded the real power for the next six centuries. Medieval Japan was divided into large autonomous feudal domains under the sometimes merely nominal suzerainty of the shogun in Edo.

© Getty Images

POMP
The Nazis used vast spectacles and parades to attract followers.

What set Japan apart from other major world powers, however, was that for almost two and a half centuries, she excluded all foreigners from the home islands, save for a few Dutch and Chinese merchants who were allowed to live on an artificial island in Nagasaki harbor. Seclusion and feudalism ended when Japan was finally forced to open its doors by American gunboat diplomacy in 1853. Determined not to go the way of India, Indo-China, and China, which had been taken over by the Western powers, Japan embarked on an accelerated program of modernization and industrialization in 1870.

In the space of two years, the world witnessed the birth of three new "empires." Of the three, the German Reich was the most politically conservative, militaristic, and autocratic. The Kingdom of Italy, because its founding fathers were progressive, was the most politically liberal and democratic. Japan, though extremely socially and politically conservative as a result of long isolation, was paradoxically the most open to outside influences. Casting around for a model to emulate, it chose the leading superpower of the day, Great Britain, whose limited electoral franchise (no one too poor, too young, insane, or female), bicameral legislature, and constitutional monarchy, she enthusiastically adopted. However, Japan's pre-World War Two system of government was not a true parliamentary democracy on the British model, but an oligarchy of former samurai officials, who ruled while the emperor, as impotent as ever, reigned.

Despite the marked cultural, socioeconomic, and political differences between Japan, Germany, and Italy between 1870 and 1918, they shared an ideological convergence in the post-World War One period that has been described as a descent into "fascism." The term originates from the Latin *fasces*: bundles of wooden sticks tied around bronze axes, which were carried by the staff of Roman magistrates as a symbol of their authority. The nineteenth-century Italian word *fascio* denoted any kind of political grouping of the right or left, but it was later associated with Benito Mussolini's (1883–1945) National Fascist Party, founded in 1922.

THE RISE OF THE TWO STOOGES

Many German right-wingers considered the Italian *Fascisti* to be too conservative, capitalist, and bourgeois, and did not adopt the term for their own political movement and ideology. Adolf Hitler (1889–1945), though he admired and often aped Mussolini, took over an existing far-right party, renaming it the National Socialist German Workers' Party in 1920 (from which we derive the name "Nazi"). In imitation of *Il Duce* (the preposterous title awarded himself by Mussolini—from the Latin *dux*, "military leader" and also the aristocratic title "duke"), Hitler elevated himself to the position of *Führer* ("guide" or "leader"), preferring this grandiloquent but empty title over that of Reich Chancellor.

Again, the situation in Japan was completely different, and many scholars would baulk at associating the Japanese state of the 1920s and 30s with Fascism (note the capital letter), while admitting that it was militaristic and politically extremely nationalistic and conservative. While Hitler and Mussolini used the democratic system to gain political power and to establish one-party states, using a mixture of demagogy and terrorism, there was no Japanese Hitler or Mussolini, and until 1940, no single political party on the model of the Nazis or Fascisti. Rather than being led astray by an extremist ideology, prewar Japan never developed solid democratic parliamentary institutions, allowing the Imperial Japanese Army (IJA) to replace the oligarchic cliques that had ruled and modernized the country in the late nineteenth century.

During the U.S. Occupation, an attempt was made to portray Japan's wartime premier, Hideki Tojo (1884–1948), as Japan's Hitler, and he was tried and executed for war crimes, but Tojo was an IJA general, not an ideologue, and he acted following the code of devotion to the emperor and the nation that had been created in 1868. Similar attempts to portray Hirohito, the Showa Emperor (1901–89), as the charismatic mastermind behind Japanese expansionism fly in the face of the reality of the individual concerned.

© United States Holocaust Memorial Museum

TWO STOOGES
The self-appointed "*Duce*" and "*Führer*" in their military finery.

These differences notwithstanding, Japanese Imperialism, German Nazism, and Italian Fascism shared many common features. As newly unified states, it is not surprising that governments used nationalism and constructed myths of racial superiority to bind their somewhat disparate subjects together. In Japan, this was expressed by discrimination and persecution of other Asian peoples and the promotion of the cultural and racial superiority of the Japanese; a similar movement in Germany was directed against all "non-Aryan" peoples, but in particular promoted to the extreme a pre-existing strain of European anti-Semitism (see pp. 149–155); this was much less marked in Italy, which did not persecute its Jewish and Roma populations until forced to do so by its Nazi allies; however, the Italians did persecute, oppress, and murder their colonial subjects in Abyssinia (now Ethiopia) and Libya.

The three empires also shared an expansionist, militaristic agenda to seize vital "living space" for the father/motherland, which the Germans did by expanding eastward into Poland and Russia; the Japanese, onto the Asian mainland; and the Italians, into North and East Africa. Finally, the Axis powers rejected their countries' earlier liberal-democratic free-market experiments in favor of corporatist, planned economies run by one-party states, predicated on ideologies promoting the collaboration of the various social classes for the common good. Although fascism was directed against the Communist ideology of continual class conflict and revolution, the Soviets under Joseph Stalin (1878–1953) were developing identical political, socioeconomic, and expansionist militaristic policies based on Marxism-Leninism. We shall see how this political disaster was soon converted into several of history's most cataclysmic man-made disasters.

EARTHSHAKER: GREAT KANTO EARTHQUAKE

1923

DISASTER

Extinction Event

Tectonic Event

Military Action

Fire

Pandemic

Famine

Political or Economic Event

Genocide

Flood or Storm

Industrial or Transport Accident

Cause: Earthquake (MMS 7.9) and tropical cyclone

Event: Destruction of much of Tokyo and Yokohama by the earthquake and subsequent firestorms; landslides; 33 foot (10 m) tsunami

Aftermath: Deaths of between 105,000 and 143,000 citizens of Tokyo and Yokohama; attacks on and murders of Korean Japanese and ethnic minorities blamed as saboteurs

We now know that Japan owes its very existence to the subduction zone. The country is an amalgam of island arcs, volcanic mountain chains that can develop offshore in regions where subduction begins beneath the ocean. Thus Japan is exposed to far higher earthquake hazard than its neighbors to the west.

Susan E. Hough and Roger Bilham,
After the Earth Quakes, 2005

In regions of the world where there is high tectonic activity, a rich mythology has emerged to explain volcanism and earthquakes. In China, the dragon has long been used to explain the many tremors that regularly shake the Middle Kingdom—a myth that she exported to her near neighbors, Korea and Japan. Japan, however, itself a country that is regularly visited by extremely powerful earthquakes, has a legend of its own to explain seismic episodes. Instead of a dragon shaking the earth, the Japanese believed that it was Ōnamazu, a monstrous catfish, who was responsible for earth tremors. The choice of the catfish, it is thought, was due to the fish's presumed ability to foretell earthquakes, and also the habit of the fish to bury itself in the mud at the bottom of ponds and rivers.

Earthquakes, as we shall see in the entry on the Tohoku Disaster of 2011 (pp. 241–245), continue to shape the somewhat pessimistic Japanese world view, in which the next major disaster is only around the corner. The country sits to the north of the tectonic boundaries where the Pacific plate subducts beneath the Philippine and Okhotsk plates. This means that the Japanese islands are not only particularly prone to tectonic disturbances but also that they are themselves products of movements of the earth's crust. In a very real sense, the Japanese are right to give Ōnamazu a dual nature, because without tectonic activity, there would be no Japan. This realization is, of course, of little comfort to the millions who have died, been injured, or lost their homes and livelihoods in earthquakes over the centuries. Unfortunately, the most densely populated regions of Japan are on its southern coastline, and are therefore the most exposed to damage from earthquakes and tsunamis occurring just off shore.

TOKYO BURNING

Japanese domestic architecture, not surprisingly, is well suited to its tectonic environment. A traditional Japanese house is basically a roofed wooden frame, which is designed to move with tremors rather like a tree bending in the wind. Only when the quake is too strong will it topple and break. There are no external walls, which are replaced by sliding shutters, and the internal sliding partitions are famously made of paper. Traditional Japanese interiors do not go in for large items of furniture or heavy artworks hung on the walls; hence, there is little danger of injury from falling objects and furniture.

Made of wood, floored with straw *tatami* mats, and roofed with tiles, shingle, or thatch, there is one thing that the traditional Japanese house is very poorly designed to resist: fire. And that is the unfortunate trade off the Japanese had to make: Although you are unlikely to be crushed to death as Aunt Bessie's Shaker chest of drawers comes crashing through the bedroom ceiling, you might be incinerated in a post-quake firestorm. By 1923, Japan had been modernizing for over half a century, and the center of Tokyo boasted a number of Western-style brick, concrete, and stone buildings, including the Imperial Hotel designed

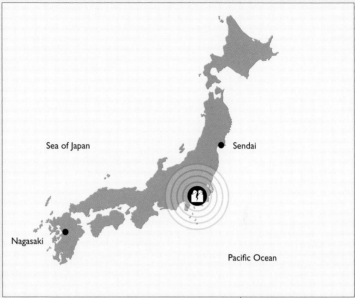

 Approximate epicenter

TECTONIC TREMORS
The Great Kanto Earthquake hit the islands of Japan on September 1, 1923.

by Frank Lloyd Wright (1867–1959), the Tokyo Central Railway Station, Central Post Office, and Tokyo Metropolitan Police Headquarters. Many of the city's neighborhoods and suburbs, however, were of more traditional Japanese construction, of the sort that can still be seen in the historical neighborhoods of Kyoto, which, as one of the few major Japanese cities to escape firebombing during World War Two, has preserved something of its prewar character.

The MMS 7.9 earthquake struck just before noon on September 1, 1923, just as many householders were preparing their midday meals over open fires and hearths. The earthquake demolished and damaged many buildings, but the high death toll of around 105,000 killed and a further 40,000 thousand missing, presumed dead, was caused by the firestorms that took hold and were fanned by high winds from a tropical cyclone that hit the city at the same time as the earthquake. Scientists have speculated that the quake and cyclone might have been linked, the huge shockwave causing a sudden drop in air pressure that triggered the storm.

In addition to reducing most of Tokyo to charred rubble, the quake and firestorm destroyed the neighboring port of Yokohama. Landslides and a

33-foot (10 m) tsunami accounted for several thousand more deaths across the Kanto region. As we saw in the entry on the Peshtigo fire (pp. 92–95), people could not escape the firestorms, many being burned alive in open ground where they had sought refuge from aftershocks, while others were stuck in asphalt melted by the heat of the flames.

If the loss of life and property were not tragic enough, the distressed, bewildered population turned on ethnic minorities in Tokyo and Yokohama, mainly Japanese Koreans and Chinese, who were accused of being saboteurs. Korea had become a colony of Japan in 1910, and the prewar relationship between the two countries could be compared to the worst periods of Anglo-Irish or U.S.–Mexican friction. Japanese citizens of Korean descent would have been indistinguishable from their Japanese neighbors, apart from their names, and the discrimination that they faced. Mobs, sometimes aided and abetted by the police and army who were supposed to protect the several thousand-strong Japanese-Korean population of the city, assaulted anyone whom they identified as Korean by making them repeat a Japanese phrase that non-Japanese were deemed incapable of pronouncing correctly. Of course, the rough-and-ready test caught people with regional accents and speech difficulties.

After the government briefly considered abandoning Tokyo and moving the capital to a safer, less earthquake-prone location, the city was rebuilt, with many suburbs and neighborhoods made of wooden houses as before. The new Tokyo would not stand for very long, however. During World War Two, the U.S.A.F., having studied the firestorms that broke out in Michigan and Wisconsin in 1871, firebombed Tokyo, reducing it to ashes once more, this time with man-made firestorms.

A TRAGEDY OF ERRORS: THE GREAT DEPRESSION

1929–39

DISASTER

Extinction Event

Tectonic Event

Military Action

Fire

Pandemic

Famine

Political or Economic Event

Genocide

Flood or Storm

Industrial or Transport Accident

Cause: Stock Market Crash of October 1929

Event: Stock prices fell; banks collapsed, leading to a credit crunch; business confidence failed, resulting in a drastic fall in world production, consumption, and trade; prices and wages collapsed, causing mass unemployment; bad government response

Aftermath: The Great Depression lasted until the outbreak of World War Two; rise of fascism and militarism in Germany, Italy, and Japan

Given the terrible violence and misery associated with the Great Depression, perhaps the saddest thing is that the whole affair could have been avoided. The Depression was the result of human errors in the area of economic policy [….] A great many mistakes were made by well-meaning people in both business and government who were grossly ignorant about the goals, tools, and impact of economic policy.

Thomas E. Hall and David Ferguson,
*The Great Depression: An International Disaster
of Perverse Economic Policies, 1998*

Economics is not an exact science like physics or chemistry, whose theories can be used to predict events in the real world. The best economics seems to be able to do is to explain why something happened after the event. The catastrophic ten-year recession now known as the "Great Depression" is a case in point. At the time, according to many leading economists, the "green shoots" of recovery were just around the next quarter. But before we explore the history of financial disasters, let's have a quick look at economic theory.

BROKE
Although it occurred long before computerized dealing, the Wall Street Crash saw an unprecedented volume of trading.

© Hulton-Deutsch Collection | Corbis

You don't have to be an economist or an economic historian to spot the key feature of economic theories that dooms most of them to failure from the start: The presupposition that human beings are capable of making rational economic choices. Although senior economics professors at Harvard and Cambridge might be models of rationality, the average consumer is just as likely to make a house purchase because, "She liked the pattern on the curtains," or choose a mode of transport because, "A Harley is the only bike for a real man," or, in a more extreme case, blow all their savings because, "The lucky green pixies told them to put it all on the lottery." In the real world, delusion, emotional engagement, and astrology are much more potent factors informing economic choices than the pronouncements of senior economic theorists.

The second major factor that gets left out of economic theories is criminality. In today's ongoing economic crisis, many of the things that had gotten us into the mess were either morally extremely dubious or downright dishonest — from mortgage lenders selling houses to people who could never afford to keep up the payments, to traders gambling with their investors' money and hiding their losses until the corporation or bank went down. Finally, what about the rationality of our political and economic masters in Washington, London, Brussels, the Fed, the Bank of England, and the European Central Bank? Is there any reason to think their decisions any more rational than our own? The well-meaning politicians for all their pious platitudes and fine hopes, still need our votes if they want to stay in power, and their freedom of action is constrained by a tangled web of contending interest groups and lobbies, and their own and advisors' ignorance about the real impact of spending $50 billion on expanding the money supply or funding a social healthcare system. As for the less well-meaning would-be world leaders, they just want to blow it all on enlarging their fiefdoms.

So for what it's worth, here is Chalinonomics—my take on the subject of economic crises past and present, which comes in three parts: (1) the short term: the human factors outlined above—greed, criminality, delusion, and gullibility; (2) the medium term: recurring structural problems within the world economy that lead to regular cycles of "boom and bust," combined with historical events (such as wars, major disasters, etc); and (3) the longer term: the broader background of population growth, the development of new agricultural techniques, and the advances in science and technology that together drive planet-wide macro-social and macro-economic changes (e.g., the Iron Age, the Industrial Revolution, the Information Age, etc).

In the case of many of the natural and natural–human disasters, there is only a limited scope for taking the "long view", apart from marveling at the ability of humans to build their homes on the slopes of active volcanoes, on top of earthquake faults, and on tsunami beach fronts, in the certain belief that nothing bad will ever happen to them. But in the case of an entirely human disaster, such as a war or a severe economic crisis, it is crucial to understand exactly what happened and why.

TIPTOE THROUGH THE TULIPS

In the entry on the Black Death (pp. 41–46), I suggested that the loss of one-third of the world's population had quite a major impact (understatement!). In Europe, it contributed to the Renaissance and to the birth of capitalism by freeing labor and monetizing the economy. In a book published in 1905 and still deservedly on many undergraduate reading lists, *The Protestant Ethic and the Spirit of Capitalism*, the German sociologist Max Weber (1864–1920) theorized that the key determinant in the development of Capitalism in northern Europe (and later in the U.S.) was the Protestant faith. An elegant and persuasive argument that has stood the test of time, which, however, does not explain the success of BMW in predominantly Catholic Bavaria, or take into account the vast supplies of coal and iron ore in the United Kingdom, Belgium, and northern France and Germany, which fortunately fueled the Industrial Revolution. Capitalism, for whatever reason, did emerge in Protestant northern Europe, and with it came the first financial crisis.

Described in Charles MacKay's (1814–89) *Extraordinary Popular Delusions and the Madness of Crowds* (1841), the world's first asset bubble is noteworthy for the choice of commodity involved: not land, ships, gold, livestock, or anything remotely useful, but tulips—yes, you read correctly—tulips, as in the rather showy flower that blooms for about a week in late spring. "Tulipomania" struck the otherwise stolid burghers of Amsterdam, Leiden, and Rotterdam in the mid-1630s, and reached its frenzied climax in 1637, when people were supposedly mortgaging their homes and selling their children to buy a promising bulb. The inevitable "Great Tulip Crash" resulted in individual and company bankruptcies, the Dutch government having to step in to shore up the financial system, and a rash of legislation to try and avert future crises (see: door, stable, horse, bolted).

What is particularly fascinating and illuminating about this piece of financial lunacy is that it developed around something as fragile and ephemeral as a flower. Of course, at the height of the bubble, many investors didn't care whether they were dealing in coal, rubies, stocks, or flower bulbs, they just saw the ever-rising price of a commodity as a way of getting rich quick; but, on the other hand, there were also enough people around who thought a single tulip bulb was worth a month's or a year's salary. This explains a lot about how humans have made their economic choices ever since.

After a slow start in the seventeenth century, financial crises, panics, bank failures, and stock and land bubbles really took off during the nineteenth century, when there seemed to be an economic disaster occurring in some part of the world every five years or so, and a real humdinger of a global recession every fifty- to one-hundred years. Cycles of boom followed by years of bust have been the rule rather than exception over the past two centuries, yet economists, politicians, and consumers seem to treat each new downturn as if it were something quite novel and unexpected.

BLACK DAYS | From relatively contained national panics, with the globalization of the economy, the crises had gotten bigger and more severe. Let me take you back to Chalinonomics for a moment, and look at what was happening in the decades leading up to the Wall Street Crash of 1929: Short term, people were always people; only, they weren't investing in tulips like there was no tomorrow, but in stocks that fuelled a six-year bull market on the NYSE and was encouraged by politicians and bankers who saw no end to the financial and electoral returns. Irving Fisher (1867–1947), a respected economic pundit of the day, felt able to assure the readers of the *New York Times* on October 17, 1929 (days before the Wall Street Crash), "Stock prices have reached what looks like a permanently high plateau [....] I expect to see the stock market a good deal higher within a few months."

In the medium term, there were the socioeconomic adjustments associated with the First World War: transferring investment and industrial capacity away from armaments and the war economy, general reconstruction, labor shortages caused by the slaughter, and re-starting consumer-oriented industrial production and world trade. And finally, in the longer term, in the late nineteenth and early twentieth centuries, the Second Industrial Revolution had radically transformed society by giving the Western world the must-haves of modern-day living: electricity in the home, domestic appliances, the automobile, airplane, radio, and telephone. Of course, these inventions were just the tip of a technological iceberg that had completely restructured industrial production, employment practices, and global trade and consumption. Years of boom also created vast surges of surplus cash that happily sloshed around the world economy, generally increasing wages, profits, and living standards, and fueling an asset bubble of unprecedented proportions in the U.S.

© Roman Slavik | Shutterstock

EPICENTER
As in the current financial crash, Wall Street was at the heart of the Great Depression.

The NYSE reached its speculative peak on September 3, 1929, when the Dow Jones (DJ) hit 381.17, registering a staggering fivefold increase in value since 1923. The bursting of the bubble, when it came, was not a single traumatic event, but one with highs and lows, rallies and collapses. The Wall Street Crash started with "Black Thursday," October 24, 1929, when a record-breaking 12.9 billion shares were traded on one day (and we're not talking computer trades here, but ticker tape, telephone, and handwritten transactions). Senior financiers and bankers met to attempt to stem the growing panic by investing heavily in the market. The strategy worked until Monday—"Black Monday," October 28—when the DJ lost 12.82 percent of its value, and on Tuesday—"Black Tuesday," October 29—it lost a further 11.73 percent. Despite the mounting evidence of impending financial Armageddon, politicians and economists kept trying to rally investor confidence by explaining that this was just a temporary blip—a minor readjustment of the market before another soaring climb.

In 1930, there was a brief rally, which saw the DJ rise to a respectable 294.07, but a combination of disastrous economic legislation and a continuing loss of investor confidence led to a catastrophic two-year decline, which stopped when the market hit its all time twentieth-century low of 41.22 on July 8, 1932, a drop of 89 percent from its September 1929 record. According to Hall and Ferguson's *The Great Depression: An International Disaster of Perverse Economic Policies*, the Great Depression in the U.S. consisted of two major recessions. The first, christened the "Great Contraction" by monetarist maven Milton Friedman, lasted from 1929 to 1933 and was the worst economic downturn in the nation's history: Real GDP fell by one-quarter and unemployment peaked at 24.9%. The second, less severe recession lasted from 1937 to 1941, and the economy returned to full employment only when the U.S. entered the Second World War.

Irving Fisher, the Pollyanna of the Wall Street Crash, set about analyzing what had gone so badly wrong. He came up with the "debt-deflation theory" to explain the nine major effects of the bursting of the stock asset bubble: (1) the liquidation of debt and distress selling, (2) contraction of the money supply as people and businesses paid off their debts, (3) a fall in asset prices, (4) a fall in the worth of businesses, leading to business failures, (5) a fall in profits, (6) a reduction in overall economic activity, (7) pessimism and loss of confidence, (8) the hoarding of cash, and (9) a fall in interest rates but a rise in deflation-adjusted interest rates.

The economic effects of the Great Depression were far-reaching, adversely affecting every region of the planet. In response, governments, as Hall and Ferguson explained, made every mistake in the economic textbook, further restricting economic activity and slowing down recovery. We shall examine the disastrous military consequences of the Great Depression on the entries dealing with the Second World War (pp. 145–164), but first, the worst floods in human history and its worst human-engineered famine.

MOTHER MONSTERS: CHINA FLOODS

1931

DISASTER

Extinction Event

Tectonic Event

Military Action

Fire

Pandemic

Famine

Political or Economic Event

Genocide

Flood or Storm

Industrial or Transport Accident

Cause: Two-year drought followed by an unusually cold winter; the snowmelt, combined with heavy spring and summer rains, caused rivers to rise to unprecedented levels

Event: Simultaneous floods of China's three main river systems: the Yellow, Yangtze, and Huai Rivers

Aftermath: Deaths of an estimated two to four million people in the affected areas

Throughout the spring, unusually heavy rains had swollen the rivers that converged at Wuhan, southwest of Nanking. Eventually, the water rushed over banks and dikes and covered the entire surrounding countryside—an area the size of New York State. The waters did not recede for two months. As many as two million died, some from drowning, most from dysentery, cholera, and famine.

Peter Conn,
***Pearl S. Buck: A Cultural Biography,* 1998**

SAVIOR
China's great rivers were tamed by legendary figures, including Emperor Yao.

In the Near Eastern flood myths that are the basis for the story of Noah's Ark, the flood is sent by the gods to destroy an impious and noisy humanity (the divine version of banging on the ceiling). In the biblical account, Yahweh orders the righteous Noah to save mankind and representatives of all land animals and birds, but in the earlier polytheistic versions, one of the gods decides to foil the planned divine destruction and snitches on his fellows to save humanity. In both cases, however, the disaster is divinely ordained as a punishment. This is a common trope of deluge myths: The Greeks, too, told of several deluges sent by the gods to destroy earlier incarnations of humanity, saving only one or two individuals to preserve the species.

The destructiveness of floods is not in doubt, but in ancient times, in Egypt and Babylonia in particular, the yearly floods of the Nile and of the Tigris and Euphrates were a necessary part of the agricultural cycle. The seasonal inundation of the Nile, for example, covered the fields in rich silt carried from the upper reaches of the river, which acted as a natural fertilizer for the following season's crops. The Nile has a predictable and relatively controlled flood, but the rivers of Babylonia, the Tigris and Euphrates, are far more dangerous, and both regularly changed their courses during antiquity, either depriving a population of water, or destroying the sun-dried mud-brick walls and buildings of a city in a raging torrent. It is not surprising that the Babylonians and Sumerians wrote of the flood as divine punishment for the sins of humankind.

China has its own version of the Great Flood that took place during the reign of the mythical Emperor Yao (whose traditional dates are given as 2356–2255 BCE). No specific area is given for the flood, nor a particular river cited as the main cause, but because Chinese civilization arose along the banks of the Yellow River on the China Plain, the legend may refer to the regular floods of that river that have been particularly destructive. In the story, the flood is a natural, not divinely inspired, disaster, and the focus of the action is on the efforts of three culture heroes, Gun, Shun, and Yu the Great (ca. 2200–2100 BCE), who attempt to control the floodwaters.

At the behest of Emperor Yao, the first of the three, Gun, tries to contain the water with dikes and dams but fails to do so; Shun, who succeeds Yao as emperor, attempts to work around the problem with administrative reforms that succeed in establishing lines of communication across the flooded areas; but it is Gun's son Yu the Great who finally solves the problem by developing a system of water management that drains surplus flow away from the affected areas. In the process of overcoming the Great Flood, the three men succeeded in creating the agricultural, irrigation, land-management, and water-control techniques on which ancient Chinese civilization was based. Yu the Great is held to be the founder of China's first imperial dynasty, the mythical Xia (ca. 2070–ca. 1600 BCE), for whom archeologists have yet to find any physical evidence. The myth, therefore, is not just about a random natural disaster or the genocidal act of a tetchy divinity but a metaphor for the emergence of human civilization from the chaos of the natural world, while at the same time it underlines the importance of rivers to early Chinese society.

WATERS OF DEATH

Three mighty rivers flow east to west across China: the northernmost is the Yellow River, and the southernmost, the Yangtze, with the Huai River and its many tributaries in between. The rivers, in particular the Yellow River, are known as the "mothers of China," for their waters have fed China's large population since ancient times. Unfortunately, the rivers are also quite capable of taking away the life that they so generously bestow. The worst natural–human disaster in the twentieth century, excluding famines and pandemics, was the series of floods that afflicted China in 1931.

The Yellow River is the most dangerous of the three, as it passes through our old friend the Huangtu Plateau, which we first visited for the entry on the Shaanxi earthquake (pp. 58–61). Loess is a loose sedimentary soil that accumulates in the region and is highly prone to erosion. Naturally, a great deal of it washes into the Yellow River as it makes its way in a vast loop westward toward to the China Plain and the sea, giving the river its name and trademark muddy, yellow water, and giving rise to the expression, "when the Yellow River runs clear," which is the Chinese equivalent of "when pigs will fly," or "when hell freezes over."

The sediment-rich waters are a natural boon to farmers, but the sediments also accumulate on the riverbed, raising its level. When conditions are right and the sediment builds up high enough and rains and snowmelt raise the water level, it can cause the river to change its course with catastrophic consequences. To counteract this, the Chinese had begun building levées to keep the river in its current course. This had led to the river being higher than the surrounding flood plain in certain areas—and we're not talking a babbling brook here, but a broad river wide and deep enough to accommodate large ocean-going vessels.

A drought, which had started in 1928, ended in 1931 with unusually high rainfall across the whole region. Combined with heavy snowmelt in the Tibetan headwaters of the rivers, the excess flow overwhelmed the existing water-management measures—dykes, levées, and canals—flooded millions of square miles of China's prime agricultural land, and engulfed several major cities, including the then capital Nanjing (Nanking). The high-water mark was reached in the city of Hankou (now part of Wuhan,

the provincial capital of Hubei Province), where the waters were 53 feet (16 m) higher than normal.

In 1931, the country was in a state of undeclared war with the Japanese Empire, and rent by internal divisions between the Nationalist Kuomintang and Mao Zedong's (1893–1976) Communist Party. In the ensuing chaos, there was little aid given to the

TENT CITY
Millions were flooded out of their homes and forced into sprawling refugee camps.

victims of the flood. Millions drowned when the rivers overtopped levées or broke through dikes and dams, and millions more starved for want of relief, and died from outbreaks of waterborne diseases such as cholera, typhus, and dysentery. After five months, the waters began to recede. Within half a dozen years, the Chinese had to face an entirely man-made disaster, the second Sino-Japanese War, which began in 1937, during which the Chinese themselves broke the levées once more in an effort to stall the Japanese advance. In this they were only partially successful, as the Japanese took Nanking, the scene of one of the worst atrocities of war (pp. 145–148).

STALIN'S HUNGER: THE HOLODOMOR

1932–33

DISASTER

Extinction Event

Tectonic Event

Military Action

Fire

Pandemic

Famine

Political or Economic Event

Genocide

Flood or Storm

Industrial or Transport Accident

Cause: Stalin's drive to modernize the Soviet economy, industrialize and collectivize agriculture with the Soviet Union's first Five-Year Plan

Event: Poor harvests and unrealistic grain quotas led to famine in Ukraine and other parts of European Russia; draconian laws passed against the "theft of Socialist property"

Aftermath: Deaths of 2 to 8 million Soviet citizens, many of them Ukrainians

Throughout the Soviet Union, the direct loss of life due to the famine and associated hunger and disease was likely to be six to eight million. Three to five million of this number died in Ukraine and in the heavily Ukrainian-populated northern Kuban, among the richest grain-producing areas in Europe. The Ukrainian word Holodomor *derives from a combination of the word for hunger "holod" and "mor," to exterminate or eliminate.*

Norman Naimark,
Stalin's Genocides, 2010

With the Holodomor, we come to another event that has been described as an act of state-sponsored genocide perpetrated against one ethnic group: In this case, by the former Soviet Union against the Ukrainian people. Like the Armenian genocide (pp. 104–8), the Holodomor is not universally recognized as a genocidal act. It is defined as such by an act of parliament in the now independent Republic of Ukraine; but the government of the Russian Federation, the successor state to the Soviet Union, unsurprisingly rejects the definition.

© Swim Ink | Corbis

"UNCLE" JOE
Reviled by much of the world as a mass murderer, Stalin remains a hero for some of his countrymen.

The identity of the man held responsible for the Holodomor, the long-time leader of the Soviet Union, Joseph Stalin (1878–1953), provides another layer of complexity to the question. As the leader of the USSR during the initial phase of the Cold War (1948–91), Stalin has naturally gotten a very bad press in the West. Hence, the opponents of Communism consider him to be the incarnation of all that is politically evil. Stalin, we now know, was responsible for a great many crimes against his political rivals and enemies, real and imagined, Russian minorities, and the citizens of neighboring countries. However, in this instance it is not only the apologists and supporters of the former Soviet Union and of Stalin, who have raised doubts about whether the famine—though most agree it was man-made—meets the ICC criteria of being "The deliberate and systematic destruction, in whole or in part, of an ethnic, racial, religious, or national group," planned and executed on the direct orders of Stalin himself.

The Holodomor presents a new type of state-sponsored persecution: one not based on religious affiliation but on ideological grounds. We have seen one similar case already in this book, in the massacres in the Vendée region of Western France during the *Terreur* (pp. 83–86), and there was a precedent in the Soviet Union during the Russian Civil War (1917–23), when the Cossacks were "ethnically cleansed" from the Don Region. Between 1919 and 1920, an estimated 300,000 to 500,000 Cossacks were murdered or exiled after siding with the czarist "White Russians" against the new Bolshevik state. The other striking difference between these earlier genocidal acts and the Holodomor is that they took place during or just after hostilities. Although war does not excuse or justify the murder and persecution of millions of people based on their ethnic or religious affiliations, it does provide the historian with some kind explanation for an otherwise grotesque act of inhumanity.

Much has been made of the parallels between the French Revolution of 1789 and the Russian Revolution of 1917. Both overthrew an established absolutist monarchical Ancien Régime, and both began with a moderate phase, although in Russia there was no period of constitutional monarchy as in France between 1789 and 1791, and the power struggle between supporters of a parliamentary system and Bolsheviks was quickly resolved by the second Revolution of October 1917. Russia withdrew from the calamitous First World War, only to be plunged into a vicious seven-year civil war, in which the White Russians received help from a coalition of foreign powers, including Japan, the UK, and the U.S., who, like the opponents of the French in the late eighteenth century, were terrified of revolutionary contagion. The Czar and his family were never put on trial for treason like the French King and Queen but were secretly murdered in 1918.

ENEMY OF THE PEOPLE

In 1918, Russia, like France in 1792, was beset with internal and external enemies, and the new regime itself was splintered into different revolutionary factions. Russia, however, did not have to find her Maximilien de Robespierre (1758– 94), as she already had an able and inspirational leader in Vladimir Lenin (1870–1924). Assisted by Leon Trotsky (1879–1940), the creator of the Red Army, Lenin turned the counter-revolutionary tide, and consolidated power in the hands of a small group of men, the *Politburo*. Like Robespierre before him, he instituted a period of terror, the so-called "Red Terror" (1918–22), to dispose of political rivals, enemies, and counter-revolutionaries. Lenin's terror, however, pales into insignificance when compared to Stalin's later "purges."

© Creative Commons

SURPLUS
Although millions starved, grain was still exported to obtain hard currency.

Although Lenin is remembered as the grand theorist of Soviet Communism, or "Marxist–Leninism," he was not a dogmatist in his approach to government and economics. Like Karl Marx (1818–83) before him, Lenin recognized that Russia, which was primarily an agrarian nation with a small industrial working class, was not an ideal candidate for a proletarian revolution, which Marx had predicted would take place in either Germany or the United Kingdom, the two most advanced industrial economies of the day. In 1921, with the civil war as good as won, the Soviet Union was facing economic meltdown. The farmers, artisans, shopkeepers, and small businessmen, who were the backbone of the economy, had little incentive to work when all the proceeds of their efforts went not to themselves and their families but to the state. A pragmatist who quickly realized that Russia's economy would need decades before it was ready to be converted into a collectivized Marxist "Brave New World," Lenin inaugurated the New Economic Policy (NEP) in 1921, which allowed for a measure of private ownership and free enterprise. As a result, the economic situation began to improve.

Lenin foresaw the need to continue with the NEP for several decades as Russia modernized and caught up with the UK, Germany, and the U.S. Unfortunately, in 1922, at this crucial moment in the history of the revolution, Lenin, exhausted from years of overwork, and weakened by a failed assassination attempt, suffered the first of three major strokes that left him completely incapacitated. He was forced to retire and finally died in 1924, leaving his one-time protégé Joseph Stalin as one of the leaders of the newly founded USSR. Winston Churchill (1874–1965), a lifelong opponent of Communism and no friend to Lenin himself, saw his death as a real tragedy for the Russian people. In his final work, the *Testament*, Lenin criticized the Soviet leadership, which included Trotsky and Stalin, whose dictatorial leanings he had begun to recognize too late. He begged his colleagues to remove Stalin from power, but the Testament was suppressed until it was too late.

© Sergey Dolzhenko | epa | Corbis

IN THE LIGHT
In Ukraine candles are lit to remember the victims of the Holodomor.

As soon as Lenin had died, Stalin made his bid for power, sidelining his rivals for power in the Politburo. His most trenchant critic and probably his most dangerous rival was Trotsky, whom Stalin finally manage to dispose of in 1927, having him exiled in 1929, and finally murdered in 1940, when Trotsky was living in Mexico. Having acquired supreme power, Stalin determined on a policy of economic modernization at home and expansionism overseas, into East Asia and Eastern Europe, two regions dominated by "fascist" powers, Nazi Germany and Imperial Japan.

In order to achieve the modernization of the Russian economy, Stalin abandoned the NEP in 1928 in favor of an accelerated program of industrialization, which he set out in the Soviet Union's first Five-Year Plan, which centralized the control of industrial and agricultural production. Because the Soviet Union could not borrow on the international markets, she depended for the hard currency that she needed to buy heavy industrial machinery on the sale of agricultural surpluses, in particular of grain, which was produced in large amounts in European Russia and Ukraine. Agriculture, according to Stalin's master plan, would play its role in creating the Socialist Utopia through collectivization and thus pay for the Soviet Union's industrialization.

Where many left-wingers have gone wrong is in the practical application of their policies to the state ownership of the means of production—factories and agricultural land. In situations such as the Israeli kibbutz movement, where the participants are not only willing but also highly committed to making a project succeed, collective enterprise can be incredibly rewarding and successful. When it is imposed from above, and mismanaged by a repressive bureaucracy that sets unrealistic targets and imposes its authority by force, the results are usually disastrous.

The Russian peasantry had only fairly recently acquired rights to the land that it farmed, in the agricultural reforms of the late Czarist period. They could not claim to own their land from time immemorial but they were extremely loath to part with it. After the October Revolution, there had been an initial drive to collectivize but this had been partially reversed by Lenin's NEP. Stalin now imposed full collectivization and set an ambitious target of a 50 percent increase in grain production. The increase would be achieved both through the collectivization and the mechanization of agriculture, but naturally, while the former could be imposed by fiat, the latter needed hard cash for new machinery, which was not available.

According to several historians, the harvests of 1931 and 1932 were not as good as usual in the Ukraine and fell short of Moscow's high expectations, but the plan had no room for flexibility, and Stalin looked for someone to blame. He picked on the *kulaks*—a class of richer peasant farmers, whom Stalin claimed were sabotaging the Five-Year Plan and resisting collectivization. In practice, the kulak class only made up 4 percent of the

FIVE-YEAR MISERY

peasantry and the people who were targeted were the minority of better-off farmers, who wanted to keep and farm their own land.

Blaming the farmers for the shortfall, the authorities sent Communist activists from the towns to requisition supplies and search for stores of illegally hoarded grain. Instead of finding a surplus that did not exist, the activists seized the farmers' own food supplies and the seed corn for the following year's crop. In desperation, farmers slaughtered their animals for food, including the horses that provided most of the heavy work in the absence of mechanized farm machinery. The result was starvation across the Ukraine and other grain-producing areas of European Russia. The authorities passed ever more draconian laws against hoarding and declared that the gleaning of grain left in the fields after the harvest was the "theft of Socialist property," a crime punishable by ten years in the *gulag* or the death penalty. Starving peasants were required to obtain internal passports to prevent them from leaving their villages, but many of those who did manage to flee to the cities died of starvation there. Just as in Ireland during the Great Famine (pp. 87–91) ninety years earlier, no aid was given to the victims, and grain continued to be exported from the region.

The famine ended in 1933 with an improved harvest, by which time between two and eight million Soviet citizens had died of starvation and famine-related diseases. There remains the question whether this was an act of genocide as defined by the ICC. Although undoubtedly the most tragic, callous assault on an innocent population in peacetime, the Holodomor does not completely accord with the criteria. Unlike the Holocaust, which we shall soon come to, there was no deliberate targeting of the entirety of an ethnic or religious group. Stalin did not order the wholesale extermination of Ukrainians living in cities, though they, too, were affected by the famine. However, he can be indicted and found guilty of the deliberate murder of an entire class of Ukrainian agrarian society, but these would be only among the first of Stalin's many millions of victims both in and outside the Soviet Union during the next two decades of his rule.

JAPAN'S SHAME: RAPE OF NANKING

1937–38

DISASTER

Extinction Event

Tectonic Event

Military Action

Fire

Pandemic

Famine

Political or Economic Event

Genocide

Flood or Storm

Industrial or Transport Accident

Cause: Xenophobic, racist ideology of the Japanese Imperial State, combined with the special relationship that had existed between China and Japan since antiquity; the outbreak of the Second Sino-Japanese War in 1937

Event: Killing, torture, and rape perpetrated against the civilian population of Nanking and surrounding communities over a six-week period by the Japanese Imperial Army

Aftermath: Deaths of an estimated 200,000 to 300,000 Chinese civilians and POWs

Verbal accounts of reliable eye-witnesses [. . . .] afford convincing proof that Japanese Army behaved and is continuing to behave in a fashion reminiscent of Attila and his Huns. Not less than three hundred thousand Chinese civilians slaughtered, many cases in cold blood. Robbery, rape, including children of tender years, and insensate brutality towards civilians continues to be reported from areas where actual hostilities ceased weeks ago.

**Harold John Timperley,
telegram, January 17, 1938**

© Yangsuping | Dreamstime

In the entry on the rise of fascism (pp. 120–124), I explained that Japan was not an East Asian equivalent of Nazi Germany or Fascist Italy. In Japan state institutions and the imperial ideology that underpinned them had remained unaltered since the Meiji Restoration of 1868. Although not trying to exonerate Japan from its responsibility for starting the Sino-Japanese and Pacific Wars (1937–45) or of the many war crimes

UNFORGIVEN
The massacre still sparks violent protests in China against Japanese militarism.

it committed, it is important to recognize that the Japanese Imperial state cannot not be equated with Benito Mussolini and Adolf Hiter's totalitarian dictatorships. On the contrary, during the late nineteenth and early twentieth centuries, Japan, her political institutions, and her rapid economic modernization were held up as shining examples for other non-Western nations to follow.

Chinese civilization reached the Japanese islands through the Korean Peninsula, but Japan itself was never incorporated into the mainland empire. Japan's enormous religious, cultural, political, and linguistic debt to its larger neighbor established a schizophrenic relationship between the two East Asian empires. During the first millennium CE, Japan modeled its state institutions closely on Chinese models. After a brief period of overseas adventurism during the sixteenth century, the Shogun Tokugawa Ieyasu (1543–1616) decided that the best policy to preserve Japan was to isolate it completely from the rest of the world. His policy of *sakoku* (closing the country) endured for over two centuries until 1853.

Japan evolved in a kind of social, cultural, and technological aspic. Removed from international discourse, trade, and regional conflicts, however, it developed—as people will when completely isolated and left to their own devices—some very strange notions about itself and the wider world. This unique world view is termed *Nihonjinron*, literally, "discourse about Japaneseness." One of the features of Nihonjinron is that it places the Japanese in the category of a unique minority "other." In most cases, making an ethnic or cultural group or the followers of a religion into the "other" is a prelude to their persecution and extermination (as in the Nazis' treatment of the Jews before the Holocaust), but for the Japanese, their minority status was a badge of honor and a symbol of their superiority over other—especially other Asian—nations.

The only references about the outside world that the Japanese had for over two centuries were about uncouth and clearly inferior European *gaijin* (outlanders), with their outlandish clothes, preposterous beliefs, unwashed bodies, yellow and red hair and beards, and overlarge noses; and the ever-present Chinese, to whom they owed so much culturally. The Japanese combined a sense of cultural uniqueness and racial superiority with a profound national inferiority complex vis-à-vis their large and powerful neighbor. The end of seclusion, imposed by a small number of Western vessels that easily overcame Japan's sixteenth-century military technology, must have come as a profound psychological shock, leading to an immediate national identity crisis.

Unlike other countries faced with the same problem—China and India, for example—Japan did not implode or disintegrate. It organized, modernized, industrialized, and armed itself to the teeth, until it could force the repeal of the unequal trade treaties imposed on it by the Western powers in the 1870s. In this, it was almost unique, as the only other Asian country to escape dismemberment or colonization was the Kingdom of Siam (modern Thailand). Having defeated the Chinese in a first Sino-Japanese War (1894–95), then Russia (1904–05), and fought alongside the victorious Allies in World War One, Japan had made it to the top table of early twentieth-century international power politics.

As highlighted in the entry on the rise of fascism, Japan wished to emulate England, France, and the U.S. in acquiring overseas possessions, for the natural resources she lacked as well as the prestige. The trouble was, most of the available territory had already been divided up, with the exception of vast swathes of China, then fought over by rival Chinese warlords, and too large to warrant much interest from the Western powers who were firmly entrenched in China's rich coastal cities.

Japan had gotten her own foothold in China, and by degrees, the Imperial Japanese Army (IJA), sometimes acting in concert with the government in Tokyo and sometimes on its own, engineered or made use of a series of "incidents"—insurrections, bombings, and attacks on Japanese nationals—to expand its holdings in China. In 1931, Japan invaded Manchuria and created the puppet state of Manchukuo, placing the deposed Qing Dynasty (1644–1912) Emperor Pu Yi (1906–67) on its throne. The West mired in the social, political, and economic crisis created by the Great Depression

GREAT JAPAN COPROSPERITY ZONE

(pp. 129–134), did little to help China, as there was no unified Chinese government to support, and Japan, after all, had been a trusted ally during the First World War.

Japan faced no significant foreign opposition. Stalin, in particular, was far more concerned about the rise of Nazi Germany than the ambitions of faraway Japan. There was no internal dissent from Japan's immature parliamentary institutions; these were unable to withstand the rise of the ultranationalists and militarists, who used the Imperial constitution to appoint conservative prime ministers. Ultimately, an IJA general, Tojo Hideki (1884–1948), became prime minister in 1940. The Second Sino-Japanese War officially began in July 1937, but for all intents and purposes had started a decade earlier. However, after the Marco Polo Bridge Incident, the IJA launched a full-scale assault, quickly capturing Beijing.

© Getty Images

INHUMAN
Nanking established the IJA's reputation for brutality against civilian populations.

The Japanese hoped to force the Nationalist leader Chiang Kai-shek (1887–1975) to negotiate with an overwhelming show of force, but Chiang opted for all-out resistance, even temporarily allying himself with the Chinese Communist Party. The IJA fought a three-month battle to take Shanghai, then as now China's commercial capital, and then moved on the Nationalist capital of Nanking, which fell in December 1937. For the following six weeks, members of the IJA engaged in the systematic murder, rape, and torture of the civilian population of the town and captured Chinese POWs. Although the "Rape of Nanking" is still denied by right-wing historians in Japan, overwhelming evidence presented to the Nanking War Crimes Tribunal makes it clear that between 200,000 and 300,000 Chinese civilians and POWs were murdered, making it the single worst atrocity of the East Asian theater.

The long relationship between China and Japan, and the mixed feelings of inferiority and superiority that the wartime Japanese felt toward their continental neighbor, may help to explain why the IJA, who treated all their POWs and subject Asian peoples with a shocking degree of inhumanity, were capable of reserving a special kind of hatred and barbarity for the Chinese.

LEST WE FORGET: THE HOLOCAUST

1938–45

DISASTER

Extinction Event

Tectonic Event

Military Action

Fire

Pandemic

Famine

Political or Economic Event

Genocide

Flood or Storm

Industrial or Transport Accident

Cause: Anti-Semitism in Europe; rise to power of Nazis under Adolf Hitler

Event: Systematic persecution, dispossession, exploitation as slave labor, and extermination of Jews in Germany and Nazi-occupied Europe as acts of state policy

Aftermath: Deaths of an estimated six million Jews in Europe; creation of the State of Israel in 1948; destruction of Jewish communities in the Near East and North Africa after the foundation of Israel; six decades of ongoing Arab-Israeli conflict

Another improvement we made over Treblinka was that we built our gas chambers to accommodate 2,000 people at one time, whereas at Treblinka their ten gas chambers only accommodated 200 people each [….] Still another improvement we made over Treblinka was that at Treblinka the victims almost always knew that they were to be exterminated and at Auschwitz we endeavored to fool the victims into thinking that they were to go through a delousing process.

Excerpt of war crimes testimony by the Commandant of Auschwitz, quoted by Robert Jan van Pelt in *The Case for Auschwitz*, 2002

I count myself extremely fortunate that my parents decided to send me to a co-ed, multi-racial school, where religious observance and teaching were kept strictly off campus. This largely prevented discrimination based on gender, race, color, and creed; however, lest my school days appear too politically correct, I'll freely admit that like other children we fought, bullied one another, and formed cliques and gangs; but we had to find our own reasons to dislike fellow pupils, such as their individual characters, abilities, and faults, and not the fact that their ancestors ten generations back had stolen someone else's land, had a different skin color, or worshipped the wrong version of the deity.

© Fred de Noyelle | Corbis

NOT FORGOTTEN
A few of the millions of names of Jewish victims of the Nazi Holocaust.

Later in life, during my freshman year at college, my friend Ginny told me that she was a Jew, and I recall asking her in all innocence what a Jew was. I can't remember what she said in reply, but through her I learned that even in liberal, tolerant, multi-cultural late twentieth-century Europe, anti-Semitism was still a force potent enough to guide her parents' choices of their daughter's high school and college. She was, like me, from a secular middle-class background but her surname identified her family as Jewish. Although we never discussed anti-Semitism in detail, I was given to understand that somehow her ancestral religion set her apart from the gentile majority.

I then belatedly realized that several of my high-school friends were Jewish, and understood why their parents, who, like my own, had lived through the Second World War, had chosen to send their offspring to a co-ed school renowned for its multi-culturalism and tolerance. Whereas my parents had been evacuated to the countryside where they spent the war in relative safety and comfort, the parents and grandparents of several of my Jewish schoolmates had quite different experiences of the war, either as refugees or as victims of Nazi persecution.

So far, this book has featured several man-made disasters that historians have classed as genocides—a description endorsed on the opening page of each entry, even if the event did not always meet the strict criteria set out by the Lemkin–International Criminal Court (ICC) definition, repeated here: "The deliberate and systematic destruction, in whole or in part, of an ethnic, racial, religious, or national group." The Great Famine in Ireland (pp. 87–91) and the Ukrainian Holodomor (pp. 139–44), for example, although they provide grotesque examples of man's inhumanity and are crimes that deserve the strongest moral condemnation, were not deliberately planned and systematically executed in the same way as the Ottoman Empire's genocide of its Armenian citizens (pp. 104–08) and the Holocaust—the two events on which U.S. jurist Raphael Lemkin (1900–59) based himself when he invented and defined the term "genocide" in 1944.

In the entry on the Holodomor, the differences and commonalities between earlier genocides were focused upon: Some had taken place during wartime, when hostilities were used as a cover and justification by the perpetrators, but others took place in peacetime, when the perpetrators had no such excuse; some were based on perceived ethnic or cultural differences, and others on religious affiliation; and finally, there were genocidal acts based on a non-religious ideology. The Holocaust is unique, however, in that it combines all these factors into one man-made tragedy: It began in peacetime and continued throughout the war years; the Jews were identified as culturally and racially "other," but with their religion providing the main identifier; and Nazi anti-Semitism was part of a new totalitarian ideology but was based on centuries of Christian European practice.

To understand Nazi anti-Semitism, it is necessary to go right back to antiquity, to the birth of organized Christianity, and examine its relationship with the religion on which it was in part based, rabbinical Judaism. Jesus Christ was, of course, Jewish, and his claims to be the Messiah—itself a Jewish concept—were based on prophesies found in the Tanakh, the Hebrew Bible, the basis for the Old Testament.

In the century after Christ's death, the Romans saw Christianity as one of many Jewish sects. But the separation of the two faiths began around the year 50 CE, at the Council of Jerusalem, where Paul of Tarsus (Saint Paul; ca. 5–67) ruled that gentile converts did not need to follow Mosaic Law. In the early centuries CE, the Romans remained deeply hostile to Jews and Christians alike because they refused to participate in the state cults of the deified emperors. They persecuted both religions equally until the Christianization of the empire in the fourth century. With

BLOOD LIBELS

Christianity as the new state religion and with paganism banned in 395 CE, the early Church had to decide how it would deal with the Jews.

The Jews could not be treated like pagan idolaters, who were believed to worship demons, or heretic Christians, who could be made to see the error of their ways and recant (while at the same time being burned alive for the good of their souls). Judaism, through the Old Testament and many borrowed Jewish precepts and practices, formed an intrinsic part

© Creative Commons

of Christianity, and, of course, all the important figures in the New Testament, including Jesus, Mary, and the Disciples, were Jewish. Early militant Christianity, however, like militant Islam several centuries later, had no room for its Jewish "fellow travelers," who shared so much with the Church but rejected her fundamental teachings and her prophet.

The Church fathers' response was to create Christian anti-Semitism: By their rejection of Christ's divinity, and their part in his trial and execution, the Jews had put themselves

LIVING DEAD
Those who were not exterminated on arrival in the death camps were worked to death.

beyond the religious pale. From being God's "Chosen People," they had become eternally cursed as "Christ killers." This indelible stain was somehow transmitted through the blood, and according to many Christian theologians, it could not be cleansed even by conversion to Christianity. Once set to this dismal pattern, the relationship between the two faiths deteriorated, with persecutions of Jews based on the imaginary twelfth-century "Blood Libel," massacres of Jewish communities during the Crusades and Black Death, and forced conversions and expulsions in every major European country between the thirteenth and fifteenth centuries. The Protestant Reformation did not improve matters, as its founder, Martin Luther (1483–1586), was himself deeply anti-Semitic. In 1543 he wrote *On the Jews and their Lies*, a classic work of anti-Semitic "hate speech" that was to influence German anti-Semites in the twentieth century.

The final piece of Germany's anti-Semitic puzzle came with her defeat in the First World War. A conspiracy of international Jewish interests, so the deluded theory went, had not only engineered Germany's defeat but also the disastrous reparations imposed on her by the Treaty of

Versailles of 1919. The Jews, it was claimed, were all internationalists and Communists, who were hell-bent on the destruction of Germany and the mythical "Aryan race." During the Weimar Republic (1919–33), these slurs were resisted and contradicted, not least by German-Jewish war veterans who had fought in the First World War. But the Great Depression (pp. 129–134) and the rise of Nazism in Germany drowned out any hope of reasoned debate. The Nazis used popular prejudices against the Jews, woven around their bizarre racist fantasies of an eternal conflict between Jews and Aryans. When Adolf Hitler (1889–1945) was elected to power in 1933, he immediately enacted measures that legalized the exclusion of Jews from public life.

In the earlier entry on the Armenian disaster, I quoted Professor Gregory Stanton's "eight stages of genocide," outlined in 1996. Stage 1, classification, defines the target group as the "other." In Christian Europe, the Jews had always been classified as different, hence Hitler merely played on existing fears and prejudices. Between 1933 and 1937, he had ample time for stages 2 and 3: symbolization and dehumanization, when the Jews were separated from other Germans by legal discrimination, and continually slandered and denigrated in the German media and the political pronouncements of the Nazi leadership.

MASS-PRODUCED MURDER

Hitler had boasted of his determination to eliminate Germany's Jewish community as early as 1922, but he had neither the popular support nor the means to do so until he consolidated his dictatorship after 1933. Stages 4 to 6, the organization of a future genocide, the polarization of the country by ever more extreme propaganda, and the preparation for mass murder by identifying the victims, were well underway by 1938. However, at that time, the plan was still the deportation and resettlement of Germany's Jewish population. Destinations for the Jews in Nazi fantasies included various parts of Africa, the island of Madagascar, then a French colony, and the British Mandate of Palestine. But even the Nazis needed a pretext to begin their plans. This they found in the murder of a German diplomat in Paris by a teenager of Polish-Jewish descent in revenge for his parents' deportation from Germany.

The Nazi response, on November 7, 1938, was to unleash its paramilitary forces and mobs against the Jews in what became known as *Kristallnacht*, the "night of broken glass," when thousands of Jewish businesses were attacked, looted, and trashed and most of Germany's synagogues were damaged or destroyed. All Jewish cultural activity was subsequently banned; Jewish newspapers were closed down; and Jewish children were excluded from government schools. Around 30,000 Jewish men were interned in concentration camps and only released when they agreed that they and their families would leave Germany. As a final step, Hitler fined the Jewish community and made it pay to repair the broken glass that his thugs had smashed. Hitler had achieved his goal of destroying the centuries-old Jewish community in Germany, but the situation was going to change again with the outbreak of the Second World War, and the early victories for Hitler's armies.

Joseph Stalin had reached an accommodation with Hitler, and when Germany invaded Poland there was no response from the Soviet Union, only shameful complicity in the destruction and partition of the Polish state. With Germany's lightning victories came vast swathes of territory, and a Jewish community in Poland two million strong. Hitler's victories in Western Europe and the Balkans in 1940 and 1941, and his invasion of Russia in 1941 (see next entry), meant that millions more Jews fell into his clutches. Before 1942, the plan remained deportation outside the expanding German Reich and its satellite states. But rather than to the fantasy island of Madagascar, Jews were deported East to ghettos in a part of occupied Poland ruled directly from Berlin, called the General Government, which included the former Polish capital, Warsaw. Jews were also used as slave laborers in factories across the German Reich, where they would face "destruction through work," i.e., be worked to death—a prelude to more direct and speedy means of extermination. In 1939, Hitler had sanctioned the formation of the *Einsatzgruppen* ("task forces"), a euphemism for SS death squads that murdered Jews in vast numbers throughout occupied Eastern Europe and Russia. The death squads were responsible for the murder of over one million people, a foretaste of the "Final Solution" through extermination that began in earnest in 1942.

According to Timothy Snyder in *Bloodlands: Europe Between Hitler and Stalin* (2010), it was the military reverses that Hitler began to experience in 1942 that triggered the final phase of the Holocaust: Stage 7 of Stanton's eight stages, extermination. The Nazis built and operated some 15,000 prison, concentration, and labor camps during the dozen years of their

"Thousand-Year Reich," but over half the killings were carried out in six extermination camps built in occupied Poland in 1942. The murders took place on an industrial scale with assembly-line methods and efficiency, combined with the latest in Nazi gas-chamber technology: Auschwitz-Birkenau, 1,100,000 killed; Treblinka, 870,000 killed; Belzec, 600,000 killed; Majdanek, 360,000 killed; Chelmno, 320,000 killed; and Sobibor, 250,000 killed, totaling an estimated 3.5 million murders out of the six million Jewish victims of the Holocaust. To this dismal figure must be added millions of Soviet POWs and civilians, Roma, homosexuals, the physically and mentally disabled, and political and religious opponents of Nazism who were sent to their deaths in the Reich's camps or were murdered by its death squads.

© Creative Commons

Despite the total defeat of Nazi Germany, and the suicide or execution for war crimes of its surviving leaders, the legacy of the Holocaust continues to trouble the peace of the world seventy years on. Shamed by its failure to intervene when it could have saved the lives of many Jews, the international community finally granted the Jewish people a homeland in the British Mandate of Palestine. However, as Martin Gilbert describes in the meticulously researched *In Ishmael's House: A History of Jews in Muslim Lands* (2011), the foundation of the state of Israel in 1948 triggered a second Holocaust: the destruction of the ancient Jewish communities of Turkey, Iraq, Syria, Egypt, Yemen, and North Africa. Fortunately, this did not involve the extermination of the Jewish citizens of Muslim countries, but their forced expulsion, without their property or money, to Israel, Europe, and North America.

MECHANIZED MURDER
Trains delivered victims from across Europe to the gas chambers of Auschwitz.

DISASTER

Extinction Event

Tectonic Event

Military Action

Fire

Pandemic

Famine

Political or Economic Event

Genocide

Flood or Storm

Industrial or Transport Accident

HITLER'S WATERLOO: OPERATION BARBAROSSA

1941

Cause: Hitler's plot to obtain Germany's *Lebensraum* (living space) in Eastern Europe and Russia, to produce food and natural resources for Greater German Reich

Event: Initial advances into Soviet territory and anti-Soviet revolts in the Baltic States; stalling of German offensive due to logistical difficulties and onset of Russian winter

Aftermath: Deaths of an estimated 14 million combatants and 20 million civilians on Eastern Front; defeat of Third Reich; Stalin's control of Eastern Europe and the Cold War

When the Soviet Union defended itself and no lightning victory could be won, Hitler and the German leadership adapted the three remaining plans to the new situation [. . . .] The Hunger Plan was abandoned in its original conception, and applied only to areas under total German control. Thus a million people were purposefully starved in besieged Leningrad and more than three million Soviet prisoners of war died of starvation and neglect.

Timothy Snyder,
Bloodlands, 2010

There are several striking parallels between the careers of Emperor Napoleon I (1769–1821) and the German Führer, Adolf Hitler (1889–1945). Both seized power from discredited democratic governments, the French Directoire (1795–99) and the Weimar Republic (1919–33), and founded regimes that they believed would endure for generations but which collapsed after no more than a dozen years: Napoleon reigned as Emperor from 1803 to 1815, and Hitler was Reich chancellor and Führer from 1933 to 1945. Both knew early military successes with lightening victories against countries that were reputed to be militarily the strongest of their day—Hitler against France, and Napoleon against Prussia and Austria-Hungary—and both failed to defeat the British, who coordinated the resistance against them from their island fortress. Finally, both were ultimately defeated, not by their human enemies but by a natural occurrence: the Russian winter.

© Creative Commons

In another series of similarities, both Napoleon and Hitler had abandoned planned invasions of England to mount their eastward campaigns; both had had alliances with Russia that broke down; and in both cases, Poland was deeply implicated in the *casus belli*. In many ways, 1941 was shaping up to be a replay of 1812—a fact not lost on many German strategists who studied the earlier French campaign and warned Hitler of the enormous risk he was taking.

In 1940, Germany had achieved many of its objectives in Europe: It had acquired the German-speaking part of Czechoslovakia (now the Czech Republic and Slovakia), achieved *Anschluss* (union) with Austria, invaded Poland, defeated the old enemy France with surprising ease, and repulsed the British, sending their expeditionary force back across the Channel—and all this without triggering a reaction from Stalin, who had signed a non-aggression pact with Hitler, with clauses outlining how Eastern Europe would be divided between Nazi and Soviet spheres of influence.

PREDECESSOR
Hitler repeated Napoleon's mistakes of 1812.

Stalin, whom we left letting the farmers of Ukraine starve during the Holodomor (pp. 139–144), continued his homicidal pursuit of absolute power by a debilitating "Great Purge" (1936–38) of the Communist Party and the Red Army. Stalin also worried about a potential foe at his back.

The Imperial Japanese Army (IJA), which was by then deeply involved in China, had already clashed with Soviet forces on the borders of the Japanese puppet state of Manchukuo (pp. 145–148). Stalin's worst fear was that the Germans would attack from the west and the Japanese from the east.

WINTER OF DISCONTENT

Had Hitler not been totally insane by then and consolidated his victories, he might have succeeded in remaining in power, but there was a kind of ghastly historical inevitability about war between Nazi Germany and Soviet Russia. Not only were they ideological opposites, but they also coveted political dominion of the whole of the European continent. Stalin saw Hitler as his cat's paw who would weaken the Western European democracies sufficiently that once Germany was defeated, the Soviets could take over the whole of Europe. In the end, Stalin achieved half of what he hoped, after 1945. He took over Eastern Europe but lost Western Europe because the Japanese attack on Pearl Harbor in December 1941, once Hitler's invasion of Russia was already in serious trouble, had finally forced the U.S. to enter the war.

For his part, Hitler knew that he could not allow the Soviet Union to continue to exist—a constant threat to the eastern borders of the Greater German Reich. There was bound to be a showdown, but on whose terms? In the end, it was the Germans who broke their pact with the Soviets and attacked, but had Stalin felt stronger, it might just as easily have been the other way around. Having dealt with the Jews, Hitler now decided to liquidate the second "inferior" race that he believed was destined to serve and ultimately make way for the Aryans: the Slavs. His plans for increasing the Reich's *Lebensraum* (living space) meant expansion into Poland, Ukraine, the Baltic States, European Russia, and the oil-rich Soviet Caucasus. The plan was to depopulate and de-industrialize this vast region and turn it into Germany's breadbasket and source of natural resources.

Operation Barbarossa was the largest military invasion of all time, involving three invading armies of over four million German and Axis troops along a 1,800-mile (2,900 km) front stretching from the Baltic to the Black Sea. Three army groups attacked simultaneously in summer 1941. The northern group aimed for Leningrad (now St. Petersburg), the central group for Moscow, and the southern for Stalingrad (now Volgograd) and the oil fields beyond. The Germans had a numerical superiority in troop numbers, but were outnumbered in terms of tanks and aircraft. However, Soviet tanks and aircraft, though vastly superior in numbers, were antiquated and in a poor state of repair. In the first weeks of the invasion, the ill-prepared and poorly led Red Army almost disintegrated under the German assault. Millions of Soviet troops and tens of millions of civilians fell into German hands: millions died, starved, shot, or worked to death in labor camps. In all, the Russian campaign claimed 14 million military lives on both sides, as well as the lives of an estimated 20 million Russian civilians.

Despite their huge gains in territory, the German armies realized too late what Napoleon had realized one-hundred-and-thirty years earlier: that Russia is vast and can call on huge reserves of resources and manpower. While Napoleon had managed to reach Moscow, the Germans only ever came within 18 miles (30 km) of the Russian capital, and they failed to capture their other objectives—Leningrad in the north and Stalingrad in the south—suffering huge casualties in their attempts. Like Napoleon's *Grande Armée*, Hitler's forces had bet on a rapid victory, leading to the collapse and surrender of the Soviet Union. But as fall rains turned into the snows of the Russian winter, Stalin was undefeated, and the Germans, unprepared for winter warfare, and their supply lines stretched to breaking point, stalled and stopped. When Stalin was sure that Japan was no longer a threat, he was able to throw his eastern reserves into the fight and begin the inexorable push toward Berlin and victory.

© 2010 Galerie Bilderwelt | Getty Images

DESTRUCTION
The Nazi plan was to depopulate Russia and give it over to German colonists.

The Second World War was not won on the beaches of Normandy any more than the Napoleonic Wars had been won at Waterloo. In 1815 and 1945, the aggressor had been fatally weakened by his invasion of Russia. The Russian winter defeated two would-be world conquerors, but in 1945 it left the world with a fateful legacy. It ensured that Stalin, fêted as the savior of the Soviet Union, would remain in power until his death in 1954, and ensured the survival of the repressive Stalinist system for a further thirty-seven years after that.

DISASTER

Extinction Event

Tectonic Event

Military Action

Fire

Pandemic

Famine

Political or Economic Event

Genocide

Flood or Storm

Industrial or Transport Accident

ATOMIC DESTRUCTION: HIROSHIMA AND NAGASAKI

1945

Cause: Development of the A-bomb by Allies who wanted to preempt the German use of atomic weapons; Americans seeking a way to make the Japanese surrender after their rejection of the Potsdam Declaration of 1945

Event: Atomic bombing of two Japanese cities, Hiroshima and Nagasaki

Aftermath: Deaths of 110,000 people from the two detonations; additional 330,000 *hibakusha* (victims of the bombings) who have died since

Up to 125,000 people will die on the day or will die soon. The wind mixes their dust with the dirt and debris. Then it sends everything boiling upward in a tall purple-gray column. When the top of the dust spreads out, it looks like a strange, giant mushroom. The bottom of the mushroom cloud is a fiery red. All over the city fires spring up. They rise like flames from a bed of coals.

> **Laurence Yep,**
> *Hiroshima,* 1996

There was nothing inevitable about the development of the atomic bomb in 1945. The structure of the atom and the existence of radioactivity were unknown until the turn of the twentieth century. It was only in 1938 that two German scientists, Otto Hahn (1879–1968) and Friedrich Strassmann (1902–80), succeeded in confirming nuclear fission experimentally. They demonstrated that once triggered, fission could be sustained through a chain reaction that would continue until all the available fuel had been used up. This proved that fission could power a nuclear reactor, and that the reaction could occur explosively in a bomb, with the instantaneous release of the huge amounts of energy locked up in the atomic nucleus of fissile uranium.

Hahn and Strassman's discoveries could have given the Axis powers the A-bomb before the Allies and changed the course of history. But it was the U.S., UK, and Canada's Manhattan Project (1941–46) that designed and built the first nuclear bombs and carried out the first successful nuclear test in New Mexico, on July 16, 1945, less than one month before the first wartime deployments of atomic weapons in August.

Defections to the Allies, expulsions, persecutions by the Nazis themselves, and acts of sabotage, such as the destruction of a critically important heavy-water plant in occupied Norway in 1943, prevented Hitler from developing the Third Reich's A-bomb, which could have been flown to London or Moscow on the world's first missile, the V–2 rocket. Berlin fell to the Red Army in April 1945, and with Hitler's suicide, German resistance quickly ended. This spared the European continent from a nuclear attack, which might have taken place had Germany not surrendered so quickly. After Victory in Europe Day on May 8, 1945, fighting continued in only one theater of war: East Asia and the Pacific, where the Allies were fast closing in on the Japanese home islands.

STILL STANDING
The Genpaku Dome was one of the few buildings left standing in Hiroshima.

© P.D.T.N.C | Shutterstock

After Japan's victories against Britain and the U.S. which matched Germany's at the beginning of European hostilities, the tide of war turned against an overextended Imperial Japanese Army (IJA) and Navy (IJN). After Allied defeats at Pearl Harbor (1941), Singapore (1942), and the Philippines (1942), the British regrouped in the West, expelling the Japanese

**THE DIVINE
WIND THAT
NEVER BLEW**

from Burma, and the U.S. pushed them back across the Pacific, destroying the IJN's carriers and thus its capacity to mount further offensives or prevent an invasion of Japan. However, while Germany crumbled under the combined attacks of the Red Army from the East and of the Allies from the West, the Japanese still believed that they could avoid defeat.

In 1945, Japan was one of the few countries in the world that could claim never to have experienced conquest and occupation by a foreign power. The last attempt, in the late thirteenth century, had ended in a disastrous and costly failure for the invading Mongols and their Chinese allies. Bred on myths of uniqueness and invincibility, the Japanese military resisted any talk of capitulation or even negotiation with the Allies, and instead preached a doctrine of resistance to the last man, woman, and child, to defend the sacred soil of the empire. The Allies knew to their cost that this was not just the idle boast of a faltering enemy.

The fierce battles for the outlying Japanese islands of Iwo Jima (February–March 1945) and in particular for Okinawa (April–June 1945), where 65,000 civilians preferred to commit suicide rather than face the uncertainties of foreign occupation, taught the Allies that the Japanese were not bluffing. In another act of desperation, the Japanese trained young pilots, the *kamikaze*, for suicide missions targeting Allied warships. The name of the force, which translates as "divine wind," was a direct reference to the huge tropical storm that had wrecked the Mongol invasion fleet in 1281. But in spite of the many casualties caused by kamikaze attacks, the divine winds would not save Japan this time.

Already exhausted by six years of war in the European and North African theaters, the Allies were prepared to offer Japan far more generous terms than she deserved. With the Potsdam Declaration of 1945, the U.S., Britain, and Nationalist China offered Japan a guarantee of sovereignty over the home islands in exchange for her unconditional surrender and disarmament. Potsdam would have meant the end of the Japanese Empire in Korea and China, but held out an assurance that the country itself would not be occupied, and its political institutions, including the monarchy, would continue as before. But there was no room in Japanese imperial ideology for surrender; the Japanese government ignored the declaration and prepared to fight on despite the certainty of defeat.

Faced with several more years of war and a growing number of Allied casualties, President Harry S. Truman (1884–1972) authorized the deployment of the still experimental atomic bombs against two Japanese targets to bring the war to a speedy conclusion. Project Manhattan had developed two different designs: the "Little Boy," a uranium-235 bomb, which had never been tested because of a shortage of the fissile uranium, but which was deemed to be the more reliable of the two; and the "Fat Man," a more complex plutonium-239 bomb, which had been successfully tested in New Mexico.

Dropped from the bomb bay of the B–29 Superfortress *Enola Gay*, Little Boy took less than a minute to reach its detonation height of 1,900 feet (600 m) over the city of Hiroshima at 08:15 a.m., on Monday, August 6, 1945. Because of strong winds, the bomb drifted 800 feet (244 m) off target, exploding directly over a hospital, causing a blast equivalent of 13,000 tons of TNT, which destroyed everything within a radius of 1 mile (1.6 km). Despite this huge destructive effect, this represented less than 1.5 percent of the bomb's fissile capability.

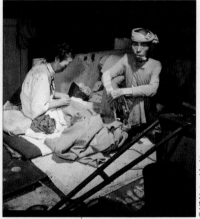

Three days later, on August 9, the B–29 Superfortress *Bockscar* set off for its designated primary target of Kokura, a small, unremarkable castle town overlooking the Shimonoseki Strait between the two large islands of Kyushu and Honshu. Because of adverse weather conditions, the *Bockscar* diverted to its secondary target of Nagasaki, the city that had traditionally been the most open to outside influences. At 11:01 a.m. a break in the cloud allowed the bombardier to sight the drop zone and release the first and only plutonium bomb ever to be dropped on a populated area. The bomb detonated 43 seconds later, at an altitude of 1,540 feet (469 m), approximately 2 miles (3.2 km) off target. The blast generated a yield equivalent to 21,000 tons of TNT, with a total destructive radius of about 1 mile (1.6 km), killing an estimated 40,000 people. By the end of 1945, a further 220,000 had died from burns, injuries, and radiation sickness. As of August 2012, the total number of deaths in the two cities directly attributable to the bombings had reached 439,713.

© US National Archives

HIBAKUSHA
The victims of the A-bombs are still dying decades later.

THE ATOMIC GENIE

After the war, Albert Einstein (1879–1955) and many of the scientists involved in the Manhattan Project petitioned the U.S. Government to dismantle the remaining bombs, ban the building of any future devices, and develop the peaceful uses of nuclear technology under the auspices of the United Nations. However, once the atomic genie was out of the bottle there was no reliable way of stuffing it back and ensuring that it would stay there. All hope of unilateral disarmament on the part of the Americans, British, and Canadians, who had built the first A-bombs, vanished when the Soviet Union, using a combination of homegrown talent and espionage, successfully tested its own nuclear device on August 29, 1949, in Kazakhstan in Central Asia.

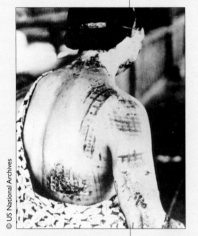

© US National Archives

FLASH
The bomb's intense light and heat scorched human skin.

The two superpowers, already fighting the undeclared "Cold War" (1948–91), entered the aptly named era of MAD, "Mutually Assured Destruction," and the nuclear arms race. The low point of the Cold War came with the Cuban Missile Crisis of 1962, when the world came closest to a full-scale nuclear war between the U.S. and NATO on one side and the USSR and Warsaw Pact on the other.

Other major powers developed their own nuclear capabilities, beginning with Great Britain (1952), followed by France (1960), and the People's Republic of China (1964). Along with the U.S. and Russia, these countries represented the first wave of nuclear proliferation. The second wave was headed by India, which detonated its first bomb in 1974, and Pakistan followed suit in 1988, creating the world's most dangerous nuclear flashpoint after the Near East. Israel supposedly tested a nuclear device in 1979, but still denies having a nuclear capability. The third wave of nuclear proliferation includes many more countries including two so-called "rogue states," North Korea and Iran. With the proliferation of nuclear technology and reactors, however, atomic weapons are now within reach not just of states but also of terrorist organizations such as Al-Qaeda, raising the specter of attacks on civilian targets as murderous as the bombings of Hiroshima and Nagasaki.

A HOUSE DIVIDED AGAINST ITSELF: PARTITION OF INDIA

1947

DISASTER

Extinction Event

Tectonic Event

Military Action

Fire

Pandemic

Famine

Political or Economic Event

Genocide

Flood or Storm

Industrial or Transport Accident

Cause: Long-standing religious and political divisions in India; end of the British Raj and partition of India into the Dominion of Pakistan and the Union of India

Event: Between 12.5 and 14.5 million people migrated from one side of the new borders to the other, sparking riots, rapes, kidnappings, and massacres on both sides

Aftermath: Deaths of between 500,000 to one million people; Indo-Pakistani War; assassination of Gandhi; breakup of Pakistan and creation of Bangladesh

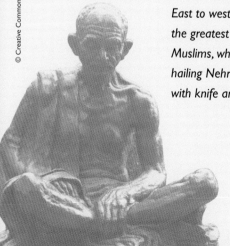

East to west and west to east perhaps ten million fled for their lives in the greatest exodus in history. The killings spread even to Delhi, where non-Muslims, who had been among the throng so cheerfully hailing Independence, hailing Nehru and Mountbatten, now turned on their Muslim neighbours with knife and club.

John Keay,
A History of India, 2000

Ancient India was a land of many faiths. During the first millennium BCE, Hinduism gave birth to two religions that were first seen as heterodox Hindu sects: Jainism (ninth century BCE) and Buddhism (sixth century BCE). Hinduism, Buddhism, and Jainism are generally tolerant of other beliefs, especially when compared to the much more militant, proselytizing Christianity and Islam. As a result, ancient India did not experience the destructive religious conflicts that disturbed the peace of Europe and the Near East during the same period.

The destruction of Sassanid Persia by the Arabs, and the Islamization of Iran and Central Asia in the seventh century CE, created an invader who saw conquest not just as an opportunity for acquiring plunder, land, and slaves, but also as a religious duty—*jihad*—to convert the infidel to the faith of the Prophet Muhammad (ca. 570–632). The Muslims, who were not versed in the subtleties of Hindu, Jain, and Buddhist theology, saw these faiths as the ultimate expression of polytheism—idolatry on steroids—with their extraordinary temples, covered in what seemed to them sacrilegious images of many-armed gods and gilded Buddhas. A confederation of Hindu rajahs, however, managed to halt the Arab invasion of India at the Battle of Rajasthan (738), ensuring that India would remain Hindu for another two centuries.

Starting in the tenth century, Central Asian Muslims achieved a more lasting conquest of northern India, establishing a series of dynasties: the Ghaznavids (tenth to twelfth centuries), the Ghorids (twelfth to thirteenth centuries), the Delhi and Lodi Sultanates (thirteenth to fifteenth centuries) and the Timurids (fourteenth to sixteenth centuries). The founder of the Timurids, Timur, better known as Tamerlane (1336–1405), ordered the massacre of 100,000 "infidel" Hindu citizens of Delhi. The Mughal Dynasty (1526–1857) that succeeded the Timurids, although also Turco-Mongol Muslims, adopted Indian customs. The Emperor Akbar the Great (1542–1605) enacted a policy of religious toleration without parallel in the Muslim world. The fifteenth century saw the emergence of the last piece of the subcontinent's religious jigsaw puzzle with Guru Nanak's (1469–1539) foundation of Sikhism.

Akbar's grandson Aurangzeb (1618–1707), a Muslim zealot, attempted to conquer and Islamicize the remaining Hindu kingdoms of southern India. Although he succeeded in vastly expanding the borders of the Mughal Empire, he also weakened it to such an extent that soon after his death it began to disintegrate, shaken internally by Hindu revolts and threatened externally by the appearance of a new threat from the far West: European merchants, missionaries, and adventurers, spearheaded by the Portuguese, who had first reached India in 1505. They were followed by the French, Dutch, and, of course, the English, whose East India Company (1600–1874) was to play a crucial role in the history of the subcontinent for the next two-hundred-and-fifty years.

The history of British rule in India is unique in the annals of world imperialism in that it began as a purely commercial enterprise. The British East India Company was established during the reign of Elizabeth I (1533–1603) and initially struggled to survive against stiff competition from the Portuguese, French, and Dutch East India companies, at a time when a "trade war" did not mean a bad-tempered exchange of strongly worded diplomatic notes and the passing of tit-for-tat protectionist legislation, but full-on military encounters with naval and land forces.

SLEEPWALKING INTO EMPIRE

During the seventeenth century, the English succeeded in holding their own against their European rivals, establishing permanent bases in India, and forming alliances with local rulers until the East India Company had become the dominant foreign power, administering vast tracts of the country, while nominally acknowledging the suzerainty of a powerless Mughal emperor in Delhi. Disasters such as the Bengal Famine of 1769–73 (pp. 79–82), however, served to discredit company rule in India; but what finally triggered India's full incorporation into the British Empire in 1858 was the disastrous Indian Rebellion (Indian Mutiny) of 1857, which was one of the bloodiest revolts of native troops against British rule during the nineteenth century. Henceforth, British kings and queens would take the grandiloquent title of Emperor or Empress of India.

The British Raj was the political equivalent of a patchwork quilt. It consisted of eight major and five minor provinces run by British administrators, appointed by the East India Company and later by the Crown, and 565 princely states, many of which were only a dozen miles across while others, such as Kashmir and Hyderabad, were country-sized—all retaining varying degrees of autonomy, while deferring to the British Crown. Unlike the Americas, Australia, and South Africa, there was never an attempt to colonize India with large numbers of white settlers, and the British population of the Raj in 1861 was 125,945, two-thirds of whom were in the military.

During the ninety years between the Indian Rebellion and independence, the British enacted a series of reforms to modernize India, built its famous railway network, and extended the electoral franchise extremely cautiously to the small emerging Indian middle class. It was not in the interests of the British to allow Indian nationalism to develop, but India soon began to search for its own national identity. However, what that identity might be was extremely complex, as India, a majority Hindu country, with large Buddhist, Jain, Sikh, and Christian communities, had been ruled in part by a Muslim minority, who dominated several of India's wealthiest northern provinces and cities, including the capital, Delhi.

In 1885, British civil servant Allan Octavian Hume (1829–1912) was one of the founders of the Indian National Congress (INC), established with British Government approval as a means to give Indian citizens a greater voice in the governance of their own country. The INC would develop into a mass political movement, becoming the present-day Congress Party, which would fight for and win independence for the Union of India, under the leadership of Mohandas "Mahatma" Gandhi (1869–1948). The Congress was home to a wide variety of political and religious groups, including secularist moderates and extremists, Hindus, and Muslims, but religious separatism was not long in appearing with the creation of the All India Muslim League (1906–1947), which would campaign for and achieve the independence of a separate Dominion of Pakistan under the leadership of Muhammad Ali Jinnah (1876–1948).

THE BEST OF INTENTIONS

The British, prodded, infuriated, embarrassed, and shamed by Gandhi, passed the Government of India Act (1935), giving India a measure of autonomy and extending the electoral franchise to 35 million of India's citizens. This fell short of full independence, for which Gandhi and the INC were campaigning. The Second World War temporarily halted moves toward independence. The Japanese, although far from democratic or anti-colonialist themselves, encouraged India's anti-British independence movement, achieving a measure of success with the creation of the collaborationist Indian Nationalist Army (INA) in 1942. After the defeat of the Japanese and their INA allies in 1945, the British, exhausted and bankrupted by years of war, recognized that they no longer had any choice, and that they would have to grant India full independence immediately. In the end, an imperial "immediately" meant two years of hard negotiating between the various interested parties.

What remained to be decided was the shape of the future country or countries that would succeed the Raj. Gandhi favored a single federated Indian nation state consisting of majority Hindu, Muslim, and Sikh states, with constitutional protections for India's religious minorities. He feared that the adoption of a two-state solution would lead to sectarian violence between India's different religious communities and war between the newly independent countries. All his attempts to persuade Jinnah to remain within the INC, however, failed. It was left to the last viceroy of India, Queen Elizabeth II's cousin Lord Louis Mountbatten (1900–79), to negotiate the grant of independence and mediate between the parties.

Even with Gandhi's considerable assistance Mountbatten could not persuade Jinnah and the All India Muslim League to abandon the creation of an independent Dominion of Pakistan. *"Pakstan"* (the "i" was added later) means "Land of the Pure" in a mixture of Persian and Urdu—the languages of Muslim India—but it is also a politically revealing acronym: "P" stands for Punjab, a large region of northern India that includes the Indian capital Delhi; "A" for Afghan Province (Northwest Frontier Province), underlining the close cultural and religious ties between Pakistan and Afghanistan; "K" for Kashmir, a Muslim-majority princely

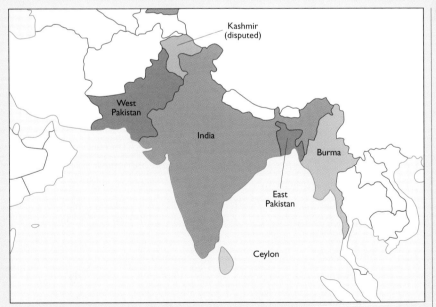

INDIA DIVIDED
Map showing the successor countries that emerged after the British Raj.

state bordering Pakistan whose Hindu ruler chose to join with India and which remains the cause of a great deal of friction between the two countries; "S" for Sindh and "-stan" from Baluchistan, for two of the four provinces of modern Pakistan.

The solution the British came up with is reminiscent of the old joke: "What is a camel?" Answer: "A horse designed by a committee." With the best intentions in the world—which we all know lead to only one place—the British oversaw the largest geographical carve-up of the twentieth century, attempting to create two viable independent states out of a hotchpotch of former imperial provinces and princely states, some with clear Muslim or Hindu majorities, a few split dangerously down the middle, and with

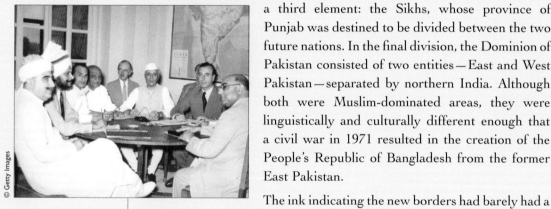

© Getty Images

a third element: the Sikhs, whose province of Punjab was destined to be divided between the two future nations. In the final division, the Dominion of Pakistan consisted of two entities—East and West Pakistan—separated by northern India. Although both were Muslim-dominated areas, they were linguistically and culturally different enough that a civil war in 1971 resulted in the creation of the People's Republic of Bangladesh from the former East Pakistan.

CONCILIATOR
Mountbatten tried and failed to make India's leader agree to a one state solution.

The ink indicating the new borders had barely had a chance to dry on the new maps of India and Pakistan when millions of Hindus, Sikhs, Jains, Buddhists, Parsees, and Christians began to migrate in one direction and millions of Muslims moved in the other. Historians estimate that between 12.5 and 14.5 million were displaced by the partition of India. Tensions between the Hindu and Muslim communities were extremely high, sparking riots and violence on both sides. Between 500,000 and one million people were killed in inter-communal fighting, and ten of thousands of women were abducted and raped. Due to the subcontinent's strict family honor codes, many of these women never returned to their families. In one final tragedy, Gandhi fell victim to an assassin's bullet as he addressed a prayer meeting in New Delhi, capital of the newly independent Republic of India. Ironically, the man who murdered Gandhi was a Hindu nationalist, who believed that the Mahatma was too pro-Muslim.

THE BITTER YEARS: GREAT CHINESE FAMINE

1958–61

Cause: Mao Zedong's modernization of Chinese economy by collectivizing agriculture and industrializing; adverse weather conditions and poor harvests in parts of China

Event: China's "Great Leap Forward" stalled and agricultural production slumped; refusal to reduce unrealistic grain quotas; failure to provide relief to farmers

Aftermath: Deaths of between 20 and 40 million people, and birth deficit of 35 million

Farmers had lost control not only of their land and harvest, but also of their own work schedules: local cadres determined who should do what and for how many work points, from collecting manure to looking after buffaloes in the fields. As the market was eliminated and money lost its purchasing power, grain became the currency of exchange. Most of it was in the hands of the state.

Frank Dikötter,
Mao's Great Famine, 2010

In total, Joseph Stalin's (1878–1953) dismal reign is thought to have caused the deaths of as many as 20 million victims in the Soviet Union and the neighboring countries under his control. Victory in the Second World War ensured that Stalin would stay in power for another eight years, during which he plunged the world into the Cold War with the U.S. and her Allies, and engineered a "hot" war against them on the Korean Peninsula. Stalin did not fight the Korean War (1950–53) directly but through his proxy, the People's Republic of China (PRC), led by Mao Zedong (1893–1976) after his defeat of the rightist Kuomintang (Nationalist Party, or KMT) in 1949.

© Hung Chung Chih | Shutterstock

DELUDED
Mao thought he could catch up with the West in five years.

Although linked as two faces of the same "Evil Empire," the Soviet Union and PRC were separated by ideological differences that began with the foundation of the Chinese Communist Party (CCP). As personalities, too, Stalin and Mao were more natural rivals than allies. Throughout the 1940s and 1950s, Maoist thought gradually distanced itself from Stalinist orthodoxy, and a split could have taken place between the two countries much earlier than it did, but the U.S. intervention in the Korean War made the two men patch up their differences. Tensions remained and Stalin did not hold good on promises to provide materiel and military assistance to help China defeat NATO forces.

THE COMMUNIST EMPEROR

For millennia China led the world, but by the early twentieth century the empire was bankrupt intellectually, economically, and politically, and under siege by foreign powers. In 1912, China became a republic, but the democratic experiment was a short-lived disaster. The country's second president followed the route taken by many Chinese strongmen and would-be reformers throughout Chinese history by declaring himself emperor in 1915. But the Chinese had had enough of emperors and dynasties, and the would-be Son of Heaven was deposed and died in 1916. Leaderless, China sank into anarchy, becoming what we would now called a "failed state," with large areas of the country under the rule of rival warlords or effectively administered by colonial powers as "international concessions."

The CCP, which looked to the newly founded Soviet Union for inspiration and support, and the conservative KMT slugged it out for power. The KMT came out on top until the outbreak of the Sino-Japanese War in

1937. During the war, the CCP and KMT agreed to an uneasy truce to fight the common enemy. However, the civil war resumed in 1940 and was won by Mao and the CCP in 1949.

The vast country that Mao now ruled was predominantly agricultural, with a few industrialized urban areas. Socially and politically, China was a gigantic pyramid, with the emperor and court at its apex above a class of landowning officials, both supported by the peasantry that accounted for 90 percent of the population. The emperor and court had been removed in 1912, but now Mao was going to replace it with the Central Committee of the CCP and its bureaucracy, with himself at its head as a latter-day Communist emperor. For ideological reasons, Mao never aspired to the imperial throne, but he had the powers and attributes of a Chinese sovereign in all but name. In life and later in death, he was revered and worshipped as much as any divinized Son of Heaven.

It is unlikely that many among China's huge rural population were communists at this stage. But after a century of civil wars and foreign invasions, they were happy to support any government that promised them peace, stability, security, and land reform. The majority of China's peasants were tenants of the old ruling class. China had a tiny urban proletariat, even smaller than Russia's in 1917. According to Marx's original theory outlined in *Das Kapital* (1867–94), Russia and China would need to be transformed socially and economically before they would be ready for true Socialism.

© Time & Life Pictures | Getty Images

ABANDONED
The Communist government abandoned the victims of the famine to their plight.

Stalin succeeded in modernizing the Russian economy, but where he failed spectacularly was in his reform of agriculture. He forced through a policy of collectivization which, coupled with the pseudo-scientific theories of the geneticist Trofim Lysenko (1898–1976), resulted in the murderous Holodomor (pp. 139–144). Mao, though wanting Stalin's position as leader of the Communist world for himself, chose to emulate Stalin's methods for his own plan to modernize China's industry and agriculture. In the process, he unwittingly repeated Stalin's mistakes, and on a much larger scale. Starting in 1949, Mao inaugurated China's first Five-Year Plan, but his task was far greater than Stalin's. European Russia in the 1920s was more developed than any region of China in the late 1940s. China, on the other hand, had its huge population and natural resources but little else. What little industrial, scientific, and commercial expertise there was had been in the hands of foreigners or of the discredited ruling class.

GREAT LEAP BACKWARD

Dissatisfied with the progress the Chinese economy was making, Mao decided on a far-reaching reform policy, which he called the "Great Leap Forward." The Five-Year Plan (1958–1963) would see Chinese industry catch up with the world's developed economies. He focused on two areas: increasing the yields of China's agriculture and her iron and steel production, which he saw as the key to the country's industrial development. His boast to the CCP congress in 1958 was that China would equal Britain's steel production by 1965.

Mao imitated Stalin in his modernization of Chinese agriculture. He embarked on a program of collectivization, taking land away from the peasants who had only recently acquired it. He also introduced new planting techniques inspired by Lysenko's bogus biological theories. Lacking the industrial infrastructure to achieve the planned increase in steel production, he promoted the building of thousands of backyard furnaces all over the country that would turn scrap metal into steel. For a brief moment it seemed that the plan would succeed. A good harvest in 1958 produced record yields, and the peasants dutifully melted pots and pans to increase China's quota of steel production. Unfortunately, what they produced was low-grade and largely useless pig iron, and the lack of transport infrastructure meant that what they produced could not be taken to the cities.

Collectivization and disastrous agricultural innovations, combined with poor weather, floods, and drought in 1959 and 1960, and the lack of manpower that had been diverted to other projects, led to a slump in agricultural production. Despite growing food shortages that were fast turning to famine, Mao continued to export grain to the cities. Estimates of the death toll from starvation for the years 1959 to 1961 range from 20 to 40 million souls. In other words, in two years, Mao had managed to wipe out anything between the current populations of Angola (20 million) and Argentina (40 million), and caused a further birth deficit of 35 million, for a total loss to China of 75 million lives.

TELEVISING FAMINE: NIGERIA

1967–70

DISASTER

Extinction Event

Tectonic Event

Military Action

Fire

Pandemic

Famine

Political or Economic Event

Genocide

Flood or Storm

Industrial or Transport Accident

Cause: Post-colonial Nigeria made up of different religious, linguistic, and ethnic groups

Event: Army coup and counter-coup triggered a secessionist movement in the southeast of the country; involvement of foreign powers prolonged the war

Aftermath: Deaths of between one and three million Nigerians from war, disease, and starvation; several decades of military government

The war had taken the lives of between 1 and 3 million Nigerians, mostly in the Eastern Region and many through starvation, leaving another 3 million displaced, but the "genocide" that the Igbos so feared did not materialize after the war. Gowon stressed that there was to be no vengeance and no reparations, and there had been no winners or losers in the "war of brothers."

Toyin Falola and Matthew Heaton,
A History of Nigeria, **2008**

Although the three-year Nigerian Civil War (1967–70; also known as the Nigerian–Biafran War) broke out seven years after Nigeria had been granted its independence by Great Britain in 1960, many of the deeper causes of the war can be found in the colonial era and the post-colonial settlement. Most of the African continent was colonized relatively late in imperial history. Although the Portuguese were the first to establish outposts in Africa in the fifteenth century, as they pushed south and east toward India and East Asia, these remained principally coastal commercial emporia from which they operated the transatlantic slave trade with their Brazilian possessions (pp. 62–66).

In this the Portuguese, and later British, Dutch, and French, found ready partners in the kingdoms and emirates of West Africa, whose own economies were based on slave labor. African slavery, though without doubt iniquitous, shared many similarities with slavery in the Classical world: A slave could earn or be granted his freedom by his master, and then integrate into Roman or Greek society. In the Americas, because of the added racial dimension, African slaves formed a permanent underclass that was given no opportunity to integrate into the dominant white culture until the abolition of slavery in the nineteenth century.

© Time & Life Pictures | Getty Images

VAIN HOPE
President Gowon hoped to resolve the Biafran problem with a quick "police action."

The British and Dutch had established extensive colonial settlements in South Africa, but this was the exception rather than the rule on the continent. The drive for the European takeover of the whole of Africa began in the late nineteenth century, in what became known as the "Scramble for Africa" (1881–1914), during which established and new colonial powers, including France, Great Britain, Germany, Portugal, Italy, and Belgium, took over vast swathes of land, artificially dividing culturally and linguistically linked groups, or creating unions between different ethnic, religious, and linguistic groups that had hitherto been ruled by very different political systems. The causes of the scramble included rivalries between the European powers, the search for raw materials for European factories, and the need to find new markets for European manufactured goods after the Long Depression, a protracted economic slump that lasted from 1873 to 1896. Britain, with its extensive existing possessions in the north and south of the continent, was a major winner, but France took over large parts of West Africa to add to its North African empire, and Germany finally obtained the colonial empire that it craved in East and Central Africa.

Decolonization started in North Africa with the independence of Libya from Italy (1951), and the first West African nation to be granted independence was Ghana. The process was sometimes peaceful and sometimes violent. Several countries had to fight wars of independence, while others were graciously granted sovereignty by European powers only too glad to be rid of troublesome and costly colonial dependencies. The British, in particular, once decolonization had begun, seemed to be in an unsightly hurry to divest themselves of their African empire. However, the viability of several of the countries that were created in the "Scramble out of Africa" was not assured.

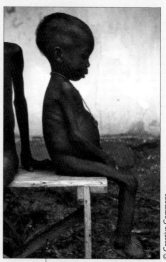

© Creative Commons

ICONIC
Biafra produced the first TV pictures of starving children.

Although India, for all its internal divisions, had been in existence for millennia before the colonial period, Nigeria was a completely artificial British construct, grouping together 250 ethnic groups, speaking over 500 languages, and belonging to many different religious faiths including Islam, Protestant and Catholic Christianity, and traditional African religions. The three dominant ethnic groups in the country were then as now the Muslim Fulani-Hausa of northern Nigeria, the Christian Igbo of southeastern Nigeria, and the Yoruba, who were evenly split between Christian and Muslim and occupied western Nigeria.

I have vivid memories of the conflict between Nigeria and Biafra, as it was also the first major famine of the television age. There was something particularly shocking about images of starving children, their eyes sunken in faces that were already skull-like, their limbs stick-thin, and their stomachs horribly distended in a terrible parody of the obesity that was already beginning to plague the overfed children of the West.

THE CAMERA NEVER LIES?

Nigeria was a federation of very different peoples, religions, and political cultures. The north, which had been ruled by Muslim emirs since the ninth century, was the most conservative and authoritarian, and the southeast, predominantly Christian, the most liberal and democratic. The economic wealth of the country, however, was concentrated in the south, in the region around the port of Lagos, and in the Igbo-majority region, which included two-thirds of Nigeria's oil reserves. The trigger for the war was a 1966 military coup led by Major Emmanuel Ifeajuna (d. 1967), Kaduna Nzeogwu (1937–67), and other junior officers, that was characterized as an Igbo plot to seize control of the country. This triggered a counter-coup by northern officers led by Lt. Colonel Yakubu Gowon (b. 1934), a Christian from a minority tribal group, who, with the support of northern Muslim officers, became the first in a long line of Nigerian military dictators.

Reprisals against Igbo members of the armed forces and civilians prompted the military governor of southeastern Nigeria, Colonel Odumegwu Ojukwu (1933–2011), to proclaim the secession of the province and the establishment of the independent Republic of Biafra in 1967. After negotiations between the federal government and the new republic ended in failure, General Gowon ordered a limited "police action" to bring an end to the conflict. Biafra was recognized by a few African countries, and received assistance from Canada, and France; the Nigerians received Soviet and British support and military assistance. The Americans remained out of the fray, providing only humanitarian assistance through the American Red Cross.

RESISTANCE
Despite desperate resistance, the rebel army was forced to surrender.

The Biafrans, though poorly armed, repulsed the advancing Nigerian columns, and later went on the offensive themselves. They advanced westward into Nigeria proper, getting within 130 miles (210 km) of Lagos. Nigerian forces counterattacked, driving the Biafran army back, but it was only after 30 long months of hostilities that the short-lived republic finally capitulated. During the hostilities, the Nigerians had blockaded Biafra, hoping that shortages would force an early surrender or trigger a rebellion among the local population against their rulers. However, the Biafran government played on Igbo fears of genocide and conducted a skillful media campaign overseas to garner support among the international community. Vast amounts of humanitarian aid were shipped to Biafra, but according to several historians, this only served to extend the conflict. In the end between one and three million people died as a result of the war, many from starvation and disease. Although the Igbo were not persecuted after the end of the war, the civil war left a legacy of political instability in the country and ensured that the rule of the military lasted until 1999.

© Getty Images

VALLEYS OF DEATH: CAMBODIAN "KILLING FIELDS"

1975–79

Cause: Takeover of Cambodia (Democratic Kampuchea) by the Khmer Rouge in 1975; extreme Communist regime

Event: Mass executions of the regime's political opponents, Buddhist monks, and members of ethnic minorities; policy of total self-sufficiency and return to the land

Aftermath: Deaths of between 1.7 and 2.5 million Cambodians; invasion of Cambodia by Vietnam, which overthrew the Khmer Rouge regime and occupied the country until 1989

The Khmer Rouge communists captured the Cambodian capital city of Phnom Penh and began their four-year reign of terror that dismembered a country. They evacuated the cities and dragged off everyone to work in the rice fields in an attempt to create a purely agrarian society.

Penne Conrad,
Out of the Killing Fields Into the Light, 2011

The Cambodian "Killing Fields," according to certain estimates, saw the extermination of one-quarter of the Cambodian population between 1975 and 1979. Rudolf Rummel (b. 1932), Professor Emeritus at the University of Hawaii, created a new term to describe this kind of human calamity: "democide," which he defines as the intentional mass murder of its citizens by a government, and which differs from genocide in that it does not target a specific ethnic or religious group. In this category, Rummel includes the killings carried out during Joseph Stalin's tenure as leader of the Soviet Union (pp. 139–144) and the deaths attributable to Mao Zedong's Great Leap Forward (pp. 171–174). Although in both cases questions can be raised as to whether the killings were intentional or just a result of criminal negligence and plain incompetence. The Killing Fields, however, clearly meet his criteria of intentional state murder of its own citizens.

In ancient times, Southeast Asia fell into two distinct spheres of influence: China to the north and India to the west, each contributing in different measure to the cultural mix of the near neighbors Thailand, Laos, Cambodia, and Vietnam. Medieval Cambodia was the home to the once powerful and extensive Khmer Empire (802–1431), which created the stone wonder that is the holy city of Angkor. The region has known its fair share of social and political tumult, with the rise and fall of empires, invasions from China, and domination by Thailand, but the genesis of the Killing Fields, as with many other world calamities, really begins with European colonization. The French entered the region in 1863 and would leave it defeated and humiliated in 1953, expelled by Vietcong insurgents, which attracted the attention of the U.S. and plunged the country into the disastrous twenty-year Vietnam War (1955–75).

During the hostilities, the entire region turned into an armed camp, with rival governments looking to Washington, Beijing, and Moscow for financial backing and military support. Southeast Asia became the largest theater of the undeclared triangular war between the U.S. and NATO, the Soviet Union and the Warsaw Pact, and the People's Republic of China (PRC). With the elimination of France from the contest, there emerged one of the most colorful figures of the region: Prince, and sometime King

© Richard Dudman | Sygma | Corbis

DYSTOPIA
Pol Pot's vision of a classless society brought death on a huge scale.

and Premier Norodom Sihanouk (1922–2012), who holds the *Guinness Book of Records* distinction of being the man who had had the greatest number and variety of political offices, ranging from constitutional monarch to Communist commissar. He was the left-leaning king of Cambodia from 1953 to 1970, until overthrown by General Lon Nol (1913–85), the founder of the short-lived pro-Western Khmer Republic (1970–75). Sihanouk fled to North Korea and the PRC, and was briefly head of state during the first year of Khmer Rouge rule (1975–76). Once Sihanouk had played his part in their takeover, however, the Khmer Rouge disposed of him—not by killing him but by exiling him to China.

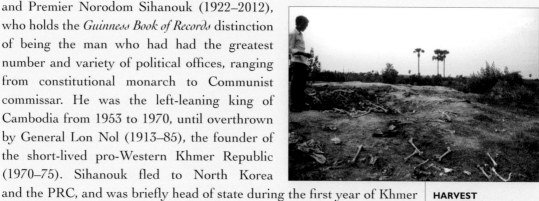

© 2007 Getty Images

HARVEST
The yearly rains uncover a bitter harvest of bones in the Killing Fields.

Lon Nol's Khmer Republic quickly became embroiled in the closing stages of the Vietnam War, experiencing bombing of its territory by the U.S. and an invasion by the North Vietnamese. The Khmer Rouge, a relatively unknown Maoist group led by Pol Pot (1928–1998), had begun their insurgency with North Vietnamese support in 1968. The popular Sihanouk, pledged his support to the Khmer Rouge, who were joined by Sihanouk's peasant royalist supporters. In the strangest alliance of modern times, monarchists fought alongside Maoists to depose a rightwing military dictator. After a seven-year insurgency, Pol Pot, with Sihanouk as a figurehead, overcame the forces of the Khmer Republic. The Americans, withdrawing from their involvement in South Vietnam, did not intervene.

BRAVE NEW AGRARIAN WORLD

The Khmer Rouge leadership put into practice across the whole country the political program they had developed on a small scale in the areas that they had already "liberated." They planned to create a Socialist utopia in one step, without going through the process of economic modernization through industrialization that had cost so many lives in the Soviet Union and the PRC. They divided the Cambodians into the virtuous "Old People," the peasants, and the "New People"—basically the educated, urban population that Cambodia, renamed "Democratic Kampuchea," no longer wanted or needed. After closing the country's borders to outside influences and interference, the Khmer rouge leadership engaged in a social experiment that was as far-reaching as it was disastrous.

The killings began immediately. Ordering the evacuation of Cambodia's cities on the pretext of U.S. bombing, the Khmer Rouge planned to return the country to a state of classless agrarianism. Private property, banking, and money were abolished, and religious institutions, hospitals, schools, universities, and private businesses were closed. Thousands died on the forced marches out of the cities, and once they arrived in the countryside, with no experience of how to feed themselves, and receiving no help from the peasants, the city-dwellers starved to death, died of epidemic diseases for which they were given no treatment, or were simply worked to death in labor camps.

But the regime also directly targeted several groups that they thought had to be eliminated. These included all former officials of the previous government; all professionals, intellectuals, artists, musicians, and writers; the religious, notably Buddhist monks, Christian and Muslim clerics; ethnic minorities including Cambodians of Thai, Vietnamese, and Chinese descent; and finally "economic saboteurs," who were those city-dwellers who had managed to survive deportation from the cities and starvation.

They faced execution in gruesome ways: poisoned, their heads beaten in with agricultural implements, or stabbed with bamboo spears in order to save bullets. The executioners killed the children and infants of their victims by smashing their skulls against tree trunks, explaining later that they did so so that they would not grow up to take revenge on their parents' executioners. The bodies were buried in mass graves around the country's deserted cities—the Killing Fields—which to this day yield a dreadful harvest of human bones and skulls.

Eventually Pol Pot overreached himself and attacked his former allies the North Vietnamese, who invaded the country and sent Pol Pot and his henchmen fleeing into the jungles of Cambodia's border with Thailand. One of the worst mass murderers in history survived until 1998, either dying a natural death or poisoned by Vietnamese agents. Although a tribunal was set up to try the perpetrators of the Cambodian democide, delays have meant that many among the senior leadership died before they could be tried, and so far only the lower tier of cadres have faced world justice.

DYING OF IGNORANCE: HIV-AIDS

1981–present

DISASTER

Extinction Event

Tectonic Event

Military Action

Fire

Pandemic

Famine

Political or Economic Event

Genocide

Flood or Storm

Industrial or Transport Accident

Cause: African Simian Immunodeficiency Virus (SIV) jumped species barrier in early twentieth century; delay of health-education campaigns by governments, churches, and NGOs, failure to license cheap generic medication in the developing world

Event: Infections and deaths in both the developed and developing world

Aftermath: Deaths of 25 million people since virus identified; 35 million people currently live with the disease; drastic falls in life expectancy in affected countries; stigma

According to estimates by WHO and UNAIDS, 34.9 million people were living with HIV at the end of 2011. That same year, some 2.5 million people became newly infected, and 1.7 million died of AIDS-related causes, including 230,000 children. More than two-thirds of new HIV infections are in sub-Saharan Africa.

"How many people are living with AIDS?,"

World Health Organization (WHO), December 2012

To begin, let's clarify the distinction between HIV (Human Immunodeficiency Virus) and AIDS (Acquired Immune Deficiency Syndrome), and give readers a brief HIV-AIDS 101. HIV is a virus, a type of micro-organism that is so primitive that it is unable to reproduce itself and needs the cells of host organisms to replicate. Over the past decades, doctors have found ways of combating infection from viruses through vaccination. HIV, however, is a "retrovirus," which constantly mutates within host cells by using the chemical reverse transcriptase. HIV's complex biochemistry and lifecycle mean that attempts to create an effective vaccine have so far failed. There are two major types of HIV: HIV 1 is the most prevalent in the world and also the most infectious, while HIV 2 is less infectious and is found mainly in West Africa.

Compared to airborne viruses such as influenza, HIV is not very infectious; it cannot survive in the outside environment and thus cannot be transmitted through casual physical contact between people or with objects and clothes belonging to an infected person. To infect a new host, HIV, which is found in blood, semen, and vaginal fluids and must have a direct route into an uninfected person's bloodstream. Once in the blood, the virus seeks out the cells it needs to reproduce. The outer coating of HIV is covered with protein receptors that target T4 cells (also known as CD4s), which play a vital role in the human immune system. CD4s "turn on" the immune system when a pathogen is detected, causing another type—CD8s—to destroy the infective agent. CD4s then "turn off" the immune response to prevent it from damaging the host's own tissues.

© John Crawford | NCI

MYSTERY
It took doctors several years to identify the virus that causes HIV-AIDS.

Once inside the T-cell, HIV injects its own genetic material into the host's DNA and sets up a "factory" to make more copies of itself. As the virus multiplies, it "buds off" or breaks out, leaving the host T-cell damaged and unable to function. With a compromised immune system, the host quickly develops AIDS, and becomes vulnerable to a growing number of secondary infections, including such rare conditions as *Pneumocystis carinii* pneumonia (PCP) and Kaposi's sarcoma (KS), which a healthy immune system would normally shrug off. Hence, HIV itself has never killed anyone; it weakens its hosts by causing a failure of the immune system (AIDS), which in turn allows opportunistic infections to develop. HIV is unusual among viruses in that it causes the death of a high proportion of its hosts; therefore, its survival strategy depends on the carriers' ignorance of their infected status, so that they can infect new hosts before they die.

There is one class of diseases for which sufferers are often blamed for self-infliction: sexually transmitted infections (STIs), including the relatively recent and deadly addition, HIV-AIDS. Of course, there are other routes for HIV infection, including mother-to-baby transmission, sharing needles for intravenous drug use or tattooing, and from using contaminated blood products and surgical instruments, all of which can deliver the virus directly into the host's bloodstream. But in the early 80s, as far as the world media was concerned, HIV-AIDS was not only an STI, it was a *gay* STI.

We now know from genetic studies that HIV originated in West and Central Africa in the late nineteenth or early twentieth century, where it began life as a simian virus (SIV) that jumped the species barrier into humans, probably through the hunting of monkeys and chimps for "bush meat." The first reliably documented case of HIV-AIDS was reported in 1959 in the Democratic Republic of the Congo. With the growth of mass air transit, the virus made its way to North America, carried by an unidentified individual from the Congo. The first cases of the unknown disease began to appear in the U.S. in the late 1970s, primarily among gay men in New York and San Francisco. A gay Canadian flight attendant called Gaëtan Dugas (1953–84) was incorrectly identified as North America's "patient zero," who was thought to be the first sufferer of a novel infectious disease christened GRID (Gay Related Immune Deficiency) in 1981 by the Center for Disease Control (CDC) and less kindly (but predictably) the "gay plague" by the tabloid press.

Of course, any disease that can affect a gay man can affect any human, but there was not much logic or rationality to be had in the early days of the HIV-AIDS "moral panic"—though, it was, "Lock up your sons!" rather than your daughters. By 1982, once cases had been reported among heterosexual men and women, hemophiliacs, and drug users, doctors renamed the condition AIDS—cause or causes still unknown. A year later, two independent research teams working in the U.S. and France isolated the virus that causes AIDS, which, after several years, was named HIV.

"LOCK UP YOUR SONS!"

With the virus identified, the FDA approved the first diagnostic test in 1985. Unfortunately, although the virus could now be identified, it was resistant to any known medical compound. Although some of the opportunistic infections could be treated, others, including KS, were fatal. The death toll in the developed world rose from the teens to the hundreds, and would soon reach the thousands. By the end of 1985, 51 countries had reported cases of HIV-AIDS, which had now become a worldwide pandemic. Without treatment, all that was known to prevent the spread of the virus was the use of condoms during anal and vaginal intercourse.

"THE PRINCESS TOOK MY HAND"

We were now in the fifth year of what potentially could have been the most dangerous disease outbreak since the Spanish Flu (pp. 115–119), yet countries all over the world seemed paralyzed and unable to fight the disease. Among the earliest and worst affected, the U.S. and UK were also among the slowest to act in the developed world. The Republican administration of President Ronald Reagan (1911–2004) and the Conservative government of Prime Minister Margaret Thatcher (b. 1925) saw themselves as supporters of traditional "family values." Reagan in particular was hamstrung by the religious right, who argued that any health information about the disease that would openly discuss "sodomy"—a medieval term originally applied to any type of forbidden sex—and promote the use of condoms was nothing short of encouraging the youth of America to engage in sexual acts.

As long as it was the members of marginalized communities who were dying—gay men, drug users, and Britons and Americans of African and Afro-Caribbean descent—governments could try to ignore the problem, but when it became clear that the heterosexual majority was at risk, both governments were shamed into action. Britain launched its "Don't Die of Ignorance" campaign in 2006, and succeeded in scaring and reassuring the British public at the same time with a description of the disease and clear safe-sex information. A year later, the U.S. became the last major Western country to launch a coordinated education campaign with the distribution of 107 million copies of *Understanding AIDS*. AIDS service organizations in Britain and the U.S. received recognition and funding, and needle exchange programs were established to prevent more drug users from becoming infected.

Alongside these belated government efforts, we should pay tribute to Diana, Princess of Wales (1961–97), who, when she opened the first specialist HIV-AIDS hospital ward in the UK, chose not to wear gloves when she shook hands with patients. Widely reported in the media, and flashed across the world's television screens, the handshake between the iconic princess and a gay man dying of HIV-AIDS did more to change attitudes to the disease than a dozen government leaflets.

We shall never know how many thousands of victims of the disease might have been spared had the education programs in the UK and U.S. started as soon as the virus had been identified, and doctors had worked out how its spread could be prevented. Male and female condoms are a cheap, 99-percent effective method, but, of course, their use raises moral and ethical dilemmas for members of certain religious groups—notably for Roman Catholics, for whom they represent not just a way of preventing disease but a means of contraception. With the same ghastly logic that sent thousands of heretics to their deaths at the stake or in the dungeons of the Holy Inquisition, the Catholic Church still holds that it is better to get pregnant and risk a slow agonizing death for yourself, your partner, and your child, than to use a condom.

© 2011 Gamma-Rapho | Getty Images

LIFESAVERS
Cost remains one of the main obstacles to tackling the epidemic in Africa.

The year 1987 saw the launch of AZT (Retrovir), the first drug known to have an effect on the virus, although it would not be until the mid-1990s that the development of several classes of antiretroviral drugs used in combinations finally slowed and even reversed the effects of the disease. However, these drugs, developed at great cost by the world's leading pharmaceutical companies, are extremely expensive. Medication costs alone per year can reach $15,000 (£10,000), and that does not include the batteries of tests and other medical procedures that are necessary to monitor and control the disease.

While special federal funding in the U.S. and socialized medicine in Europe and other parts of the developed world have shouldered this financial burden for their citizens, this is impossible in the developing world, where the only hope for sufferers is either through the charitable donations of richer countries or the manufacture of cheaper, generic versions of patented drugs. At the time of writing, litigation over patent infringements continues between the big pharmaceutical corporations and national governments and companies in the developing world—again at the cost of millions of lives.

BLEEDING TO DEATH

One final group that has suffered from the HIV-AIDS pandemic is the world's hemophiliacs, who are dependent for their survival on blood factors—blood-clotting proteins extracted from the plasma of donors. From the late 1970s until testing for HIV was introduced in 1985, thousands of hemophiliacs were given blood products contaminated with HIV. In 1984, Ryan White (1971–1990), an American teenager who had received contaminated factor VIII, was diagnosed with HIV-AIDS, at the height of the moral panic about the disease. Although doctors assured his teachers and the parents of his classmates that he presented no risk, he was excluded from school. His parents took the school to court, and White became a national celebrity and spokesman for AIDS awareness and education. Sadly, he died aged 19, a few years before antiretroviral therapy (ART) became available in the U.S.

Allegations have since surfaced that pharmaceutical companies recruited donors from high-risk groups, including gay men, drug users, and prisoners, to manufacture blood-clotting proteins, even after the risks of HIV contamination had become known. But worse was to come, as it has subsequently been discovered that the same blood products were also infected with another sexually transmitted viral infection, hepatitis C, a particularly dangerous form of the disease that can cause accelerated cirrhosis of the liver and liver cancer, conditions that are invariably fatal unless treated with a liver transplant.

With no drug cure or preventative vaccine in sight, HIV-AIDS continues to disable and kill millions in the developing world, where a combination of treatment costs, religion, and stigma still presents a major obstacle to halting the pandemic. In the developed world infection rates are creeping up as younger people who were not exposed to the deadly first years of the pandemic and the health-education campaigns, and have been lulled into a false sense of security by the existence of ART, engage in unsafe sex practices, risking not just infection from HIV-AIDS, but confection with HIV, hepatitis C, and the latest addition to the STI family, HPV (Human Papilloma virus).

STICKING PLASTER: ETHIOPIAN FAMINE

1983–85

DISASTER

Extinction Event

Tectonic Event

Military Action

Fire

Pandemic

Famine

Political or Economic Event

Genocide

Flood or Storm

Industrial or Transport Accident

Cause: Emperor Haile Selassie I overthrown by army coup; policies of the new Ethiopian government following dogmatic Marxist-Leninist principles; drought

Event: Civil war and government's use of starvation against rebel areas; forced resettlement of farmers from affected areas and "villagification"; misappropriation of relief funds by both sides; failure to distribute food aid equitably or at all

Aftermath: Eight million victims of famine; between 500,000 to one million died

War, famine, pestilence—and doctrinaire Marxist-Leninist dictatorship: these are the four horsemen of the modern Ethiopia's particular apocalypse. They have combined with one another into a brew more poisonous even than the sum of its parts.

James Finn,
Ethiopia: The Politics of Famine, 1990

The Ethiopian famine was the first all-singing, all-dancing multimedia disaster-event, complete with worldwide rock concerts, hit singles, and harrowing TV documentaries featuring the desperate, the starving, the dying, and the dead. Band Aid (1984) and the following year's Live Aid that was specifically targeted at relieving the Ethiopian famine, were the brainchildren of Bob Geldof (b. 1951), lead singer of the Boomtown Rats.

What was overlooked in the rush to provide relief for the starving of Ethiopia was the true causes of the disaster, which, as we shall see below, were only marginally natural (the drought) but mainly human, in the ongoing civil war in the region, and the policies of the Ethiopian military dictatorship. Additionally, there was quite a complex subtext to the outpouring of charity and concern for our fellow men and women, much of which was undoubtedly genuine, though a great deal of it, one suspects, had to do with a sense of collective guilt.

The developed world was experiencing a period of unprecedented growth and a steady rise in living standards. By the mid-1980s, despite the occasional recession and oil shock, Westerners, to quote former British Premier Harold Macmillan (1894–1996) in 1957, "Had never had it so good," and for us, living in our affluent bubble, to quote the campaign slogan of Prime Minister Tony Blair (b. 1953) exactly forty years later, "Things could only get better." But this was far from the case for the citizens of the countries sub-Saharan Africa, who since independence had experienced decades of civil war and famine.

Hence, the first layer of guilt was that felt by anyone on the up suddenly being confronted by someone down and almost out—the kind of feeling that makes the wealthy commuter give a few dollars to the beggar outside the subway station in the morning. This charitable act, while it will no doubt assuage the commuter's conscience at having so much more than his fellow man, may have unexpected consequences—possibly in allowing the beggar to buy a fatal dose of the drug that may have put him or her on the street in the first place. But it is easier to give a few dollars than to address the huge and seemingly insurmountable individual and social problems that put that individual on the streets.

Below this initial layer of guilt was the suspicion that we, the capitalist, Western, liberal-democratic and, not forgetting, the oh-so-politically-correct, former colonial masters of Africa, were responsible for the tragic plight of the continent's starving millions because of the way our grandfathers and great-grandfathers had exploited their colonial subjects in the nineteenth and early twentieth centuries, skewing Africa's economic development for their own benefit. This led us to believe that our increasing affluence was a direct consequence of their enduring impoverishment.

Finally, I suspect that the deepest layer of guilt was racial in origin. The victims of the famines were black Africans, whose ancestors our forebears had enslaved and forcibly transported to the New World, where they had become a racial underclass. This is not to deny that our ancestors bear much of the responsibility for the historic imbalances in the world economy, and the inequalities between the developed and developing worlds, but it would be a gross oversimplification to heap all the blame for the plight of the African poor on affluent (white) Westerners, let alone white North Americans who never took part in the nineteenth-century "Scramble for Africa."

BIG ISSUE
Crisis aid does not address the issues of underdevelopment in Africa.

The outpouring of concern and giving that produced the catchy if rather schmaltzy "Do They Know It's Christmas" (1984) were the world equivalent of our commuter giving a beggar a few dollars, with which, the commuter hopes, the beggar will buy himself food and not a fatal dose of crack or heroin. Unfortunately, there is no way of knowing what the money will be used for. An alternative would be to buy the beggar a sandwich and a hot beverage, which at least will ensure that he or she gets a decent breakfast, but while it will help the beggar survive another day, it will not get him or her off the streets.

Certain readers might be outraged if they conclude that I am equating a beggar strung out on drugs with the peoples of Africa, but my intention was to equate the feelings of the Live Aid and Band Aid donors with those of the commuter. Before we deal with the famine itself, let us look more closely at the different layers of guilt that triggered a lot of the charitable giving of the 1980s.

THE EXCEPTION TO THE RULE

Was the West's affluence in the postwar period built on exploitation of its colonial possessions? While it is true that colonialism brought great rewards to the imperial powers, it also entailed great costs. In the end, empires were too expensive to maintain; bankrupted by the Second World War, and facing mounting military costs to maintain their rule, most preferred to withdraw, sometimes with unseemly haste. Where the colonial power attempted to fight the historically inevitable, as the French did in Indo-China and Algeria, the consequences were dire both for the ruling colonial power and the local population.

Although there are several truly shocking examples of colonial exploitation in Africa—in particular in the Belgian Congo, where the colonial regime of King Leopold II (1835–1909) pursued genocidal policies that killed millions of Congolese—Ethiopia was exceptional in that it was the only country on the continent that did not become a European colony during the Scramble for Africa. It succumbed to Benito Mussolini's imperial ambitions only in 1936 and regained its independence nine years later. But this was not the only thing that set Ethiopia apart from its neighbors. The empire adopted Christianity in 324 CE, making it the second country to do so after Armenia, and some thirty-six years before the Roman Empire. It remained a Christian kingdom surrounded by Muslim states, with an extraordinary dynastic history that reads like something out of *A Game of Thrones* (1996).

The last Ethiopian emperor, Haile Selassie I (1892–1975), regained power in 1945, but he was deposed in 1974 by a group of junior officers led by Mengistu Haile Mariam (b. 1937). The former emperor and members of his family and government were summarily executed that same year, leaving the new regime ostracized by the West, and increasingly reliant on the Soviet Union and its ally Cuba for support in fighting a civil war against Eritrean separatists. Within the territory it controlled, the junta began implementing a Soviet-style reform of agriculture, which predictably led to falls and not increases in food production. In a region already always on the brink of food insecurity because of recurring droughts and lack of long-term investment in infrastructure and agricultural machinery, it would only take a few bad harvests to tip parts the country into severe food shortages.

However, although there were droughts in parts of Ethiopia in 1983 and 1984, researchers, including Nobel Prize-winning Harvard economist Amartya Sen (b. 1933), claim that natural factors were not the causes of the famine, and that there was in fact only a small overall reduction in the national harvests for those years. The Mengistu junta was able to hold back the insurgents only with Russian military aid and Cuban troops, while at the same time it was using starvation as a weapon of war against insurgent areas. However, Mengistu managed to portray himself as the victim of aggression and not the aggressor, and most international aid was channeled through his government. Much of the food aid, instead of being distributed equitably between both sides in the civil war, was used by the government to feed its own supporters and militias, while a huge amount was left undistributed to rot in government warehouses. To present a balanced picture, there are also allegations that a great deal of the aid that went to insurgent areas for famine relief was diverted to fight the war.

At the same time the Mengistu regime was pursuing ever more radical policies in the areas under its control: the resettlement of several million people with the excuse of moving them from drought-stricken areas, but really aimed against the insurgents, and a "villagification" program—the forced movement of people from isolated homesteads into villages, again with the excuse of being able to provide the population with food and healthcare, but in reality to ensure closer political control.

Ultimately, it seems that Western donations, including the millions raised by Live Aid, allowed Mengistu to stay in power and prolonged the civil war. In doing so, they actually worsened the famine that is now believed to have killed between 400,000 and (according to the UN) as many as one million people. There were two disasters here, and both of them affected the most impoverished and disadvantaged people on the planet: The first was the famine itself, that was artificially created and prolonged for ideological and military ends; the second is that it took years for the international community to realize that what was really needed to help Africa out of disaster was not a sticking plaster, but a complete overhaul in how emergency aid was administered and distributed, long-term development aid to prevent such crises from recurring, and pressure from aid donors, NGOs, and the UN to insist on much better standards of governance from regimes whose only real interest was remaining in power.

© Alain Keler | Sygma | Corbis

POLITICS
The real causes of the famine are now thought to have been more political than natural.

DISASTER

Extinction Event

Tectonic Event

Military Action

Fire

Pandemic

Famine

Political or Economic Event

Genocide

Flood or Storm

Industrial or Transport Accident

HEALTH AND SAFETY GONE BAD: BHOPAL GAS LEAK

1984

Cause: Inadequate health and safety protocols; staff reductions to save money; poor maintenance and training; plant built too close to densely populated area

Event: Catastrophic release of a cloud of toxic chemical gas over Bhopal

Aftermath: Deaths of between 4,000 and 8,000 victims from the initial gas release; a further 8,000 over the next two weeks; over 550,000 gas-related injuries

After the eyes and lungs, the organs most affected were the brain, muscles, joints, liver, kidneys and the reproductive and immune systems. Many of the victims sank into such a state of exhaustion that movement became impossible. Many suffered from cramps, unbearable itching or repeated migraines.

Dominique Lapierre and Javier Moro,
Five Minutes Past Midnight in Bhopal, 2002

© Moori | Dreamstime

In the developed world, workplaces are now so secure that we have forgotten that in the early stages of industrialization, the demands of labor reformers were not only for fair wages but also for adequate occupational health and safety regimes. During the First Industrial Revolution, the major safety issues in factories were the machinery itself, fire, and boiler explosions, but with the opening of chemistry's "Pandora's Box" during the Second Industrial Revolution, hitherto unknown chemical compounds became part of everyday industrial processes, adding to an already deadly list of historic industrial poisons such as arsenic, lead, mercury, and asbestos,

and creating new dangers for an uninformed and unprotected workforce. One industrial disaster that led to labor safety legislation in the U.S. was the tragedy of the "radium girls," who between 1917 and 1926 painted luminous watch dials with a substance containing the radioactive element radium. Exposure to radiation caused extreme facial disfigurement and painful deaths from cancer. Later in the century, many of the most complex and long-lasting class-action suits

© Chris Rainier | Corbis

UNREGULATED
Lax safety rules in India contributed to the accident at the plant.

concerned the diseases caused by the mining, manufacture, and use of asbestos—asbestosis and mesothelioma—which have cost an estimated $200 billion (£125 billion) in the U.S. alone.

Among the most dangerous industries, because of the many toxic compounds that it uses and combines, is the chemical industry, making products with a huge number of applications in daily life. Unfortunately, these have resulted in several of the worse instances of environmental pollution, such as Minamata disease that affected coastal communities in Japan between 1932 and 1968, caused by the pumping of chemical waste containing mercury into the sea. After Minamata, Japan joined the rest of the developed world in setting high standards of industrial environmental protection and occupational health and safety.

Faced with the huge costs of litigation in case of accidents, and occupational health and safety legislation in the developed world, many Western companies have moved their more dangerous plants and manufacturing processes to countries where this legislation does not exist or is not enforced fully, and where litigation and compensation costs are lower for accidents leading to deaths and injuries to workers, their families, and the general public.

KILLER CLOUD

The Union Carbide (UCC) plant in Bhopal, capital of the central Indian state of Madhya Pradesh (MP), was set up to produce the pesticide carbaryl, sold under the UCC brand name of Sevin. From 1979, the plant

used a manufacturing process that included the use of the toxic chemical methyl isocyanate (CH_3NCO; MIC)—a colorless, inflammable liquid that reacts dangerously with water—part of the manufacturing process. Another chemical process to make carbaryl, that does not involve the use of MIC as an intermediate, is used in plants in the developed world. However, that process is more expensive.

The Bhopal plant had a history of pollution and safety issues, starting in 1976. Particular problems associated with the MIC production plant and storage facility in 1981, 1982, 1983, and several times during 1984, resulted in the hospitalization of dozens of staff who did not have adequate protective clothing or breathing apparatus. Worse, the plant was staffed at half strength to save on salaries, and the Indian personnel were not sufficiently trained to ensure the maintenance and safe operation of the plant, and certainly not to deal with a major emergency.

COCKTAIL
Scientists still do not know the composition of the deadly gas cloud.

Many of the fail-safe systems, including the MIC storage tank refrigeration that would have mitigated some of the worst effects of the disaster, had been disabled, again to save money. Due to a slump in demand for Sevin, the plant's MIC storage facility was filled beyond its recommended capacity, and the MIC tank alarm that should have warned staff of an impending disaster had been out of commission for four years. Compared to the multiple fail-safe mechanisms demanded by U.S. legislation, there was only one manual backup system at Bhopal. But a month before the disaster, most of the safety systems were not functioning and the plant was in a poor state of repair.

During the night of December 3, 1984, water leaked into a storage tank containing 42 tons of toxic MIC. This started the chemical equivalent of a nuclear "meltdown," causing a runaway reaction between the MIC, water, corroded iron from steel pipes, and other contaminants, which raised the temperature in the tank to over 392°F (200°C), while the recommended storage temperature for MIC was 40°F (4.5°C). This raised the pressure in the tank to such an extent that it vented 33 tons of gas into the atmosphere in less than an hour.

The gas cloud, in addition to the MIC, may have carried a lethal cocktail of phosgene, hydrogen cyanide, carbon monoxide, hydrogen chloride, and carbon dioxide over densely populated shantytowns that had grown up around the plant. The cloud was heavy and stayed close to the ground, mostly affecting children and those already confined to bed. The initial effects of exposure were coughing, vomiting, eye irritation, and suffocation. The causes of death were choking, circulatory collapse, and pulmonary edema (fluid in the lungs). In the aftermath of the disaster, there were an unusually high number of stillbirths among mothers affected by the leak, as well as a 200 percent increase in neo-natal deaths.

In what was by far the worst industrial accident in history, an estimated four to eight thousand died from the initial gas leak, with an estimated additional eight thousand deaths in the first two weeks after the accident. It was impossible to reach a confirmed death toll because many living in the area did not appear in any official records. Several environmental campaign groups claim that even the upper figure of eight thousand deaths from the release is a gross underestimate, and that the true figure is closer to 20,000 victims. In addition 500,000 people were treated for gas-related injuries. The final compensation, fought every step of the way by UCC's legal team in India, averaged a paltry $455 (£280) for a personal injury claim and $1,128 (£696) for a death. It goes without saying that if the disaster had occurred anywhere in the developed world, and especially in the U.S., the senior executives of the company would now be in jail, and the company would have been bankrupted by compensation payments of many billions of dollars.

DISASTER

Extinction Event

Tectonic Event

Military Action

Fire

Pandemic

Famine

Political or Economic Event

Genocide

Flood or Storm

Industrial or Transport Accident

MELTDOWN: NUCLEAR CHERNOBYL

1986

Cause: Flaws in reactor design and operating procedure; insufficient backup cooling; INES level 7 major accident

Event: Failed emergency shutdown led to two explosions that ruptured reactor containment and sent radioactive steam over the Soviet Union and Europe

Aftermath: 56 people died; estimated 4,000 died since of cancer and many at risk; 350,000 people evacuated from most contaminated areas

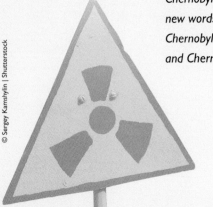

Chernobyl has become synonymous with human suffering and brought new words into our lives—Chernobyl liquidators, children of Chernobyl, Chernobyl AIDS, Chernobyl contamination, Chernobyl heart, Chernobyl dust, and Chernobyl collar (thyroid disease).

Alexey Yablokov *et al* **(eds.),**
Chernobyl, 2010

In 1955, Great Britain opened the world's first commercial nuclear power plant at Calder Hall, Cumbria, equipped with Magnox reactors that generated energy for the UK national grid and secretly produced weapons-grade plutonium for Britain's nuclear deterrent. When the first nuclear power plants came online with their ultra-modern buildings and sleek concrete smokestacks producing nothing more polluting than white steam, they must have seemed like the shape of things to come, especially when compared to the low-tech, dirty, coal-fired power stations belching out choking black fumes, which still provided most of the developed world's energy in the 1950s.

Billed as clean and safe, capable of producing limitless energy from comparatively small amounts of fuel, nuclear reactors are among the most dangerous machines ever devised and built by humans, as was to become increasingly clear as accidents multiplied. A nuclear reactor is a sloweddown version of an atomic bomb, with the same atomic fission reaction taking place within its core under controlled conditions. Fission generates huge amounts of heat, used to superheat steam, which, like coal, gas, or oil in conventional plants, drives steam turbines that generate electricity. However, if something goes wrong, it's not possible to turn off a nuclear reactor like a conventional power plant by flicking a switch. Control rods have to be inserted into the reactor core to dampen and ultimately stop the nuclear reaction.

Reactors can be cooled with air or gas, or with "heavy" ($2H_2O$) or "light" water (H_2O), but if for some reason the cooling system fails, the core will begin to melt and may escape the containment vessel built around it. At this point, radioactive material will be released into the environment with disastrous consequences for any human, animal, or plant life in the vicinity, and not just for the duration of the emergency but, within the most contaminated areas, for up to 20,000 years.

Although there is no danger of the fuel in a reactor setting off a nuclear explosion, fires and meltdowns have ejected large amounts of radioactive material into the environment. The first serious incident occurred in the UK, at Windscale (later renamed Sellafield), where a military reactor caught fire in 1957. The blaze was kept secret for decades, but as nuclear accidents became more frequent and occurred near to populated areas, it became impossible to keep them hidden from the public.

In 1990, the International Atomic Energy Agency (IAEA), the UN body charged with monitoring all nuclear activities on the planet, devised the International Nuclear and Radiological Event Scale (INES) to grade the seriousness of nuclear accidents. The seven-level scale is modeled on the Moment Magnitude Scale for measuring earthquakes (see p. 60), with each level being ten times more severe than the previous one. These are in order of severity: level 7: "Major Accident"; level 6: "Serious Accident"; level 5: "Accident with Wider Consequences"; level 4: "Accident with Local Consequences"; level 3: "Serious Incident"; level 2: "Incident"; level 1: "Anomaly"; and level 0: "Deviation."

Windscale was retrospectively rated a level 5 Accident with Wider Consequences because the fire had caused "severe damage to the reactor core" and had led to "release of large quantities of radioactive material within an installation with a high probability of significant public exposure," including several fatalities from radiation. The Three Mile Island accident near Harrisburg, PA, on March 28, 1979, also merited a level 5, as a loss of coolant caused a partial core meltdown and a release of radioactive gases into the atmosphere (fortunately no fatalities were reported). There have been five level 5 accidents, including the two mentioned above, one level 6 Serious Accident, and two level 7 Major Accidents: the Fukushima Daiichi Nuclear Disaster in 2011 (pp. 241–245), which is the penultimate entry in this book, and the Chernobyl nuclear disaster. A level 7 is defined as a "major release of radioactive material with widespread health and environmental effects requiring implementation of planned and extended countermeasures," which is IAEA-speak for "Run for your life!"

CORE BREACH IMMINENT, MR. LAFORGE

The description of the Chernobyl nuclear disaster that took place during the night of April 26, 1986, reads like something out of an episode of *Star Trek: The Next Generation*, with "containment failure" and a major "core breach." Unfortunately, there was no Geordi La Forge or Data on hand to come up with a clever solution five seconds before the reactor went into meltdown. Chernobyl Nuclear Power Plant (now in the independent Republic of Ukraine, but in 1986 in the Ukrainian Soviet Socialist Republic) operated four RBMKs ("High-Power Channel-type Reactors"), an early Soviet design, which is the oldest still in use. It was RBMK No. 4 that went critical and literally blew its top in 1986.

There were two investigations into the causes of the Chernobyl disaster. The first, just after the accident in the bad old Soviet days, blamed operator error for the tragedy; the second, carried out in 1991, when the Soviet Union was about to implode, concluded that the disaster had been caused by flaws in the original design of the RBMK and its operating procedures that the operators could not have anticipated or dealt with. For the operators on the night of April 26, who had finally been exonerated of all blame, the matter was pretty irrelevant, as all of them had been killed in the explosions that wrecked the reactor. The reconstruction of what actually happened is based on a certain amount of hard evidence and a large amount of guesswork, as investigators picked over the extremely dangerous radioactive ruins of the reactor before and after it was encased in a giant concrete sarcophagus.

© Oliver Sved | Shutterstock

The dreadful irony of the Chernobyl accident was that it was caused by a test of the steam turbines to make sure that they would operate the cooling system in the event of a SCRAM—an emergency shutdown of a reactor. The RBMK is a light water-cooled reactor, and in the event of a SCRAM, the power operating the cooling pumps would go offline along with the reactor. There were three backup diesel generators that would automatically cut in to power the pumps, but these would take between one minute and one minute 15 seconds to get up to full power. With the tremendous heat generated by the reactor, a one-minute delay might prove fatal. However, it had been calculated that the residual energy from the steam turbines as they wound down would be just sufficient to bridge the gap. The theory had to be confirmed by a live test on the reactor itself, which was due to take place during a routine maintenance cycle of Reactor 4, when its output would be lowered from 1,000 MW to 700 MW prior to a complete shutdown.

However, what the experiment's designers had not foreseen was that the particular configuration of the RBMK made it particularly prone to "reactor poisoning," a process which meant that during the test the power dropped below 700 MW. At 500 MW the operators tried to correct the

ANTIQUE
Chernobyl operated the oldest Soviet design for commercial reactors.

problem, but their actions caused a further power drop to 30 MW—bringing the reactor to a near-shutdown state. Unbeknownst to the operators, the RBMK becomes extremely unstable at very low power levels. Nevertheless, they decided to continue with the test and succeeded in bringing the reactor up to 200 MW. At this point, it is thought there was a sudden power surge in the reactor, which initiated a SCRAM procedure—either by the operators by pressing the SCRAM button in the control room, or automatically, by the emergency protection system in response to the surge.

GHOST TOWN
Several towns in the vicinity of the plant had to be abandoned.

The control rods that would shut down the reactor move at 15 in/sec (40 cm/sec), so that they would take about 20 seconds to travel through the 23-foot (7 m) core. But instead of dampening the nuclear reaction, the insertion caused a further power spike. The core overheated, causing a first explosion that damaged the core so that the control rods became jammed one-third of the way in, and broke cooling pipes. This caused a reactor surge to 530 MW, which causing a huge increase in temperature and pressure within the core. A second explosion destroyed the reactor casing, lifting the 2,000-ton upper plate, killing the operators in the control room, and releasing a plume of radioactive steam into the atmosphere. In addition to the deaths in the immediate vicinity, and the thousands of cancers it has already caused and is predicted to continue causing, the radioactive cloud drifted over large parts of Belarus, Ukraine, and European Russia, reaching as far north as Scandinavia, as far south as Greece and Italy, and as far west as Switzerland.

The accident put the future of nuclear power in doubt, at least in the West, but with the repeated oil shocks and concerns over energy security, there have been calls for the re-examination of the nuclear option.

BLACK TIDE: *EXXON VALDEZ* OIL SPILL

1989

DISASTER

Extinction Event

Tectonic Event

Military Action

Fire

Pandemic

Famine

Political or Economic Event

Genocide

Flood or Storm

Industrial or Transport Accident

Cause: Insufficient crew and poor working conditions aboard the supertanker; poor maintenance meant that collision avoidance system was out of commission

Event: *Exxon Valdez* ran aground, spilling between 11 million U.S. gallons and 32 million U.S. gallons of crude oil

Aftermath: Death of between 250,000 and 400,000 seabirds, 3,000 sea otters, 3,000 harbor seals, 250 bald eagles, and 22 orcas

Scientists are still studying the long-term effects of the oil spill on Prince William Sound. Today, many of the beaches again look beautiful, but some of the oil spilled in 1989 can still be found up to 400 miles from the place where the Exxon Valdez *ran aground. Beneath the shore's rocks, sand is covered with oil that has hardened like asphalt.*

Philip Margulies,
The **Exxon Valdez** *Oil Spill,* **2003**

As the old saying goes, good things come in threes, but unfortunately, it seems, so do bad things. With the *Exxon Valdez* oil spill, the largest accidental release of oil into American waters until the *Deepwater Horizon* accident in the Gulf of Mexico in 2010, we come to the third of the major environmental disasters that took place in the 1980s. After the genocides and democides of the first half of the twentieth century, this next trio of human disasters was the result of abuses by private capitalist corporations and Communist state enterprises. In all three cases, the disaster was a result of poor or insufficient occupational health and safety and environmental protection legislation, combined with greed on the part of organizations that were more concerned with cutting costs and maximizing profits than safeguarding the lives of their employees, ensuring the safety of the public, or protecting the natural environment.

It is one of those geopolitical ironies that crude oil is found in places where there is not much demand for it, and thus it has to be transported thousands of miles across the globe where it is refined to power automobiles and heat

homes, and made into thousands of plastic wares. Where possible, crude oil is transported across continents through snaking pipelines, but where hostile politics, insurmountable geography, or oceans get in the way, the only feasible way of moving it is by ship. The first oil tankers were iron-hulled sailing ships such as the *Falls of Clyde*, launched in 1878, which had a capacity of 19,000 barrels (but of paraffin for lamps rather than crude). In comparison, the world's current record holder, an "Ultra Large Crude Carrier," such as the MT *Hellespont Alhambra* launched in 2002, can carry 3,166,353 barrels of crude oil. The *Exxon Valdez*, launched in 1986, had the relatively modest capacity of 1.48 million barrels—quite fortunately for Alaskan wildlife, as it turned out.

TRANSPORTER
The *Exxon Valdez* carried oil from Alaska south to the U.S.

© Karen Kasmauski | Corbis

At the time of the spill, the *Exxon Valdez* was owned and operated by a subsidiary of the world's largest oil company by revenue, and the biggest of the six oil "supermajors," ExxonMobil. ExxonMobil was heavily criticized over the cleanup of the *Exxon Valdez* spill.

In addition, the lawyers that you can afford can postpone hefty fines and compensation payments for years or even almost indefinitely. In the event, when an Anchorage jury awarded punitive damages of $5 billion against the company for the *Exxon Valdez* spill, amounting to one year's profits for the company at the time, ExxonMobil appealed all the way to the Supreme Court, which ruled that punitive damages should be limited to just over $500 million. Another accusation laid at Exxon-Mobil's sizeable and well appointed corporate doors is that it currently funds nine out of the ten scientists who are willing to deny climate change (see pp. 246–251).

© Jean-Louis Atlan | Sygma | Corbis

WILDERNESS
The isolated location made tackling the spill much more difficult.

But how many people died in the disaster? How many bodies were mangled in the shipwreck? How many wives widowed and children orphaned? Actually none—not one human life was lost. But between 250,000 and 400,000 seabirds died slow painful deaths, as did 6,000 sea otters and harbor seals, 250 bald eagles, and 22 orcas.

The *Exxon Valdez* carried crude extracted from the Prudhoe Bay Oil Fields in northern Alaska and transferred along the 800-mile (1,300 km) Trans-Alaska Pipeline (1977) to the southern port of Valdez, where the crude was loaded aboard the tanker at the Valdez Marine Terminal. From there it would be taken along the Pacific coast south to the U.S., as the Canadian government had not agreed to the defilement of several thousand miles of virgin wilderness for an extension of the pipeline. In this case, we have plenty of evidence that implicates the Exxon Shipping Company as the main culprit responsible for the disaster.

HIGH BUT NOT DRY

The *Exxon Valdez* did not have a sufficient crew, and those on board were expected to work 12- to 14- hour shifts. Because of overwork, the officer of the watch did not take evasive action to avoid the tanker running aground on Bligh Reef (named for Captain Bligh of *Mutiny on the Bounty* fame). However, the vessel's Raytheon Collision Avoidance System, which would have warned the crew of an impending collision, was out of commission and had not been repaired to save on money.

The design of the tanker also played its role in the disaster. Like the RMS *Titanic* (pp. 100–103), the *Exxon Valdez*'s hold was divided into several watertight compartments—in the tanker's case full of crude oil—contained within a single steel hull. When *Titanic* collided with the fateful iceberg, one compartment too many was breached to allow her to stay afloat for more than two hours; in the *Exxon Valdez* accident, the reef holed some compartments, several of which emptied between 11 million U.S. gallons and 32 million U.S. gallons into Prince William Sound. There was no danger of the giant ship sinking, but she continued to leak oil into the ocean until the remaining oil in her damaged tanks was pumped into other vessels, which took several days.

© Creative Commons

SEA DEATH
The main victims of the spill were seabirds and mammals.

Single-hulled vessels, such as *Titanic* and *Exxon Valdez*, were the rule for much of the nineteenth and twentieth centuries. However, it had long been recognized that a double-hulled design is much safer. The SS *Great Eastern* of 1854, designed by the visionary engineer Isambard Kingdom Brunel (1806–59), was the first great double-hulled iron ship. Her double hull saved her from sinking after a collision that was potentially more serious than the *Titanic*'s iceberg encounter. Although experts agree that a double hull would not have prevented the *Exxon Valdez* oil spill altogether, it would have greatly reduced its severity. Readers will appreciate, however, that a double hull consumes twice the amount of steel as a single hull. Though in view of the disasters that single hulls have caused, the savings in money seem to be something of a false economy.

Recently the oil-tanker industry has smugly commented that there are now significantly fewer tanker spills than there were in the 1970s and 1980s, although much more oil is transported in tankers. However, there is a very good reason for this improvement: after the *Exxon Valdez* and other tanker disasters, neither the U.S. nor the EU will allow single-hulled oil tankers to dock in their ports.

CAIN AND ABEL: RWANDA GENOCIDE

1994

DISASTER

Extinction Event

Tectonic Event

Military Action

Fire

Pandemic

Famine

Political or Economic Event

Genocide

Flood or Storm

Industrial or Transport Accident

Cause: Division between Tutsi and Hutu communities; invasion by rebel Tutsi Rwanda Patriotic Front (RPF); assassination of Juvénal Habyarimana and Cyprien Ntaryamira

Event: Planned genocide of the Tutsi population by Hutu-led government; mobilization of Hutu militias who started to massacre the Tutsi and moderate Hutu sympathizers

Aftermath: Deaths of between 500,000 and one million Rwanda citizens; overthrow of Hutu government by RPF; two million Hutu fled Rwanda; continuing hostilities

The first explorers who reached Rwanda and Burundi were immediately struck by the fact that the population though linguistically and culturally homogeneous, was divided into three groups, the Hutu, the Tutsi and the Twa [....] They shared the same Bantu language, lived side by side with each other without any "Hutuland" or "Tutsiland" and often intermarried. But they were neither similar nor equal.

Gérard Prunier,
The Rwanda Crisis, 1997

The kingdom of Rwanda was founded in the fifteenth century by Bantu-speaking peoples, now referred to as the Hutu and Tutsi. Genetic and linguistic studies have shown that they do not form two distinct ethnicities—even if they did at one point in their early history, there has been so much intermingling between them over the centuries that any ethnic and cultural differences have disappeared. As Gérard Prunier explains in *The Rwanda Crisis*, the divisions between the two groups were largely artificial and social and emerged in the centuries after the establishment of the kingdom of Rwanda. In addition, the differences between the two communities were encouraged by the colonial authorities—both German and Belgian—whose misguided racist theories led them to divide the population into these three fictitious groups: Hutu, Tutsi, and Twa.

GREEN LAND
On the surface, Rwanda was a peaceful, homogeneous society.

The Rwandan monarch *Mwami* Kigeri IV Rwabugili (r. 1853–95) pursued an expansionist policy, absorbing neighboring kingdoms to encompass most of modern Rwanda. He then reorganized his realm, dividing it into military provinces and districts principally administered by the Tutsi minority aristocracy, who governed the Hutu majority of peasant farmers. However, during this period, a sizeable group of Hutu held high-ranking positions in the state, and relations between the two communities seem to have been mostly peaceful. Rwanda was not part of the first phase of the "Scramble for Africa" (1881–1914). But in 1890, a conference held in Brussels decided that Rwanda and its neighbor Burundi would fall within the German sphere of influence, in exchange for Germany's renunciation of any claims over British Uganda and the Belgian Congo.

Short of manpower, the Germans, who were trying to consolidate their rule further east, in Tanganyika, chose to rule their newly acquired Central African possessions through the existing political institutions. They supported the Mwami's Tutsi minority rule, and injected their own particular racist ideology into the mix by claiming that the Tutsi, whom they saw as taller, fairer-skinned, and "more noble" than the Hutu, were thus racially superior, and therefore the "natural" rulers of the country—following the same logic that dictated that the white race was destined to rule the world. This ideology was backed up by spurious pseudo-scientific theories and research into physical appearance, height, and skull size. Later biometric research has shown that the physical differences between the Hutu and Tutsi can be explained by their different diets: the Tutsi, who raise cattle, have a much more nutritious diet—especially in childhood when they supplement mother's milk with cow's milk—than the Hutu who are primarily crop farmers.

After Germany's defeat in World War One, Rwanda and Burundi became a protectorate administered by Belgium, the European power that had shown itself to be among the worst colonial exploiters in the neighboring Belgian Congo. The Belgians continued the German policy of governing the country through the Tutsi Mwami. To make Rwanda pay its way, they introduced cash crops, in particular coffee, which was cultivated through a *corvée* system of forced labor, which was imposed on the Hutu agrarian majority by the Tutsi administration.

In 1935, the Belgian authorities went as far as introducing a system of "ethnic identity cards" that indicated whether an individual was Tutsi, Hutu, or Twa; however, as these ethnicities had no basis in reality, the Belgians decided on the expedient of defining anyone who owned more than ten head of cattle as a Tutsi, and anyone else as either a Hutu or a Twa. Through various educational, political, and religious policies, the colonial authorities reinforced and maintained the social and political differences between the three communities.

For once we cannot blame colonialism entirely for the genocide that took place in Rwanda in 1994, in which death squads of extremist Hutu killed between 500,000 and one million Tutsi and moderate Hutus, who wanted no part in a campaign of mass murder. However, what the policies of the Belgian colonial administration had succeeded in doing was codifying centuries-old tensions and rivalries between the Hutu and Tutsi, and turning them into an economic, political, and social reality.

THE HUTUS' "FINAL SOLUTION"

As in other parts of the continent, the 1950s and 1960s saw increasing pressure on the colonial power, Belgium, for independence. The Belgians had ruled through the Tutsi monarchy, and they were now faced by two different rival independence movements—the Tutsi demanding an independent Kingdom of Rwanda, and the Hutu emancipation movement that favored a republic. The two groups quickly became militarized and began what was to be a thirty-five-year civil war that would culminate in the Rwanda genocide. Even before the Belgians granted Rwanda her independence in 1962, there were assassinations on both sides, and the first massacres of between 20,000 and 100,000 Tutsi took place in 1959.

Independence saw the final eclipse of the monarchy and its replacement by a Hutu-dominated republic. In 1963, Tutsi guerillas who had fled to Burundi attempted an invasion of Rwanda, triggering another massacre of some 14,000 Tutsi. Throughout the Rwandan Civil War, Burundi played a crucial role. Although Burundi, like Rwanda, has a Hutu majority, until the early 1990s the country was dominated by a Tutsi-majority army, which provided shelter and support for Rwandan Tutsi refugees and rebels. The Rwanda Hutu government and the rebel Tutsi Rwandan Patriotic Front (RPF) signed a peace accord in 1993, but by then relations between the Hutu and Tutsi had been damaged beyond repair. High-ranking Hutu in the Rwandan government and army had been planning a Nazi-style "final solution" of the country's ethnic problems by exterminating the Rwandan Tutsi and any moderate Hutu who sided with them.

© David Turnley | Corbis

REFUGE
The genocide caused major refugee crises, both Hutu and Tutsi.

The trigger for the genocide was the assassination of the Hutu presidents Juvénal Habyarimana (1937–94) of Rwanda and Cyprien Ntaryamira (1955–94) of Burundi, who died when their plane was shot down as it was about to land at Kigali airport. The murder of the two leaders signaled the beginning of the genocide on April 6. The Tutsi RPF immediately resumed operations against the genocidal Hutu government, but the massacres and civil war lasted until July, when the Tutsi took over most of the country. There was to be one final tragic twist to the story, however. Although the genocide stopped in the Tutsi-controlled areas, France, the only foreign power to recognize the genocidal government, sent troops to secure the remaining Hutu territory, which perversely allowed the genocide to continue in areas under French "protection."

BEGGAR THY NEIGHBOR: SREBRENICA MASSACRE

1995

DISASTER

Extinction Event

Tectonic Event

Military Action

Fire

Pandemic

Famine

Political or Economic Event

Genocide

Flood or Storm

Industrial or Transport Accident

Cause: Long-standing division of the Balkans between Muslim Bosniak, Greek Orthodox Serbian, and Catholic Croat communities; collapse of Yugoslavia

Event: Invasion of Serbian areas of Bosnia-Herzegovina by Serbia in alliance with the Bosnian Serbs; ethnic cleansing of Bosnian Muslims; failure of UN force to intervene

Aftermath: Murder of 8,373 Bosniak civilians, mainly adult men and boys in Srebrenica and surrounded towns and villages, including 500 under the age of 18

Today, we pay tribute to the victims of a terrible crime—the worst on European soil since the Second World War [....] We can say—and it is undeniable—that blame lies, first and foremost, with those who planned and carried out the massacre, or who assisted them, or who harbored and are harboring them still. But we cannot evade our own share of responsibility.

UN Secretary General Kofi Annan, speech on the tenth anniversary of the Srebrenica massacre, 2005

Before embarking on this entry, I would advise readers with a shaky grasp of Balkan geography to consult a detailed atlas of the region. Now consisting of Greece, Albania, Slovenia, Croatia, Serbia, Montenegro, Kosovo, Former Yugoslavia Republic (FYR) of Macedonia, Bosnia-Herzegovina, Bulgaria, and European Turkey, the Balkans were the flashpoint that triggered the First World War. But as the main crossing point between Asia and Europe, the Balkan Peninsula has been a political and military hotspot since remotest antiquity.

The outbreak of World War Two added an ideological dimension to what was already known to be an extremely complex ethnic and religious situation. The postwar settlement awarded Yugoslavia, Bulgaria, and Albania to the Soviet sphere of influence. The Socialist Republic of Yugoslavia, led by Marshal Josip Tito (1892–1980), quickly broke with Russia, preferring to remain "non-aligned"— the better to play the Communist East against the capitalist West—Albania also broke with Moscow after Joseph Stalin's death, choosing the Communist rigor of Maoist China over Nikita Khrushchev's (1894–1971) more "liberal" Soviet Union; Bulgaria remained a staunch Soviet ally until the collapse of the USSR in 1991.

© Creative Commons

EXECUTION
The Bosnian Serbs realized that their plans entailed the genocide of Bosniak Muslims.

Tito's atheistic, Communist, non-aligned regime temporarily suppressed the religious and ethnic conflicts in Yugoslavia, but the end of Central and Eastern European Communism allowed centuries-old rivalries and nationalistic aspirations to re-emerge. Central to the conflicts that broke out between the republics of the former Yugoslavia were the ambitions of the Serbs, whose empire had ruled much of the central Balkans during the fourteenth and fifteenth centuries, until it had been conquered by the Ottoman Turks in 1459. However, the notion of a "Greater Serbia," not dissimilar to Adolf Hitler's "Greater German Reich," emerged reinvigorated from the wreck of post-Communist Yugoslavia.

THE PERILS OF BALKANIZATION

The complexities of the region, have given us the pejorative geopolitical term "Balkanization," meaning the fragmentation of a state or region into small and mutually hostile entities. For its size, the region is cursed with many rival entities. Currently the Balkans are divided between 13 nation-states, whose territories are wholly or only partly included within the peninsula, which covers an area of 189,000 square miles (490,000 km^2), and which is only slightly larger than the state of California (163,000 square miles/423,970 km^2).

Although Yugoslavia was not part of the Soviet hegemony in Eastern Europe, it remained a non-aligned Socialist state until the collapse of the Soviet Union and the disbanding of the Warsaw Pact. The former socialist republics (SR) of Croatia, Slovenia, Macedonia, and Bosnia-Herzegovina declared their independence from the SR Yugoslavia in 1991, and were recognized by the U.S. and most European countries the following year, triggering a military response from Serbia and Montenegro, the only two former SRs that chose to remain within Yugoslavia.

The motives of the Serbs, led by indicted war criminal President Slobodan Milošević (1941–2006), were not to maintain the integrity of the defunct Yugoslavian SR, recreated as the Federal Republic of Yugoslavia (FRY), but to use what remained of the Yugoslav national army to secure the dominance of Serbia over the other former Yugoslav republics—or, failing that, to detach the regions of Croatia and Bosnia-Herzegovina where Serbs were in the majority to create a "Greater Serbia." Bosnia-Herzegovina was in the most precarious military position, having a long border with Serbia, and with 31 percent of its population identified as ethnic Serbs.

After launching an attack on Croatia, Milošević, aided and abetted by his Bosnian Serb allies, Radovan Karadžić (b. 1945), former president of Republika Srpska (the Bosnian Serb region within the federated state of Bosnia-Herzegovina), and the Bosnian Serb military commander General Ratko Mladić (b. 1942), attempted to detach a large section of Bosnia-Herzegovina and incorporate it into the Serbian-led FRY. The problem the Serbs faced, however, was that the territories they wished to annex from Croatia and Bosnia-Herzegovina were not all contiguous with Serbia. Areas populated by Muslim Bosniaks and Croatian Catholics separated the Serb areas from one another and from Serbia proper.

Unlike previous conflicts in the Balkans that had led to hostilities between the great powers of the day, the Yugoslav wars did not flare up into a more generalized European or world war. The creation of the EU meant that the former European antagonists over the region—Italy, Austria, and Germany—were now NATO allies and EU partners, who attempted (but did not always manage) to speak with one voice, with the support of U.S. President Bill Clinton (b. 1946), who was elected to office in 1993. Russia, and her Eastern and Central European allies Bulgaria, Hungary, and Romania, which might have intervened on the Serb side, were in chaos after the collapse of the Soviet Union. Thus the world was spared a drawn-out proxy war in southern Europe, which otherwise might have developed into a very terminal nuclear World War Three.

The world in 1992 was very different from the world in 1938, when Nazi Germany had occupied Czechoslovakia's German-speaking areas, with the acquiescence of Britain and France, triggering only impotent protests from the UN's predecessor, the League of Nations (1919–46). But initially it seemed that there might be a repeat of the tragedy, with the U.S., EU, and UN unable to act decisively to prevent Serbian expansionism. In 1992 the UN established UNPROFOR (United Nations Protection Force) to attempt to keep the peace, but its efforts were hampered by the sheer complexity of the situation on the ground, with hostilities between Serbs, Bosniaks, and Croats leading to the massacre and "ethnic cleansing" of civilians on all sides.

The most shocking of these war crimes, however, took place in Bosnia-Herzegovina in July 1995, in the Muslim Bosniak region of Srebrenica. The Serbs needed to control the region to link several of their Bosnian enclaves, which meant that the majority Muslim population of the area would have to be removed. It is now clear that the Bosnian Serb leadership realized that this would involve the "ethnic cleansing" of the area, amounting to genocide, as defined in earlier entries. In 1992–93, Serb offensives and their policy of destroying Bosniak villages had driven 70,000 refugees into Srebrenica, and claimed over 3,000 lives. In April 1993, the UN Security Council declared Srebrenica a "safe area," guarded by a small and lightly armed detachment of Dutch UNPROFOR troops.

All attempts to negotiate with the Bosnian Serbs were unsuccessful, and relations between UNPROFOR and Republika Srpska deteriorated rapidly to a state of undeclared war when Bosnian Serb forces took UNPROFOR troops hostage and used them as human shields against NATO attacks. The Bosnian Serbs had effectively blockaded the 400 to 600 Dutch troops in Srebrenica, preventing their resupply or reinforcement. In July 1995, they mounted a full-scale offensive. The Dutch fell back to their HQ or surrendered, and Bosnian government forces were unable to prevent the capture of the region. Thousands of Bosniaks tried to seek refuge in the Dutch compound but most were locked out on the orders of the Dutch commander.

The massacres began on July 12 in the village of Potocari and ended ten days later. Although the victims were supposed to be men of fighting age, some 500 boys under the age of 18, as well as men over 65, and a number of women and girls were murdered and buried in mass graves. Bosnian Serb troops and paramilitaries raped many Bosniak women and girls. A column of several thousand refugees left the enclave making for Bosnian-held Tuzla some 35 miles (55 km) away. The Bosnian Serbs ambushed, shelled, and attacked them with chemical weapons. Many were captured, but, half-starved and disorientated, some reached the safety of Bosnian lines, to be greeted by representatives of the world press who could not believe what they were seeing. The most shocking was that these acts of genocide, mass rape, and ethnic cleansing, which the Western world had witnessed countless times in the developing world during the past fifty years, were happening on the doorstep of affluent, liberal-democratic Europe.

© Creative Commons

DEATH TOLL
Muslim men and boys were the primary targets of the massacre.

News of the massacre of 8,373 Bosniaks finally galvanized the EU and U.S., which succeeded in isolating the Bosnian Serbs from their allies, and forced them to negotiate after a bombing campaign combined with logistical and financial support for a joint offensive by the forces of Croatia and Bosnia-Herzegovina. For the first, and probably for the last time, the U.S., EU, and Russia cooperated in brokering the Dayton Peace Accord of 1995. Although the war in Bosnia-Herzegovina ended in 1995, the tensions and conflicts between the Serbs and their neighbors have not been resolved; and with the independence of Kosovo in 1999 and Montenegro in 2006, the dangerous "Balkanization" of the region continues.

DISASTER

Extinction Event

Tectonic Event

Military Action

Fire

Pandemic

Famine

Political or Economic Event

Genocide

Flood or Storm

Industrial or Transport Accident

TERROR FROM THE SKIES: 9/11

2001

Cause: Development of fundamentalist Islamic ideology seeking to overcome Western dominance of the Near East and establish "world caliphate;" radicalization of Muslims after the Arab–Israeli wars, Soviet invasion of Afghanistan, and Yugoslav civil war

Event: Al-Qaeda-trained operatives hijacked four passenger airliners: three reached targets in New York and Arlington, while the fourth crashed en route to Washington

Aftermath: Deaths of 3,388 people, over 6,000 injured; declaration of "War on Terror"

Today, our fellow citizens, our way of life, our very freedom came under attack in a series of deliberate and deadly terrorist acts. The victims were in airplanes, or in their offices; secretaries, businessmen and women, military and federal workers; moms and dads, friends and neighbors. Thousands of lives were suddenly ended by evil, despicable acts of terror.

**President George W. Bush,
speech, September 11, 2001**

The idea of flying a plane into the tallest buildings in the world's financial capital seems more far-fetched than the plot of many disaster movies. But this was not a disaster movie in which the hero saves the day. Although many were saved, and many rescuers, survivors, and victims displayed extraordinary heroism and fortitude, this was real life, and 2,977 people died on Tuesday, September 11, 2001, including the 246 passengers and crew of the four hijacked planes and 125 employees of the Pentagon. In addition, 411 New York rescue workers died in the collapse of the World Trade Center (WTC).

In 1992 the American political scientist Francis Fukuyama (b. 1952) published *The End of History*, in which he concluded that the collapse and disintegration of the Soviet Union in 1991 signified the triumph of Western capitalism and liberal-democracy over "Bolshevism," and represented the "end of history," that is, the end point of humanity's social, political, and economic development. However, even in the heady days when jubilant German crowds were dismantling the Berlin Wall, Fukuyama failed to account for the spectacular success of Communist China that was challenging established political economy by following a completely different developmental model from the Western world.

A PREMATURE ENDING

As we have seen even more clearly in the past decade, there is no real reason why a totalitarian Communist regime cannot sustain a thriving capitalist economy. The predictions that increasing wealth would lead the emerging Chinese middle class to demand greater political rights have so far failed to materialize. So far the Communist leadership's policy of redistributing the fruits of China's huge economic success to its middle class while maintaining absolute power has proved resistant to all social-media-based activism. However, Fukuyama was not wrong in asserting that we had reached the end of one chapter of human history—the end of the ideological conflict between Soviet Bolshevism and Capitalist liberal-democracy. What he had not seen coming was the next great ideological conflict: that between the West and a resurgent militant fundamentalist Islam, which declared *jihad*, holy war, to destroy the West.

The world's great religions share many of the same general precepts and commandments, but none more so than the three "religions of the book"—Judaism, Christianity, and Islam. Perhaps because they share so much, these three faiths have long been historic rivals. For proselytizing faiths such as Christianity and Islam, the ideal endpoint would be the conversion of the whole world, which, in theory, would remove one major cause for human conflict. However, reading any history of the Christian Church and of the Muslim community of the faithful will reveal that, like any organization, with the passing of the founder, they developed rivalries, factionalism, and doctrinal disagreements. And when the argument is over the word of God or Allah, disagreements are redefined as "heresies," and rival factions as heretical sects to be persecuted and destroyed.

Many of history's worst disasters, as we have seen, have an important religious dimension. While Christianity took three centuries to attain the status of a world religion, it took Islam less than a century. The first wave of Arab-Muslim conquests in the seventh and eighth centuries converted the Near East, Persia (Iran), Afghanistan, Egypt and North Africa, and Spain, but it was the second wave starting in the fifteenth century, spearheaded by the Ottoman Turks, that established an Islamic empire in the Near East, Africa, and Europe rivaling the Roman Empire. Turkic-Mongol nomads took the faith to India, western China, and Southeast Asia. For centuries, the Islamic world led in every field of human endeavor. The Muslim courts of Constantinople, Tehran, and Delhi were the richest, the most cultivated, and the most socially and ethnically inclusive during the Middle Ages and early modern period. Islam triumphant seemed destined to become the universal faith of the Eurasian continent and possibly of the entire world.

But in the seventeenth century Islam went into retreat. Mughal India succumbed to a combination of a Hindu Renaissance and British imperial ambitions; the Ottoman advance was halted in Europe; and the Ottoman Empire, badly governed and turned onto itself, began to stagnate and disintegrate. Nationalist aspirations among the provinces of the empire and revolution at home ended the Sultan's dictatorial rule, and ushered in the secularist regime of Mustafa Kemal Atatürk (1881–1938), the founder of the modern Turkish state. The European provinces of the empire had won their independence before World War One, and in its aftermath the Western powers moved in to dismember what was left of the Ottoman Empire outside Turkey: The French, who already ruled much of North Africa, occupied Syria, and the British took Egypt, the UAE, Aden, Palestine (now Israel, Jordan, and the Palestinian territories), and Iraq.

Externally, Western colonialism had defeated traditional Ottoman rule, and a homegrown secularist movement, which saw Westernization as Turkey's only hope of survival, completed the process. The postwar period saw the emergence of similar secular, socialist, pan-Arab Ba'athist regimes in Iraq, Egypt, and Syria, which aligned themselves with the Soviet Union against the West and repressed Islamist movements at home. For the duration of the Cold War (1948–91), and after the foundation of the State of Israel, the U.S. and USSR fought proxy wars through their respective allies in the Near East. But in 1979, a third force entered Near Eastern politics with the Islamic Revolution in Iran.

Islam, like Christianity, is divided into several sects, the two largest being the Sunni and Shi'a. Hence, the influence of Shi'ite Iran was reduced in a largely hostile Sunni Near East. However, even among Sunni Muslims, the example of Iran's revolution provided an example to follow—especially in its dealings with the U.S. and USSR. The Islamic world was finally awakening after centuries of stagnation and retreat. The Soviets embarked on their disastrous occupation of Afghanistan in 1979, hastening the demise of the USSR when they were forced to withdraw in 1989. Saddam Hussein's (1937–2006) Iraq invaded the oil-rich state of Kuwait in 1991, and was only ejected by forceful American and NATO intervention in the First Gulf War. Although held in check, a resurgent Islam and Arab nationalism were beginning to make themselves felt and heard on the world stage.

CHOKING
The streets of lower Manhattan choked with debris, smoke, and ash.

As is well known, the 9/11 attacks were planned and executed by Al-Qaeda, the fundamentalist Islamist terror network founded and initially funded by Osama bin Laden (1957–2011). Although Al-Qaeda remains one of the most famous and feared terrorist groups on the planet, its name is not derived from some grand religious, social, or political ideal. In English it translates as "The Base," as in a military base. But in this case, and quite appropriately, it refers to a specific terrorist camp set up in 1988 to train *mujahideen* insurgents fighting Soviet occupation of Afghanistan.

THE BASE

The origins of Al-Qaeda's ideology, however, developed long before the Soviet invasion in the work of the Egyptian Islamist Sayyid Qutb (1906–66), who was a leading member of Egypt's Muslim Brotherhood during the 1950s and 1960s. The aims of the Brotherhood and other fundamentalist Islamist groups were to establish a world Caliphate (religious government) based on the precepts found in the Quran and the Sunnah (the acts of the Prophet Muhammad, ca. 570–632), such as *shari'ah* law.

This kind of extreme religious fundamentalism can be seen as an ideological response to a perception that a religion and a culture are under threat.

Hence, in an increasingly secular world, we have seen the emergence of fundamentalist Islam, Christianity, Judaism, Hinduism, etc. And while Islamist parties have made considerable progress in the past decade, winning national polls in Turkey and Egypt, there has been a simultaneous push for modernization, liberalization, and secularization, during the ongoing events known collectively as the "Arab Spring."

RESPONSIBILITY
Bin Laden's plot to destroy the West led to his and his organization's destruction.

That secularism and democracy will always prevail is not a foregone conclusion. Which way a country goes will depend on its social makeup: for example, the presence of an educated middle class that can counteract more conservative elements in society. In Egypt and Turkey, for example, a large conservative agrarian population has ensured the election of moderate Islamist regimes, but a large, urban middle class is vocal in its opposition to the introduction of shari'ah and other measures that would restrict the role of women in society and suppress democratic institutions and civil rights. However, in countries such as Afghanistan, where there is a tiny middle class, discredited by its association with the U.S. and NATO occupation, it seems unlikely that Western-style democracy will survive the withdrawal of foreign troops in 2014.

Osama bin Laden and many of his early collaborators and operatives were born in Saudi Arabia. Although an ally of the West, the kingdom of Saudi Arabia is an undemocratic fundamentalist Islamic monarchy, grown fantastically wealthy on the sale of crude oil to the developed world. The home of the holy cities of Medina and Mecca, which host the yearly Hajj pilgrimage, the country is also the center of the Sunni Islamic world, and is socially extremely conservative. It is a country of contrasts and contradictions: While it boasts some of the world's most modern and sophisticated technological, commercial, and industrial infrastructure, at the same time it forbids women from driving cars. The religious police enforce a legal code little changed since the medieval period, which includes the death penalty for adultery and the amputation of hands for theft.

Bin Laden is typical of the contrasts and paradoxes of his native land. Educated a Wahhabi (Saudi fundamentalist) Muslim, he also studied engineering, played soccer, and supported the British soccer team Arsenal. Among his idols were two military figures of the Second World War, the leader of the Free French and later French president, Charles de Gaulle (1890–1970), and British field marshall Bernard Montgomery (1887–1976), the Allied commander who defeated the Germans in North Africa. In his style of dress and speeches, however, he presented himself as a traditional Arab Muslim, complete with white robes, turban, and bushy moustache and beard. This man whose education, lifestyle, and personal wealth owed so much to the Western world swore to expel the U.S. from Saudi Arabia, destroy Israel, and set up a world state based on fundamentalist Islamic principles.

Al-Qaeda's strategy to achieve its ambitious plan for world domination was simple: A series of high-profile terrorist attacks that would provoke the U.S. and her allies into invading the Near East, which would ruin it economically and lead to the social and financial collapse of the West. In the aftermath, Muslims would rise up and establish a universal Caliphate run on strict Islamic lines. While the 9/11 attacks achieved the organization's aim of triggering a massive NATO response—the invasion of Afghanistan and the War on Terror—it also resulted in the elimination of the Al-Qaeda leadership that had planned the attacks. Although the West totters on the brink of financial disaster, our economic woes, as we shall see in the entry on the Lehman Brothers bankruptcy (pp. 234–240), were not engineered by Al-Qaeda but were self-inflicted.

DECLARING JIHAD AGAINST AMERICA

© Gary Yim | Shutterstock

REMEMBER
Ground Zero will be the home of a permanent memorial to the victims of 9/11.

DISASTER

Extinction Event

Tectonic Event

Military Action

Fire (or Heat wave)

Pandemic

Famine

Political or Economic Event

Genocide

Flood or Storm

Industrial or Transport Accident

FRENCH FEVER: EUROPEAN HEAT WAVE

2003

Cause: Global warming; record temperatures during the summer of 2003; increasing number of older people living on their own without family support

Event: Extremely high temperatures in France during July and August

Aftermath: 14,802 heat-related deaths in France; further estimated 35,000 to 70,000 deaths across Europe; shortfall in European harvest; drought; forest fires

According to British scientists, Europe's scorching heat wave of 2003 will be considered typical seasonal weather by the middle of the twenty-first century, and may be below average in a century. The British team made a case that the summer of 2003 was Europe's hottest in southern, western, and central Europe in at least five centuries. From the eastern Atlantic to the Black Sea, the mercury was 2.3°C (4.14°F) above average. According to their models, by the 2040s at least one European summer in two will be hotter than in 2003.

Bruce Johansen,
The Encyclopedia of Warming Science
and Technology, 2012

Northwestern Europe—northern France and Germany, southern England, Belgium, Luxemburg, and the Netherlands—is not associated with unusually warm weather. The five centuries between 1350 and 1850 were known as the "Little Ice Age," when temperatures often dropped low enough to freeze over rivers and the sea in southern England, something inconceivable in the twenty-first century. It is thought to have been a natural climatic event, related to higher than average volcanic activity or minor changes in the sun's output; it affected only the northern half of the planet, and although called an "ice age," did not have the severity of the glacial periods that saw ice sheets reaching the south of England, causing a substantial drop in sea level. The last glacial period ended around 12,000 years BP, and we are now living through what is known as an "interglacial"—a long-term but finite warm period within the ongoing ice age. In the long run, human civilization will come to an end when the ice sheets return, making the most densely populated regions of the planet—northern Europe, Russia, North America, and northern China—as inhospitable as today's Arctic or Antarctic.

FRENCH TOAST

Map of France showing the maximum temperatures in August 2003 (in Fahrenheit).

The French, were ill-prepared for the unusually high temperatures that afflicted the country during July and August 2003. Although France has its Mediterranean region where the summer temperatures regularly hit between 80°F and 90°F (20°C and 30°C), the country north of the central mountain range known as the *Massif Central* has much cooler summers, with temperatures averaging 70°F (20°C). Above-average temperatures typical on the beaches of *Côte d'Azur* were not expected in a city such as Paris.

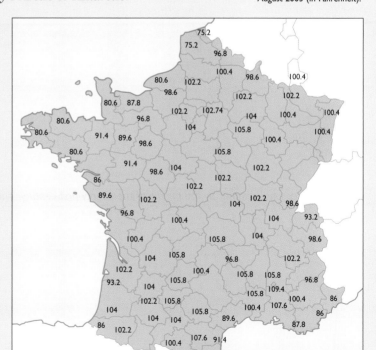

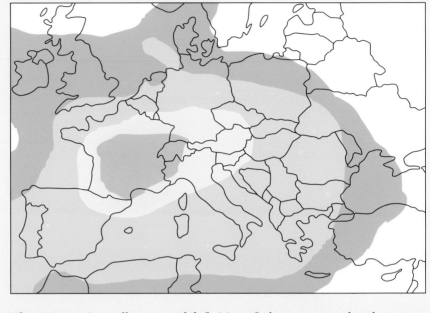

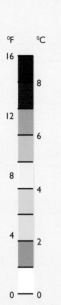

°F	°C
16	
	8
12	
	6
8	
	4
4	
	2
0	0

EUROPE HEATS UP
The heat wave was at its hottest in France, but other parts of Europe experienced unusually high temperatures.

There is no universally accepted definition of a heat wave, and each country sets its own parameters to define an unusually hot period. In France a heat wave is declared if daytime temperatures exceed 91.4°F (33°C), and nighttime temperatures exceed 68°F (20°C) for three consecutive 24-hour periods. In the southern and southeastern U.S., and vast tracts of Asia, Australia, and Africa, 91.4°F (33°C) might be considered a quite pleasant temperature, especially if it weren't too humid. However, people in those regions will have houses either fitted with air conditioning or designed to dispel heat naturally with large windows and doors, terraces, flat roofs, and reflective wall coverings, and their lifestyles and clothing will be well adapted to hot conditions. This was not the case for the population of France's capital and northern cities.

DOG DAYS

A heat wave is caused when an area of high pressure settles over a landmass, preventing air circulation and gradually heating up the atmosphere below. As the air becomes stiller, there is little chance of rain clouds developing and thus the water evaporating from rivers and lakes is not replenished. This leads to drought and increases the likelihood of forest fires. Although heat waves are not uncommon, the events of the past decade have broken temperature records all over the world. Most climate scientists see this as further evidence of global warming. A team of British researchers (see quote on p. 222) has predicted that in twenty-five years, far from being exceptional, summers as warm or warmer than 2003 might occur every two years.

"Heat wave" in French is *canicule* ("dog days"), and in addition to the architectural and lifestyle factors listed above that are common to the whole of northwestern Europe, there are particular reasons why France reported the greatest number of heat-related deaths in Europe in the summer of 2003. In the first two weeks of August, daytime temperatures in Paris were in excess of 95°F (35°C) for nine days, topping the previous daytime record of 102°F (39°C), and the nighttime record of 80°F (25.5°C) on the night of August 10–11. The densely packed houses and apartment blocks of Paris, which is a city with relatively few parks and open spaces, need cooler nighttime temperatures to dissipate the heat that builds up during the day. With the high August temperatures, the nightly cooling did not occur, making the interiors of well-insulated French homes unbearably hot.

© 2009 AFP | Getty Images

HOME ALONE
Many of the victims were seniors left behind by their vacationing families.

August is traditionally the month when France — including many of its factories, government agencies, municipalities, shops, and medical services — closes down and heads south for the yearly seaside break. In years gone by, the whole family, including the grandparents, would rent a holiday home on the coast and vacation together. In the twenty-first century, however, family breakdown, shorter vacations, and economic constraints have meant that many older people have been left home alone during the vacation season. Unaccustomed to the extreme temperatures, and with no family or medical support network to fall back on, many older people became disoriented and severely dehydrated, and suffered from heat stroke.

The French, who have long prided themselves on the strength of the traditional extended family, especially when compared to the Anglo-Saxon nuclear family, were shocked to discover that almost 15,000 vulnerable older people had died in France's metropolitan areas. Unfortunately, with so many older people living alone in Europe, and with the increasing likelihood of more extreme weather events, the death toll among the most vulnerable in our societies is likely to keep on rising.

DISASTER

Extinction Event

Tectonic Event

Military Action

Fire

Pandemic

Famine

Political or Economic Event

Genocide

Flood or Storm

Industrial or Transport Accident

THE DAY THE SEA ROSE: INDIAN OCEAN EARTHQUAKE AND TSUNAMI

2004

Cause: MMS 9.2 earthquake off the coast of Sumatra, Indonesia

Event: Tsunami hit the coasts of Indonesia, Thailand, Burma, the Indian Ocean islands and Indian Subcontinent, Sri Lanka, Madagascar, and East and South Africa

Aftermath: Deaths of an estimated 230,000 to 280,000 victims; enormous economic dislocation and damage to tourism, fisheries, and agricultural infrastructure; permanent rise in sea levels affecting shipping

The areas that were hit hardest were Indonesia and the Andaman and Nicobar Islands. On the island of Sumatra, the tsunami reached close to 2 miles (3.2 km) inland, wiping the land clean of life. Some reports estimate that almost 70 percent of the population of coastal villages on Sumatra were killed by the tsunami.

Greg Roza,
The Indian Ocean Tsunami, 2007

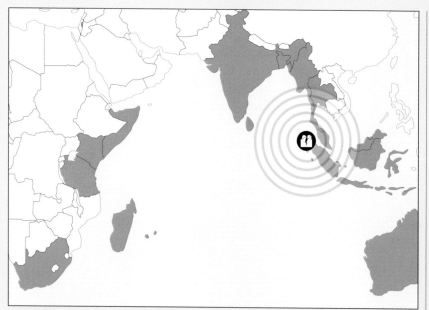

Approximate epicenter

Affected areas

SUBDUCTION ZONE
An earthquake off of the coast of Sumatra, Indonesia, struck on December 26, 2004, resulting in a devastating tsunami.

We return for the third and final time to a region we have visited before for two of the world's worst volcanic eruptions: Lake Toba (pp. 16–20), which almost wiped out humanity in 70,000 years BP, and Krakatoa (pp. 96–99), which produced the loudest bang ever heard. Not only do we return to the same region of the Pacific Ring of Fire, but also to cover the most destructive and costly human–natural disaster of the twenty-first century so far. The area south of the Indonesian islands is a subduction boundary where the Indo-Australian plate moves north and slides under the Eurasian plate. In addition to creating new land and volcanoes, the tremendous pressure generated triggers massive earthquakes along the convergent boundary, which is out to sea in the Indian Ocean. This mitigates the damage from the quake itself as the density of soil and rock is relatively good at absorbing shock waves, but conversely it exposes the population for thousands of miles around to something that is potentially even more devastating: a megatsunami that can travel all the way across the Indian Ocean to strike the shores of Africa.

The Indian Ocean earthquake and tsunami is a good example of the kind of natural–human disasters that threaten the world population in the twenty-first century. Now that the population of the planet has reached seven billion, all the most desirable real estate has been occupied. Most desirable of all, along with river systems such as the Nile, Ganges, and Yellow River, which saw the birth of the first settled agrarian civilizations, are coastal areas, which are rich in natural resources, and offer an easy means of transport by boat along coastal shipping lanes.

Indonesia, consisting of over 17,000 large and small islands, is now the fourth-largest country in terms of population (238 million in 2011). The island of Sumatra, which has a population of 50 million, is the largest island to be entirely within Indonesia. The island is perched above the 1,600–mile (2,600 km) Sunda Trench, a subduction zone that moves at around 2.1 inches (5.5 cm) a year. The coast of Sumatra is lined with the Bukit Barisan mountain range, a series of lofty volcanoes, a dozen of which have been active in the past two hundred years.

THE CRUEL SEA

In addition to the large populations living in the immediate vicinity of the Sunda Trench, there are other human factors that may have led to the huge loss of life caused by the tsunami. Firstly, the date and time of the quake were significant. The earthquake struck on the morning of December 26, an important holiday season in Europe, when many northern Europeans escape to Western and Southeast Asia—especially the beach resorts of Thailand and Sri Lanka—for winter-sun vacations.

© Beawiharta | Reuters | Corbis

GREAT FLOOD
Debris was washed miles inland by the tsunamis triggered by the earthquake.

Among the largest overseas contingent were some 20,000–30,000 Swedes vacationing in Thailand and Sri Lanka, which explains why Sweden lost most citizens in the disaster with 543 killed, and another 1,500 in need of emergency medical assistance and repatriation. The second-highest casualties were reported by Germany, with 539 confirmed dead, and thousands more who had to be rescued from flooded areas. France lost 95 citizens, the United Kingdom, 150, the U.S., 33, and Australia 26. In total 2,307 foreign nationals visiting the affected areas either died or are missing and presumed dead.

Environmentalists have suggested that other human-related factors played a part in increasing the severity of the damage caused by the tsunami. Many offshore reefs off the coasts of Thailand, Indonesia, Bangladesh, India, and

Sri Lanka have been destroyed with dynamite to facilitate shipping or to make way for aquaculture farms, and large areas of mangrove swamps that once lined the coasts of the region have been cleared to make way for industrial, tourist, and residential developments. Together, the mangroves and reefs provided a natural barrier to tsunamis, which might have considerably lessened the severity of the disaster.

The loss of life sustained by European tourists is dwarfed by the number of casualties suffered by the countries in the path of the tsunamis: Indonesia lost an estimated 205,000 people, and a further 500,000 were displaced; Sri Lanka suffered 35,000 deaths and 516,000 displaced; India, 26,000 dead and over 600,000 displaced; and Thailand, around 8,000 dead. The total number of deaths is between 230,000 and 280,000, with a further 1.6 million people displaced, placing it among the top ten deadliest human–natural disasters since 1900.

© 2012 AFP | Getty Images

DRY DOCK
The *Apung 1*, flung 1.5 miles inland, is now a somber tourist attraction.

Like other disasters of the video camera and cellphone age, the tsunami was captured live, and a great deal of footage of both the earthquake and the ensuing tsunami as it reached the coasts of Indonesia, Thailand, and Sri Lanka is available on the Internet. But perhaps one the best illustrations of the strength of the tsunami is told by the fate of the PLTD *Apung 1*, an electric generator ship that was offshore near Banda Aceh, Indonesia, when the tsunami struck. The 2,600-ton *Apung 1* was flung about 1.5 miles (2–3 km) inland, where it came to rest on top of two houses, killing everyone inside. The stranded ship is now a bizarre memorial to the events of December 26, 2004.

While the tsunami caused enormous damage to the natural environment, fishing communities and costal farming areas, as well as the tourist infrastructure of Thailand and Sri Lanka, perhaps the most enduring and serious damage was to the Indian Ocean itself. The massive earthquake raised the sea floor in several areas, creating new hazards for shipping and altering established shipping lanes. We humans believe that we can control and remake nature to suit our needs, but while humans can claim to have remade much of the natural environment, planet earth in its most violent tectonic manifestations will never ever be completely tamed.

DISASTER

Extinction Event

Tectonic Event

Military Action

Fire

Pandemic

Famine

Political or Economic Event

Genocide

Flood or Storm

Industrial or Transport Accident

THE BIG DIFFICULT: HURRICANE KATRINA

2005

Cause: Category Five hurricane

Event: Storm surge through levées protecting New Orleans

Aftermath: Flooding of 80 percent of Metro New Orleans; the costliest natural disaster in the U.S., estimated at $108 billion; deaths of 1,836 people across seven U.S. states

A massive storm surge sends water over the Mississippi River–Gulf Outlet (MRGO) and the Industrial Canal, causing immediate flooding in St. Bernard Parish and the eastern neighborhood of New Orleans. Water levels in most areas are 10 to 15 feet. In some places, the water is so deep that police officers in boats have to steer carefully around streetlights. Ninety-five percent of the parish is underwater.

> **Douglas Brinkley,**
> ***The Great Deluge, 2006***

Storms often feature in the myths of ancient Greece. The plot of Homer's (fl. mid-eighth century BCE) *Odyssey*, for example, hinges on several storms in which the hero Odysseus is shipwrecked and forced to use his considerable wits to extricate himself and his crew from the clutches of sundry monsters, enchantresses, and sirens, before the gods, having had their fun, allow him to return home from Troy to Ithaca—a journey of 600 miles (950 km) as the porpoise swims, that should have taken a few weeks at most, but takes the hero ten years. Although the Mediterranean storms Odysseus encounters occasionally sink his wooden galley, mostly his vessels run aground or are wrecked but are quickly repaired and afloat once more, or they ride out the storms in the safety of the many sheltered anchorages in the region.

© NASA

CENTRIFUGE
A hurricane is a gigantic heat engine driven by the temperature of the ocean.

Compare the rather wimpy storms of Mediterranean myth with those of the pre-Colombian Americas, and an entirely different picture emerges, which also may explain why there was no Maya Christopher Columbus or Aztec Ferdinand Magellan. For six months of the year, from the beginning of June to the end of November, tropical cyclones form over the Atlantic, from where, as we shall see in the last entry that features Hurricane Sandy (pp. 246–251), they can travel north to make landfall on the Eastern Seaboard, or travel westward, drifting over the islands of the Caribbean, across Florida, and over the Gulf of Mexico, where, encountering warm waters, they can grow in intensity to become fully fledged hurricanes.

An average tropical cyclone season will feature on average 12 tropical storms and six hurricanes—a name derived from an ancient god of the Maya and also the Taino Native Americans of the Caribbean, Huracán or Juracán. As we saw in the entry on demographic collapse in the Americas (pp. 52–57), the Taino and other Caribbean peoples were wiped out soon after the arrival of the Spanish, so what we know of their beliefs comes from unsympathetic Spanish sources; however, it seems that the god of storms Huracán was also one of the Maya creator deities, who had attempted and failed twice to make a satisfactory humanity—the first time from clay and the second time from wood. According to the

© Patricia Marroquin | Shutterstock

BLOWN AWAY
Hurricanes generate winds
that can lift up cars and
boats and demolish buildings.

Popol Vuh, a colonial-era record of much earlier Maya myth cycles, Huracán destroyed the second creation with a great flood.

A tropical cyclone is an incredibly powerful heat engine, capable of producing extraordinary amounts of energy. One estimate of the energy they release is 200 times the entire world's electrical generating capacity, or the equivalent of detonating a 10-megaton nuclear bomb every 20 minutes. If we could harness this unlimited clean power source, our energy worries would be over for ever. In layman's terms (and believe me, I am the ultimate layman), the sun heats up the surface of the ocean, which begins to condense and rise up as water vapor. The condensation triggers higher wind speeds, whose action increases the condensation. Thus, the basic mechanism of a tropical cyclone, as long as conditions are right, is a positive feedback loop that keeps on building in intensity. The spin of a hurricane is provided by the rotation of the earth (the Coriolis effect). Physically, a hurricane consists of outlying bands of thunderstorms and rain clouds that rotate around a circular "eye," a column of clear, calm air at the center of the storm. These can be 19 to 40 miles (30–65 km) in diameter, though eyes as small as 2 miles (3.9 km) and as large as 230 miles (370 km) have also been recorded.

IN THE EYE OF THE STORM

Like earthquakes and volcanic eruptions, tropical cyclones are graded in terms of their strength. The Saffir–Simpson hurricane scale (SSHS) defines seven levels according to wind speed, including five hurricane categories. Starting at the bottom of the scale, a tropical depression has winds of less than 38 mph (62 km/h), and a tropical storm has wind speeds of 39 to 73 mph (63 to 118 km/h), before we get to hurricanes proper; a Category One hurricane has wind speeds of 74 to 95 mph (119 to 153 km/h); a Category Two, 96 to 110 mph (154–177 km/h); a Category Three, 111 to 129 mph (178–208 km/h); a Category Four, 130 to 156 mph (209 to 250 km/h); and finally, a Category Five, winds in excess of 157 mph (252 km/h).

Records began in 1851, and in the past one-hundred-and-sixty-two years the Atlantic basin has experienced 35 Category Five hurricanes, including a record four in 2005: Emily (July 16) that hit the Maya homeland, Yucatán, and then went on to Mexico; Katrina (August 28–29), and the costliest hurricane in U.S. history; Rita (September 21–22), which made landfall in western Louisiana; and Wilma (October 19), that veered away from the Gulf of Mexico, over southern Florida, and on over the North Atlantic where it dissipated without causing further damage. Of the four, Katrina was the costliest in terms of lives and material damage, as it flooded the greater part of New Orleans.

As I was born in "old" Orléans in France, I've always had a great fondness for my hometown's namesake across the Atlantic. But whereas Orléans straddles the River Loire, which, though broad and historically deadly, has never flooded in my lifetime, New Orleans, built in the Mississippi Delta, surrounded by lakes and wetlands, is gradually sinking into the soft sedimentary soils by the year. A recent survey revealed that about half of the city is now below sea level, and therefore is dependent on an extensive system of embankments, or levées (from the French verb *lever*, to raise), along the banks of the Mississippi, ranging in height from 24 feet (7.3 m) to 50 feet (15 m) to keep the city dry (if not high).

© Creative Commons

The Mississippi levée system is the most extensive in the world with 3,500 miles (5,600 km) of embankments built by the U.S. Army Corps of Engineers, which began work on the levées in the late nineteenth century. Unfortunately, the levées around New Orleans were insufficient for a storm of the size and intensity of Hurricane Katrina. A combination of poor design and maintenance, and insufficient height for the storm surge caused by Katrina, caused 53 failures of the levées protecting the city. The worst civil-engineering failure in U.S. history, the disaster left 80 percent of Metro New Orleans flooded, claiming the lives of 1,577 victims in Louisiana, many of them in New Orleans, and costing a record $108 billion dollars.

AWASH
The levée breaches led to the flooding of 80 percent of Metro New Orleans.

DISASTER

Extinction Event

Tectonic Event

Military Action

Fire

Pandemic

Famine

Political or Economic Event

Genocide

Flood or Storm

Industrial or Transport Accident

THE MATRIX RELOADED: LEHMAN BROTHERS BANKRUPTCY

2008

Cause: U.S. real estate bubble burst in 2007; subprime mortgage crisis; risky and criminal behavior on the part of leading financial institutions, including Lehman Brothers; failure of regulatory and oversight mechanisms nationally and internationally

Event: Lehman Brothers' share price collapsed and the firm filed for bankruptcy

Aftermath: Largest bankruptcy in U.S. history; Lehman's global reach meant that all major financial markets were affected; near-failure of leading world banks

Banks were compelled to jump into line, and soon they were making thousands of loans without any cash-down deposits whatsoever, an unprecedented situation. Mortgage officers inside the banks were forced to bend or break their own rules in order to achieve a good Community Reinvestment Act rating, which would please the administration by demonstrating generosity to underprivileged borrowers even if they might default.

Lawrence McDonald and Patrick Robinson,
A Colossal Failure of Common Sense, 2010

© Orna Ydur | Shutterstock

In *The Matrix* (1999) Agent Smith (Hugo Weaving) tells the hero, Neo (Keanu Reeves), that the original "Matrix" in which humans were kept prisoners by their machine masters was a simulation of a perfect world. But, Smith explains, humans could not accept Utopia, and their minds rebelled and tried to wake up from something that they instinctively sensed was too good to be true. Although the *Matrix* trilogy contains a great deal of pseudo-philosophical claptrap, this one point, at least, does have verisimilitude—not that we live in a computer-driven simulation, but that humans find ways of resisting and fighting what would be in their own long-term best interest.

Although history has shown us over and over again that our self-interest is actually best served by cooperation and sharing, we never seem to learn the lessons of history but just repeat its mistakes: wars, failed revolutions, financial crises, etc. Earlier entries on the socioeconomic experiments of both the extreme right and extreme left amply demonstrate the dismal failure of totalitarian regimes of any ideological complexion. The countries that combine what is now called "compassionate" capitalism with a form of democratic government are the most able and likely to provide for the material welfare, health, and mental wellbeing of the majority of their citizens. True, no system is perfect, but, to adapt a famous quote about democracy by British wartime premier Winston Churchill (1874–1965), the following argument appears correct: "Capitalism is the worst economic system, except for all the others that have been tried from time to time."

When its excesses are controlled by legislation protecting the rights of individuals, capitalism has proved itself capable of growing economies, expanding trade, raising living standards, and providing universal education and healthcare, while at the same time safeguarding the environment. When the brakes are off, however, capitalism, as we have also seen in the entries on the Bhopal (pp. 194–97) and *Exxon Valdez* (pp. 203–206) disasters, can be destructive of individuals, societies, and the whole planet. But to those who gleefully claim that capitalism has failed and needs to be replaced, I'd like to ask, by what exactly? Unless you want to try another "Great Leap Forward," Soviet (pp. 139–44) or Maoist style (pp. 171–74), or follow the Khmer Rouge in their attempt to recreate an agrarian utopia (pp. 179–182)? With seven billion humans on the planet, utopian solutions are not realistic, unless you're ready to sacrifice half to two-thirds of humanity.

Our current economic woes, however, do present us with a strong indictment of capitalism. But before we throw out the baby, the bath, the bath water, the faucet, and the bathroom in an easy condemnation of an economic system that has put hamburger and fries on most tables, credit cards in most pocket books, and smart phones in most back pockets, let's try to reconstruct exactly what had gotten us to a global financial crisis whose duration and severity might match or eclipse the greatest global downturns.

In the past one-hundred-and-forty years, the world economy has experienced many minor and three major global financial crises: the Long Depression of 1873–96, the Great Depression of 1929–41 (pp. 129–134), and the Great Recession (2007–present). Does this indicate that there is something structurally wrong with capitalism? Your guess is as good as mine or as the Fed's chairman's or of the Bank of England's governor's. At this point, the reader might be asking him- or herself what this has to do with the Lehman Brothers bankruptcy of 2008, but bear with me, and all will become clear.

NEO IN WONDERLAND (WHAT WE THOUGHT HAPPENED)

It's 2007, and Neo wakes up, realizing that the economic reality he's been experiencing isn't quite the one he thought it was. He's lived through the 1990s, when the world appeared to be in pretty good shape: He's seen the end of Soviet Communism, victory in the First Gulf War, and peace breaking out in the former Yugoslavia (pp. 211–15); the financial deregulation that had begun in the 1970s seems to be paying rich dividends; and apart from a few bumps on the financial yellow brick road, stock markets and house prices are on the up and up. The dawn of the new millennium, however, is slightly clouded: 9/11 (pp. 216–221) leads to the War on Terror, and the West is in collective hock to China, which is lending us the money to buy the goods it can produce much more cheaply than workers in Birmingham, Alabama, or Birmingham, England. But even if we have maxed out the family's and the country's credit cards, we feel rich because our assets are increasing in value.

Pop! The sound of the worldwide property and asset bubble bursting in 2007 wakes Neo up, and flushes him down the garbage tube into the real world of Zion (aka the post-Apocalypse economy). He tries to piece together what has really been happening over the past twenty years. So, at the risk of mixing my metaphors and movies: How did we go from being "on top of the world" to being two hours away from a disastrous shipwreck? After all, the world economy has not hit a financial iceberg.

In fact, from 2007 onwards, as far as most of the world was concerned, it was going to be plain sailing in the sunset with champagne for everyone. In his budget speech that year, British chancellor of the exchequer and later prime minister Gordon Brown (b. 1951) confidently assured his audience, "We will not return to the old boom and bust"—a sentiment echoed in the statements of governments and financial institutions worldwide. In an eerie replay of Irving Fisher's rosy predictions on the eve of the Wall Street Crash of 1929 (pp. 132–133), governments, banks, and consumers in the developed world persuaded themselves that we had finally managed to overcome the structural instabilities of the capitalist free market that regularly triggered local or global recessions. Initial analyses of the financial crisis of 2007–08 underplayed the gravity of the situation, and tried either to spread the blame around or not apportion blame at all.

© Espion | Dreamstime

FALLEN
Once thought to be "Masters of the Universe," Lehmans were giants with feet of clay.

The first explanation Neo was asked to believe was that the crisis had been caused by the bursting of the U.S. property bubble (true), which had been aggravated by structural problems in the world economy: imbalances that left the developed world reliant on financial services and on China making all the consumer goods; problems with the regulatory framework after the repeal of the Glass–Steagall Act (1933–99); the end of a quarter-century of the technological innovation that had put a PC in every office and home, and a cellphone and MP3 player in every pocket and pocket book; the monetarists' favorite—too much liquidity in the money supply; my personal favorite—the new financial products and derivatives such as CDOs (collateralized debt obligations), MBSs (mortgage back securities), and CDSs (credit default swaps), which were so complex that even the poor little bankers who had dreamed them up in the first place could not fully understand them; and finally, of course, there were a few bad apples whose reckless risk-taking had jeopardized the whole system—rogue traders like Nick Leeson (b. 1967) and out-and-out crooks like Bernard Madoff (b. 1938), who gave the hardworking, honest financiers a bad name (all partly true, but not yet the whole story).

Hence, we—national governments, Wall Street, and Joe Schmoe on Main Street—were equally to blame, or equally the victims of economic circumstance, that is, something that was "bigger than all of us." However, we were assured that normal service would be resumed in a year or two and that we would pick up where we had left off. Whoopee! Throw another roll of hundreds on the fire, and let's get a subprime mortgage for an even bigger house! Six years on, although there are signs of recovery in the U.S., much of the world is still in recession, with the sovereign-debt crisis, Euro crisis, fiscal cliff, and debt ceiling enforcing austerity in the developed world. Even China is experiencing a bad case of growing pains, because no one can afford to buy quite as many of her goods as before.

NEO THROUGH THE LOOKING GLASS (WHAT REALLY HAPPENED)

We finally reach the Lehman Brothers bankruptcy. Remember them? No, well: old-established financial pillar of the NYSE and Wall Street, home to the "Masters of the Universe," and a company once so profitable that its bonus pool was the size of the GDP of a small country. They were profitable beyond the dreams of most people's avarice, and guess what: that still wasn't enough, and they, individually and corporately, wanted more. That is not to say that Lehman single-handedly triggered the financial crisis of 2007–8, but they were an exemplar of its underlying causes and regrettable consequences.

On p. 234 a former Lehman employee, Lawrence McDonald, is quoted, who in his account of the collapse of the bank, *A Colossal Failure of Common Sense* (2010), blames everyone apart from the company for its downfall. It was stupid consumers who borrowed much more than they could ever pay back, and the government who forced poor Lehman to take too many risks, and then failed to step in with the checkbook when it all went belly-up. Well, Mr. McDonald, your defense of Lehman does not stand up to even the most cursory scrutiny.

What we (and Neo) have learned since 2008 is that the financial crisis and ensuing Great Recession were not acts of a malevolent financial god but that a great deal of it can be laid at the doors of the world's major financial institutions. Let's begin with a look at the real-estate bubble in the U.S. and much of the developed world. House prices were rising not just in the U.S.

but all over the developed world. Buy a house, and even if you can't secure a regular mortgage, we can get you a cheap subprime mortgage, and the increase in house prices will ensure that by the time your repayments go up, you can sell at a profit, move, and buy a new and even bigger home on another subprime deal. In another words, a huge Ponzi (pyramid) scheme using houses instead of cash. It was all so easy—as long as house prices kept on rising. But just lending to "underprivileged borrowers" wasn't enough for Lehman and the other Wall Street branches of Caesar's Palace. They found new ways of making money out of consumer and company debt—mortgages, bank loans, credit cards—the CDSs, MBSs, and CDOs listed above—by "securitizing" them and selling them on as investments.

Now, let's think about this in extremely simple terms—yes, more Chalinonomics (see pp. 129–34). An honest farmer has a pig, which he slaughters and turns into 100 lb (45 kg) of bacon, which he takes to market and sells at $1.50/lb, for earnings of $150 (minus expenses). Very simple so far: real pig, real bacon, real sales, and 100 consumers get their bacon sandwiches. On the road, the honest farmer meets the clever tinker, who says, "Why not breed two pigs next year? And you'll make more money." But the honest farmer replies: "There aren't enough rich people in the town who can afford to buy bacon. I wouldn't be able to sell it all, and I'd make a loss." "Simple," says the tinker. "Reduce the price to $1/lb, and you'll get more customers, and you'll make $200." "I don't know," says the honest farmer, "It'll be a lot more work, and I'm happy with my $100." "Then let me give you the $200 now for the two pigs," suggests the tinker, who can borrow the money from the rich merchant, and plans to sell the bacon to 200 poor customers who will pay him 12 cents a month for twelve months, netting him $288. The tinker has just invented the bacon futures market, which is the simplest form of derivative.

But this is only the beginning of his moneymaking schemes. He wants some cash to invest in another pig, so he goes to the rich merchant and says, "I have 100 people paying me 12 cents a month for twelve months, but I will sell you their 12-cent debt for a dime, so you'll make $2.00 on the year." He's kept back 100 customers at 12 cents, so he knows he's still ahead of the game. And if his third pig scheme pays off, then he's in clover. At this point, the tinker has made a quantum leap in investment by securitizing the debts of 100 people and selling them on as an investment vehicle. Let's call it the

PWF derivative, for "Pigs Will Fly." Now, boys and girls, what happens next? Yes, you guessed it, the farmer's pigs die of swine flu, and there are no pigs, no bacon, and no bacon sandwiches for anyone. His customers lose their money, the rich merchant loses his money, and because he's rich, he has the tinker arrested and thrown into prison.

But over-complex financial products that were designed to make money out of debt were only the beginning of what Neo was finding out about the world's financial system. Far from being unwilling lenders forced by governments to lend to "underprivileged borrowers," predatory mortgage providers were pushing consumers to take loans that they could never hope to repay, even if the real-estate bubble hadn't burst. OK, so far, we the consumer and they the bankers were equally to blame, because, if we hadn't been greedy, we wouldn't have let them talk us into borrowing money and investing in their promises, but we now know that Lehman and other financial institutions were engaging in some very creative and questionable accounting practices to make their products more desirable and improve their balance sheets.

And, far from there being the odd rogue trader taking risks with the investors' money, the whole industry was geared to wild corporate risk-taking, secure in the knowledge that they were "too big to fail," as well as quite a lot of downright criminality—called "malfeasance" in the genteel financial world—such as fixing inter-bank lending rates (LIBOR, TIBOR, and SIBOR). And why did they do it? Clearly, at some point it's no longer about your salary and bonus's purchasing power, but just a wild ride—an addiction to risk-taking that is no different from the small-time gambler who bets on the racetrack. And what about the governments and regulators charged with safeguarding the financial system? Worldwide, they embodied the attitudes of the three wise monkeys: "Hear no evil, see no evil, and speak no evil": As long as the electors were happy and the taxes were rolling in, they kept quiet and hoped for the best.

It's incorrect to claim that capitalism is the Root of All Evil—long-term, with the right safeguards, it could prove to be the savior of humanity. However, though capitalism needs economic innovators, entrepreneurs, and risk-takers, what it doesn't need is gambling addicts and crooks.

DOUBLE TROUBLE: TOHOKU EARTHQUAKE AND NUCLEAR ACCIDENT

2011

DISASTER

Extinction Event

Tectonic Event

Military Action

Fire

Pandemic

Famine

Political or Economic Event

Genocide

Flood or Storm

Industrial or Transport Accident

Cause: Earthquake (MMS 9.03) and nuclear accident (INES 7)

Event: Tsunamis that traveled up to 6 miles (10 km) inland; meltdowns in three nuclear reactors at the Fukushima Daiichi Power Plant

Aftermath: Deaths of 15,680 people from tsunami and two deaths from reactor meltdown; evacuation of 140,000 residents; extensive damage in the Tohoku region; main Japanese island of Honshu moved 8 feet (2.4 m) east and earth's axis altered slightly

The sound becomes a gathering roar. The roar grows louder and more imminent, pressing invisibly on the scene we're witnessing. And now the first small cries of alarm can be heard inside the great space. A woman wheeling a carry-on whirls around to face the huge window. [....] The camera moves to catch them; then, perhaps sensing something, it scurries back to the great glass wall, and freezes there in terror.

Elmer Luke and David Karashima,
March Was Made of Yarn, **2012**

The Tohoku disaster combined a natural phenomenon—a powerful earthquake and tsunami—with an industrial accident, a nuclear reactor meltdown. Japan has the unenviable distinction of being the only country whose civilian population has been bombed with nuclear devices (pp. 160–64), and the country has an understandably complex relationship with the nuclear dilemma. On the one hand, 80 percent of Japanese polled in 2012 don't want anything more to do with a technology that continues to cause deaths from radiation-related cancers sixty-eight years after the dropping of the atomic bomb; on the other, the country is poor in natural resources, especially coal, natural gas, and oil, and nuclear power has provided a more secure form of power generation than trusting to either Russia or China to supply its energy needs, especially during the protracted Cold War (1948–91). Until 2011, nuclear power plants provided one-third of Japan's energy requirements, which was planned to increase to 40 percent until the Tohoku earthquake and nuclear accident temporarily closed existing nuclear plants and suspended the commissioning of new ones.

TSUNAMI DEVASTATION
While Fukushima could survive a quake, it failed when hit by the tsunami.

Energy supply and security, however, is only one of several nuclear issues that the Japanese are faced with. In 1945, only one country, the U.S., had an offensive nuclear capability, but by the turn of the new millennium there were over a dozen nuclear powers in the world, including two of Japan's near neighbors, Communist China and North Korea. Recent tensions with China over uninhabited islands claimed by both countries, and North Korea's development of missiles capable of delivering nuclear payloads to Japan's cities, have led the extreme right to call for Japan to build its own nuclear deterrent, which is well within its technological reach. So far, Japanese governments have resisted the pressure, and they will probably continue to do so as long as they can count on the nuclear capability of the U.S. to deter attacks by other powers in the region.

The third nuclear issue Japan has to consider, along with all other countries with a civilian nuclear program, is the danger of nuclear terrorism. After the collapse of the Soviet Union in 1991, and the decommissioning of many nuclear weapons left in the newly independent former Soviet republics, the fear was that enough radioactive material would fall into the hands of terrorists that they could make a "dirty bomb," that is, not a nuclear device capable of detonating, such as the bombs dropped on Japan in 1945, but a conventional explosive device packed around radioactive material that would be detonated in New York or London, spreading a radioactive cloud over the city, which would then face the kind of contamination experienced in Chernobyl after the reactor meltdown of 1986 (pp. 198–202).

While so far the world's intelligence agencies have managed to prevent this kind of attack, after 9/11 a member of the Al-Qaeda leadership admitted that the organization had initially considered crashing planes into four nuclear reactors in the U.S. He claimed that they changed their minds because of the indiscriminate nature of such an attack; however, it is hard to believe that a group that is willing to crash a plane into a building at the cost of the lives of their own agents and of thousands of innocent victims, including fellow Muslims, was really concerned about how it killed people. They may have reasoned that if they had targeted nuclear power plants, they would have been shot down before reaching them, or had they succeeded, they might have faced massive nuclear retaliation by the U.S., turning parts of their impregnable Afghan refuge into a nuclear wasteland. Al-Qaeda's restraint, however, might not be shared by other groups, including Japan's homegrown brand of terrorist/cult fanatics, such as Om Shinrikyo, which carried out a poison-gas attack in the Tokyo subway in 1995.

The final reason why Japan has to ask itself serious questions about the future of its nuclear power industry is its tectonic position on the upper left-hand side of the Ring of Fire. The Japanese islands are located very close to convergent boundaries between the Pacific, Philippine Sea, and North American plates. Subduction creates a very active tectonic region with ten percent of the world's active volcanoes and around 1,500 earthquakes every year, including major tectonic disasters such as the Great Kanto earthquake that destroyed Tokyo and Yokohama in 1923 (pp. 125–128).

The Japanese lead the world in earthquake-proof technologies. They have to, and visitors to Tokyo will marvel at the Japanese's audacity in building towering skyscrapers and deep tunnels underground in an area that is so seismically unstable. For example, a 20-second MMS 6.9 quake hit the port city of Kobe in western Japan in the 1990s, killing 6,434 people. It is a

WATER

testament to the qualities of Japan's quake-proof buildings that the quake did not kill many more people.

In March 2011 Japan was struck again, this time by an MMS 9.03, the fifth-largest quake ever recorded and the largest ever in Japan, off the coast of Tohoku, northeastern Japan. The position and size of the rupture of the ocean floor meant that the damage from the quake itself was dwarfed by the destruction wrought by the tsunami that it generated. Waves in the open sea reached 133 feet (40.5 m), creating tsunamis between 8 feet (2.4 m) and 28 feet (8.5 m) high that traveled up to 6 miles (10 km) inland in the worst-affected areas. Anyone who has been to Japan will have seen the sea defenses that have been erected along the coast to protect towns from tsunamis and typhoons (tropical cyclones, or Pacific hurricanes). The fact that these were so easily overcome testifies to the enormous power of this particular tectonic event.

Entire towns and villages were completely wiped out; roads, bridges, and railroads were washed away or mangled into twisted heaps of concrete and steel; hundreds of ships were tossed and crushed in their harbors like a child's toy boats. In all 15,680 people, many of them over the age of 60, perished—mainly from drowning as walls of water surged over the coastal towns and villages. In addition to formidable sea defenses that lessened the impact of the tsunamis, Japan also has one of the most sophisticated earthquake and tsunami warning systems in the world. Thousands were able to get to higher ground or climb to the upper floors of structures that withstood the floodwater, and thus survived the tsunami.

FIRE Unfortunately, the earthquake was only the first part of the dual disaster: The tsunami triggered an INES Level 7 "Major Accident," only the second ever recorded after the Chernobyl disaster (pp. 198–202). Although, when compared to the elderly Soviet design, Japanese nuclear reactors are much safer and built to resist the most severe earthquakes, three of the six BWRs (Boiling Water Reactors) at the Fukushima Daiichi Power Plant suffered catastrophic meltdowns, killing two plant workers and seriously injuring 37, and releasing large amounts of radioactive material into the environment.

American-designed BWRs in service at Fukushima were, like the Chernobyl RBMKs, light water (H_2O)-cooled reactors, but they have many more safety features and backup systems than the Russian model, and they did not suffer from core instability at low power levels. What both reactor designs shared, however, was their absolute dependence on permanent cooling to prevent the core from overheating and melting. All reactors in Japan are programmed to shut down automatically in case of a major quake, and the four power plants in the region did so. Even when shut down, the core still needs to be cooled. As in Chernobyl, Fukushima Daiichi was equipped with back-up diesel generators that would power the cooling system as soon as the reactors were shut down, cutting off all power. In Fukushima, there was not a one-minute lag between the shut-down and the back-up system kicking in.

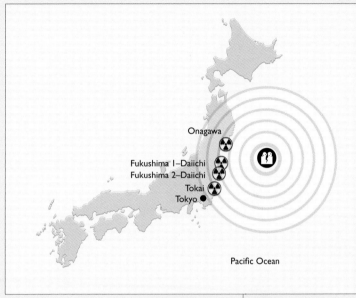

What the designers of the plant had not prepared for, however, was the height of the tsunami that hit the low-lying coastal plant after the quake, while the three active reactors were cooling down. The water flooded and disabled the diesel generators. At this point flooding the reactors with seawater might have prevented the meltdowns, but as this would mean writing the reactors off, this was left as an option of last resort if all else failed. As the water boiled away in the reactor cores, hydrogen gas was released, triggering explosions that breached containment. By the time seawater was allowed to flood into the reactors, the damage had been done, and large amounts of radioactive material had been released into the atmosphere, causing the evacuation of 140,000 residents in the immediate vicinity of the plant, and spreading over the whole of Japan.

 Nuclear Accident

 Approximate epicenter

DUAL DISASTER
The tsunami triggered by the Tohoku earthquake hit four Japanese nuclear power plants along the coast.

DISASTER

Extinction Event

Tectonic Event

Military Action

Fire

Pandemic

Famine

Political or Economic Event

Genocide

Flood or Storm

Industrial or Transport Accident

THE DAY BEFORE YESTERDAY: HURRICANE SANDY

2012

Cause: Category Two hurricane

Event: Largest Atlantic hurricane ever recorded, measuring 1,100 miles (1,800 km) across; it merged with an arctic front, changing from a tropical storm into a blizzard

Aftermath: Deaths of 253 people in seven countries; estimated cost of $65.6 billion dollars; re-election of President Barack Obama

Warm oceans are jet fuel for hurricanes, so it's fair to say that these warmer temperatures are revving Sandy's engine. And while many factors shape sea surface temperatures in a given place, the overall trend—directly linked to climate change—is toward hotter oceans. Thus, while Sandy's particular path could be considered a matter of chance, the warm temperatures beneath it allow the storm to be stronger, for longer, than it might otherwise have been.

**"Was Hurricane Sandy Supersized
by Climate Change?"**
The Guardian, **retrieved January 4, 2013**

In 2004 I went to the movies to see the latest in a long line of disaster and Apocalypse movies, *The Day After Tomorrow*, which was the first movie to dramatize the possible disastrous effects of climate change. The paradoxical premise of the film is that global warming, by melting the ice caps and dumping a lot of cold water in the Atlantic Ocean, would disrupt the Gulf Stream—the warm current that ensures that countries at quite northerly latitudes benefit from a temperate climate—which in turn would trigger the end of the current inter-glacial and the catastrophic return of the ice sheets over northern Europe and most of the continental U.S.

True to Hollywood tradition, the action had to be compressed into a few weeks (and 90 minutes of screen time), so the ice age returns thanks to continent-sized megastorms that look like hurricanes, but, instead of using the heat of the oceans as an engine (see Hurricane Katrina, pp. 230–33), are somehow generated over land. The "eye" of these giant negative hurricanes produces temperatures so low that they freeze the fuel in helicopters (around -100°F or -73°C) sent to rescue the British royal family and turn humans into giant novelty ice cubes. The two heroes of the movies are the unlikely father and son pairing of Kevin Costner as the concerned climate scientist who predicts the disaster, and his son Jake Gyllenhaal, who survives the flooding and deep freezing of New York City in the New York Public Library, no doubt burning the books of climate-change skeptics.

Climatologist William Hyde of Duke University refused to see the film unless someone paid him $100. When the money was raised, Hyde commented in his review that the movie was "to climate science as Frankenstein is to heart transplant surgery." High praise, as *Frankenstein, or the Modern Prometheus* (1818), is one of the best horror novels ever written. The science may be bogus, but as the news conveyed on October 29, when Sandy surged over the Jersey Shore and into Lower Manhattan, it was easy to compare Sandy's effects to the plot of *The Day After Tomorrow*. Not only had the giant hurricane seemingly come out of nowhere on October 22, right at the end of the tropical cyclone season, but also, instead of staying south to ravage the warm Caribbean and southeastern U.S. as Katrina had done, Sandy headed north to an already cooling Eastern Seaboard, with Atlantic City and New York in its sights (maybe even storms get bored and look for a good time in the Big bad Apple).

Not only was Sandy out of place in choosing not to devastate Florida, Louisiana, and Texas by heading north, but it was also the largest Atlantic tropical cyclone ever recorded at 1,100 miles (1,800 km), which, photographed from the International Space Station, obscured a greater part of the North Atlantic and Eastern Seaboard. Next, just like in the movie, Sandy hit coastal New Jersey and Manhattan with a vengeance. It wasn't quite the tsunami that chases Gyllenhaal and his friends along Fifth Avenue into the New York Public Library, but an impressive amount of water overtopped Manhattan sea defenses, flooding tunnels, subways, and basements, and shorting power supplies to blackout large parts of the city for days. The greatest, wealthiest, and most vibrant city on the planet had been paralyzed by a single extreme weather event. It wasn't the stuff of disaster movies, but, being real life, it was more impressive and a lot scarier.

© NASA

BEST LAID PLANS
FEMA officials working to deal with the aftermath of Hurricane Sandy.

In the movie, the flooded city of New York then freezes over. Although this did not happen with Hurricane Sandy, as the storm moved inland over the Appalachians and the Midwest, it merged with a cold front coming down from the Arctic. In a final echo of *The Day After Tomorrow*, Sandy dumped up to 33 inches (84 cm) of snow on West Virginia, with blizzard conditions causing power outages all over the state, and in Ohio and Michigan. Watching from the comfort and warmth of my rain-swept London apartment, it seemed that, although the climatic factors that had created Sandy were different from the pseudo-science of the movie, the outcome was strangely similar (while, of course, in the real world, not signaling the start of another ice age).

Despite its awesome size and power, and the disruption and material damage it caused (estimated at $65.5 billion), fortunately, Hurricane Sandy only killed 253 people in the countries it afflicted between October 22 and 31. Its long-term impact will hopefully be much greater, because its timely coming probably clinched the presidential election, and gave a lot of people who were either unconcerned about climate change or in total denial something to think about—the largest hurricane ever recorded, in the wrong place, at the wrong time. Climate scientists did not immediately jump up and say: "We told you so! Now who's sorry?" But they soberly suggested that the observable rise in the temperature of the oceans may have contributed to making Sandy a lot bigger and more severe—not conclusive evidence that would convince the climate skeptics, but maybe a niggling doubt that would grow over time.

For President Barack Obama (b. 1961), Hurricane Sandy could not have come at a more opportune time; it may very well have saved his presidential bacon. However, this should not detract from the real concern the president showed in the aftermath of the disaster, especially when compared to President George W. Bush's lackluster performance after Hurricane Katrina. The hurricane also put the issue of climate change back on the agenda. The Great Recession has been a mixed blessing for the future of our planet's climate. Although it has reduced carbon emissions from oil- and coal-fired power plants because of the economic downturn in the developed world, it has also reduced investment in expensive renewables, and encouraged the exploitation of shale gas through fracking, which is not an environmentally sustainable technology.

SAVING OBAMA

© Creative Commons

WINNER
President Obama benefited electorally from his handling of Hurricane Sandy.

Although Hurricane Sandy was an extremely unusual climatic event, it does not conclusively prove that climate change is taking place. Science does not work that way. One or more scientists posit a hypothesis about an aspect of the physical world, and it may take decades to confirm or deny the hypothesis experimentally. We only managed to prove some of Albert Einstein's (1879–1955) theories decades after his death, which didn't make them any less correct—it was just that our experimental science needed all that time to catch up with Einstein's theoretical genius. In exactly the same way, though climate scientists cannot confirm their own theories experimentally, as it would mean creating an experiment the size of planet earth, this does not mean that their predictions and theories are wrong. In this case, however, the only way climate change can be confirmed 100 percent is when the world as we know it comes to an end, when global warming caused by greenhouse gases boils our oceans away.

The triggering of an ice age was first proposed in the 1970s, but fortunately did not happen within the 20- to 30-year time scale predicted. We cannot rule it out, although it would take centuries. As pointed out in the earlier entry on the French heat wave (pp. 222–25), the most likely cause of the demise of our civilization will be the end of the current temperate interglacial period. But that could be tens to hundreds of thousands of years in the future, so forget about buying blankets and stockpiling kerosene.

SAVING GAIA   In the 1970s British environmentalist James Lovelock (b. 1919) developed the concept of "Gaia"—the ancient Greek name for Mother Earth—which defined the planet as a closed, self-regulating system that, given the chance, will always be able to return to a state of balance. In the Gaia hypothesis, humanity is both the baddy and the fall-guy, because our actions have created a sustained disequilibrium that will have dire consequences both for the planet and for us. If we could find ways of living more harmoniously with the natural environment, we would not only save the planet but also our own long-term future. If we do not, we condemn most of humanity to death from famine, pestilence, and war—in other words, an ecological apocalypse, as opposed to the military apocalypse (nuclear war), the natural-disaster apocalypse (asteroids, supervolcanoes, and megaquakes), or the medical apocalypse (the killer pandemic).

© NASA

PREDICTION
Climate scientist believe Sandy's record size and strength can be attributed to climate change.

But if you study the history of the earth since its creation, and of our neighbors Mars, Venus, and Mercury, the Gaia hypothesis falls apart. It is just an environmentalist's pipe dream and one not based on the facts. Life on earth has been almost wiped out on five occasions—the most recent featured as the opening entry of this book: the Cretaceous–Paleogene extinction (pp. 10–15). Granted that we have slaughtered countless species in our time as top predator on the planet (pp. 67–70), but we are mere serial shooters when compared to the mass murders committed over the past several billion years by dear old Mother Nature. The dinosaurs dominated our planet for 135 million years, yet they were snuffed out in a matter of years by a giant ball of flaming rock falling from the sky. Where is the balance, fairness, justice, mercy, or sense in that? We, too, might meet the same absurd, instantaneous extinction from an interplanetary collision. Alternatively, nature might leave us alone for another 100 million years, and then it is our own actions that will decide whether and when the human species survives or dies.

The "Mayan Apocalypse" was probably the most laughable non-apocalypse in history, with the media outnumbering believers at key end-of-the-world sites. The reality of the Maya, as we saw in the entry on the collapse of their civilization (pp. 36–40), is that, far from existing in balance with the cycles of Gaia, they destroyed their environment not once but twice, and survived to face a third human apocalypse in the shape of the Spanish Conquest. The Maya, despite having suffered three major disasters, are still with us. They continue to use their complicated ritual calendar, though they abandoned the Long Count version many centuries back. On December 21, 2012, I watched a group of modern Maya dance in the turning of the solar year at the foot of the classic-era pyramids of Tikal, Guatemala, resurrected from the jungle a millennium after the city had been abandoned.

We are not so very different from the ancient Maya (our pyramids are just a lot taller and our mathematics are even more complex) in that the real threat to the survival of our civilization is the human disaster created by our runaway success: man-made global warming. Thus far, despite the millions who have perished in the thousands of natural, natural–human, and human disasters over the past 70,000 years, humanity has not only survived but also thrived, reaching the extraordinary population of seven billion in 2012. In the end, however, in about a billion years, if we are still around, we will face the certain destruction of our home planet, as the increasing output of the sun (in this case nothing to do with man-made global warming) boils away the oceans and the earth's life-giving atmosphere.

WE, THE LATTER-DAY MAYA

FURTHER READING

There are many good general reference works available in printed form or online covering the entries featured in this book. Still one of the most authoritative is the *Encyclopaedia Britannica*, available for free at most large public and school libraries, and online at britannica.com as a subscription service. Another reference source that is increasingly used by authors and journalists is the ubiquitous Wikipedia (en.wikipedia.org). The content of Wikipedia, however, is user-generated, and is not independently verified. As a result there are inaccurate or biased articles included in the Wiki database. Nevertheless, it provides a good starting point to find references on a wide range of topics.

In addition to books and articles, web addresses of general and specialist sites have been included whenever appropriate. All URLs were correct at the time of writing, but it is the nature of the Internet that these change as sites migrate to new service providers or are taken down. If a website is no longer active or has moved, please conduct a search on the topic in a search engine such as Google.com.

The reference materials listed below fall into two categories: in certain instances they provide detailed accounts of the topics covered in the entries; in others they give the reader a general background on the period, person, or topic. When a source listed is strongly biased either for or against the topic under discussion, a balancing work supporting the opposite point of view is offered where available. Materials about entries in other media, such as videos and film and TV documentaries or dramatizations of the events, are included, though these do not necessarily stick faithfully to the facts, and take Hollywood liberties with storylines and characters.

Whodunit?:
Cretaceous–Paleogene Extinction

Frankel, C. *The End of the Dinosaurs: Chicxulub Crater and Mass Extinctions.* Cambridge: Cambridge University Press, 1999.

"Asteroids—The Good, the Bad and the Ugly." *Horizon*, BBC Television, first broadcast. September 25, 2012.

Going It Alone:
Toba Population Bottleneck

Dawson, A. *Ice Age Earth: Late Quaternary Geology and Climate.* London: Routledge, 1991.

Havilland, W. *et al. Anthropology: The Human Challenge.* Andover, Hants: Cengage Learning, 2010.

Without a Trace:
Santorini-Thera Eruption

Plato. *Timaeus and Critias.* Ed. A. Gregory, trans. R. Waterfield, New York: Oxford University Press, 2009.

Guide to Santorini Island: www.travel-to-santorini.com

The First "Dark Ages":
Bronze Age Collapse

Drews, Robert. *The End of the Bronze Age: Changes in Warfare and the Catastrophe ca. 1200 BC.* Princeton, NJ: Princeton University Press, 1995.

The End of Eternity I:
Alaric's Sack of Rome

Gibbon, E. *History of the Decline and Fall of the Roman Empire.* London: Penguin, 2001.

Illustrated History of the Roman Empire: www.roman-empire.net

Lost:
Collapse of Classic Maya

Chase, A. and Chase, D. "Classic Maya Warfare and Settlement Archaeology at Caracol, Belize." *Estudios de Cultura Maya.* XXII, pp. 33–51, 2002.

Grube, N., Eggebrecht, E., and Seidel, M. *Maya: Divine Kings of the Rain Forest.* Cologne: Köneman, 2000.

Stephens, J. and Catherwood, F. *Travels in Central America, Chiapas, and Yucatan.* New York: Harper & Brothers, 1841.

"A Third of the World Died":
Black Death

Gottfried, R. *Black Death: Natural and Human Disaster in Medieval Europe.* New York: Simon and Schuster, 1985.

Barnett, S. Anthony *The Story of Rats: Their Impact on Us, and Our Impact on Them.* London: Allen & Unwin, 2002.

The End of Eternity II:
Mehmet the Conqueror Takes Constantinople

Crowley, R. *Constantinople: The Last Great Siege, 1453.* London: Faber and Faber, 2005.

Norwich, J. J. *Byzantium: The Decline and Fall.* London: Penguin, 1996.

The Black Reality:
Demographic Collapse in the Americas

Casas, Bartolomé de las. *The Devastation of the Indies: A Brief Account.* Trans. H. Briffault, Baltimore, MD: Johns Hopkins University Press, 1992 (1542).

Prescott, W. and Foster Kirk, J. *History of the Conquest of Mexico.* New York: Barnes & Noble, 2004.

Building on Sand:
Shaanxi Earthquake

Information on geological faults:
www.see.leeds.ac.uk/structure/faults

USGS Earthquakes Hazards Program website:
www.earthquake.usgs.gov/earthquakes

The Fatal Middle Way:
Triangular Trade

Klein, H. S. *The Atlantic Slave Trade.* Cambridge: Cambridge University Press, 2010.

The Human Touch:
Holocene Extinction

Martin, P. *Quaternary Extinctions: A Prehistoric Revolution.* Tucson, AZ: University of Arizona Press, 1989.

The IUCN Red List of Threatened Species:
www.iucnredlist.org

Deathtrap:
Great Fire of London

Ackroyd, P. *London: The Biography.* London: Chatto & Windus, 2000.

The Diary of Samuel Pepys website:
www.pepysdiary.com

Shaking Faith:
Lisbon Earthquake and Tsunami

Shrady, N. *The Last Day: Wrath, Ruin, and Reason in the Great Lisbon Earthquake of 1755.* New York: Penguin, 2008.

A Question of Supply:
Bengal Famine

Eraley, A. *The Mughal Throne: The Saga of India's Great Emperors.* London: Orion, 2003.

Le Déluge:
French Revolutionary *Terreur*

Doyle, W. *The Oxford History of the French Revolution.* Oxford: Oxford University Press, 2003.

McPhee, P. *Robespierre: A Revolutionary Life.* New Haven, CT: Yale University Press, 2012.

Blighted Land:
The Great Famine

Bartoletti, Susan Campbell. *Black Potatoes: The Story of the Great Irish Famine, 1845–1850.* New York: Houghton Mifflin Harcourt, 2005.

Woodham-Smith, C. *The Great Hunger: Ireland 1845–1849.* London: Penguin, 1992.

The Year of Fires:
Peshtigo Fire

Guess, D. and Lutz, W. *Firestorm at Peshtigo: A Town, Its People, and the Deadliest Fire in American History.* New York: Holt Paperbacks, 2003.

Wisconsin Historical Society website:
www.wisconsinhistory.org

Biggest Bang:
Krakatoa Eruption

Thornton, I. *Krakatau: The Destruction and Reassembly of an Island Ecosystem.* Cambridge, MA: Harvard University Press, 1997.

Winchester, S. *Krakatoa: The Day the World Exploded*. New York: HarperCollins, 2005.

Ship of Nightmares:
Sinking of the RMS *Titanic*

Adams, S. *Titanic*. London: Dorling Kindersley, 2009.

Titanic. Dir. James Cameron; starring Kate Winslet and Leonardo DiCaprio, 1997.

The First Genocide:
Armenia

Freedman, J. *The Armenian Genocide*. New York: Rosen, 2009.

Kevorkian, R. *The Armenian Genocide: A Complete History*. New York, I. B. Tauris: 2011.

Going Forth:
Battle of the Somme

Buchan, J. *The Battle of the Somme*. New York: George H. Doran & Co., 1917.

Prior, R. and Wilson, T. *The Somme*. New Haven, CT: Yale University Press, 2006.

Blackadder Goes Forth. BBC Television; starring Rowan Atkinson, 1989.

All Quiet on the Western Front. Dir. Lewis Milestone, 1930.

Mass Killer:
Spanish Flu

Barry, J. M. *The Great Influenza: The Story of the Deadliest Pandemic in History*. New York: Penguin, 2005.

Crosby, A. *America's Forgotten Pandemic: The Influenza of 1918*. Cambridge: Cambridge University Press, 2003.

The Will to Power:
Rise of Fascism

Carsten, F. L. *The Rise of Fascism*. Berkeley, CA: University of California Press, 1982.

Newton, M. E. *The Path to Tyranny: A History of Free Society's Descent into Tyranny*. Phoenix, AZ: Eleftheria Publishing, 2010.

Earthshaker:
Great Kanto Earthquake

Hough, S. E. and Bilham, R. G. *After the Earth Quakes: Elastic Rebound on an Urban Planet*. Oxford: Oxford University Press, 2005.

A Tragedy of Errors:
The Great Depression

T. E. Hall and D. Ferguson *The Great Depression: An International Disaster of Perverse Economic Policies*. Ann Arbor, MI: University of Michigan Press, 1998.

Keynes, J. M. *The General Theory of Employment, Interest and Money*. New York: Harcourt, Brace & World, 1965.

Rauchway, E. *The Great Depression and the New Deal: A Very Short Introduction*. Oxford: Oxford University Press, 2008.

Mother Monsters:
China Floods

Fort, E. and Stevens, D. *Ten Deadliest Natural Disasters in the Past Century: The 1931 China Floods*. Webster's Digital Services, 2010.

Stalin's Hunger:
The Holodomor

Naimark, N. *Stalin's Genocides*. Princeton, NJ: Princeton University Press, 2010.

Snyder, T. *Bloodlands: Europe Between Hitler and Stalin*. London: The Bodley Head, 2010.

Japan's Shame:
Rape of Nanking

Chang, I. *The Rape of Nanking: The Forgotten Holocaust of World War II*. New York: Penguin U.S.A., 1998.

Timperley, H. *What War Means: The Japanese Terror in China*. London: Victor Gollancz, 1938.

Lest We Forget:
The Holocaust

Feig, K. *Hitler's Death Camps: The Sanity of Madness*. New York: Holmes & Meier, 1981.

Gilbert, M. *In Ishmael's House: A History of Jews in Muslim Lands*. Toronto, Ontario: McClelland & Stewart, 2011.

Lemkin, R. *Axis Rule In Occupied Europe: Laws of Occupation, Analysis of Government, Proposals for Redress.* New York: Lawbook Exchange, 2005.

Niewyk, D. and Nicosia, F. *The Columbia Guide to the Holocaust.* New York: Columbia University Press, 2000.

Hitler's Waterloo:
Operation Barbarossa

Glantz, D. *When Titans Clashed: How the Red Army Stopped Hitler.* Lawrence, KS: University Press of Kansas, 1995.

Snyder, T. *Bloodlands: Europe Between Hitler and Stalin.* London: The Bodley Head, 2010.

Atomic Destruction:
Hiroshima and Nagasaki

Allen, T. and Polmar, N. *Code-Name Downfall.* New York: Simon & Schuster, 1995.

Ogura, T. *Letters from the End of the World: A Firsthand Account of the Bombing of Hiroshima.* Tokyo: Kodansha International, 2001.

A House Divided Against Itself:
Partition of India

Akbar, A. *Jinnah, Pakistan and Islamic Identity: The Search for Saladin.* London: Routledge, 1997.

Keay, J. *India: A History.* London: HarperCollins: 2010.

Ghandi. Dir. Richard Attenborough, starring Ben Kingsley, 1982.

The Bitter Years:
Great Chinese Famine

Dikötter, F. *Mao's Great Famine: The History of China's Most Devastating Catastrophe. 1958–62,* London: Bloomsbury, 2010.

Televising Famine:
Nigeria

Falola, T. and Heaton, M. *A History of Nigeria.* Cambridge: Cambridge University Press, 2008.

St Jorre, J. de *The Nigerian Civil War.* London: Hodder and Stoughton, 1972.

Valleys of Death:
Cambodian "Killing Fields"

The Killing Fields. Dir. Roland Joffé, 1984.

Tully, J. *A Short History of Cambodia: From Empire to Survival.* London: Allen & Unwin, 2008.

Dying of Ignorance:
HIV-AIDS

Centers for Disease Control and Prevention website, HIV/AIDs:
www.cdc.gov/hiv

UNAIDS website:
www.unaids.org

World Health Organization (WHO) website, HIV/AIDs:
www.who.int/topics/hiv_aids

Sticking Plaster:
Ethiopian Famine

Clay, J. and Holcomb, B. *Politics & the Ethiopian Famine: 1984–1985.* Piscataway, NJ: Transaction, 1987.

Sen, A. *Poverty and Famines: An Essay on Entitlement and Deprivation.* New York: Oxford University Press U.S.A., 1983.

Health and Safety Gone Bad:
Bhopal Gas Leak

D'Silva, T. *The Black Box of Bhopal: A Closer Look at the World's Deadliest Industrial Disaster.* Victoria, BC: Trafford Publishing, 2006.

Lapierre, D. and Moro, J. *Five Minutes Past Midnight in Bhopal.* New York, Warner Books: 2002.

Meltdown:
Nuclear Chernobyl

Mara, W. *The Chernobyl Disaster: Legacy and Impact on the Future of Nuclear Energy.* New York: Marshall Cavendish, 2010.

Yablokov, A. *et al* (eds.) *Chernobyl: Consequences of the Catastrophe for People and the Environment.* Hoboken, NJ: John Wiley & Sons, 2010.

Black Tide:
Exxon Valdez Oil Spill

Margulies, P. *The Exxon Valdez Oil Spill: When Disaster Strikes!* New York: Rosen, 2003.

Streissguth, T. and Chandler, G. *The Exxon Valdez: The Oil Spill Off the Alaskan Coast.* Mankato, MN, 2003.

Cain and Abel:
Rwanda Genocide

Ensign, M. and Bertrand, W. *Rwanda: History and Hope.* Lanham, MD: University Press of America, 2010.

Prunier, G. *The Rwanda Crisis: History of a Genocide.* New York: Columbia University Press, 1997.

Beggar Thy Neighbor:
Srebrenica Massacre

Honig, J. W. and Both, N. *Srebrenica: Record of a War Crime.* New York: Penguin, 1997.

Rohde, E. *Endgame: The Betrayal and Fall of Srebrenica, Europe's Worst Massacre Since World War II.* New York: Penguin, 2012.

Terror from the Skies:
9/11

The 9/11 Commission Report: Final Report of the National Commission on Terrorist Attacks Upon the United States. (Official Edition.) CreateSpace Independent Publishing Platform, 2010.

DiMarco, D. and Kean, T. *Tower Stories: An Oral History of 9/11.* Santa Monica, CA: Santa Monica Press, 2007.

French Fever:
European Heat Wave

Braasch, G. and McKibben, B. *Earth under Fire: How Global Warming Is Changing the World.* Berkeley, CA: University of California Press, 2009.

Johansen, B. *The Encyclopedia of Warming Science and Technology.* London: Sage Publications, 2012.

The Day the Sea Rose:
Indian Ocean Earthquake and Tsunami

Lüsted, M. A. and Lay, T. *The 2004 Indian Ocean Tsunami.* Edina, MN: ABDO Publishing, 2008.

Roza, G. *The Indian Ocean Tsunami.* New York: Rosen, 2007.

The Big Difficult:
Hurricane Katrina

Brinkley, D. *The Great Deluge: Hurricane Katrina, New Orleans, and the Mississippi Gulf Coast.* New York: HarperCollins, 2006.

Horne, J. *Breach of Faith: Hurricane Katrina and the Near Death of a Great American City.* New York: Random House, 2008.

The Matrix Reloaded:
Lehman Brothers Bankruptcy

McDonald, L. and Robinson, P. A. *Colossal Failure of Common Sense: The Inside Story of the Collapse of Lehman Brothers.* New York: Crown, 2009.

Ward, V. *The Devil's Casino: Friendship, Betrayal, and the High Stakes Games Played Inside Lehman Brothers.* Hoboken, NJ: John Wiley & Sons, 2011.

Double Trouble:
Tohoku Earthquake and Nuclear Accident

Architectural Institute of Japan *Preliminary Reconnaissance Report of the 2011 Tohoku-Chiho Taiheiyo-Oki Earthquake.* Tokyo: Architectural Institute of Japan, 2012.

Luke, E. and Karashima, D. (eds.) *March Was Made of Yarn: Reflections on the Japanese Earthquake, Tsunami, and Nuclear Meltdown.* New York, Vintage, 2012.

The Day Before Yesterday:
Hurricane Sandy

Archer, D. and Rahmstorf *The Climate Crisis: An Introductory Guide to Climate Change.* Cambridge: Cambridge University Press, 2010.

Seymour, S. *Hurricanes.* New York: HarperCollins, 2003.